Tampering with the Machinery

LESTER O'SHEA

Tampering with the Machinery

ROOTS OF ECONOMIC

AND POLITICAL MALAISE

McGRAW-HILL BOOK COMPANY

New York   St. Louis   San Francisco
Düsseldorf   Mexico   Toronto

Library of Congress Cataloging in Publication Data

O'Shea, Lester.
Tampering with the machinery.
Bibliography: p.
Includes index.
1. United States—Economic policy—1961-
2. United States—Politics and government—1945-
I. Title.
HC106.7.082   338.973   80-24432
ISBN 0-07-047749-3

1 2 3 4 5 6 7 8 9 D O D O 8 7 6 5 4 3 2 1

Book design by Anita Walker Scott

Published in association with
SAN FRANCISCO BOOK COMPANY.

To Barbara

TAMPER

. . . a: to interfere so as to weaken or change
for the worse   b: to try foolish or dangerous
experiments.

—*Webster's New Collegiate Dictionary*

Contents

Foreword

BY WILLIAM E. SIMON

During my four years in government, I witnessed Big Government in action from the inside. I left Washington convinced of the crucial importance of generating a public awareness among Americans that our country has careened away from the fundamental precepts of American society that made our country the most advanced civilization in history toward collectivism, coercive centralized planning, and a statist dictatorial system. I am glad that Lester O'Shea has written this book, for while I may not agree with all his thinking or emphases, it is, I believe, overall a worthwhile contribution to that effort.

We must make the American people aware that the fundamental principles of American society have been reversed. Those principles, when the nation was expanding healthily, included giving the highest priority to individual liberty, a conscious prejudice against intervention by the state into our lives, recognition of the interdependence of economic wealth and political liberty, and respect for productivity and producers. It is evident today that our nation is being ruled by precisely the opposite principles. Mr. O'Shea exposes, in a detailed, straightforward manner, many facets of this reversal, which is at the very heart of our growing political and economic degradation.

The United States, today, is a redistributionist state, characterized by a nonstop assault on our productive classes. And this politics of stealing from productive Peter to pay nonproductive Paul—the coercive leveling of egalitarianism—could not, despite vote-conscious politicians and special interest groups, have swept the country and become the political curse of our era that it is but for the powerful political intelligentsia, the vocal intellectual superstructure of this country.

For that reason, I am pleased that Mr. O'Shea has seen fit to devote part of his book to a study of these moral and economic despots and their liberal biases (*liberal*, as I use it here, refers to today's misdefinition, that once noble term having been appropriated by those who favor *restriction* of liberty). In laying bare much of the irrationality and nightmarish hypocrisy of this intelligentsia and discussing the origins of their bias in a straightforward manner, he makes a contribution to the cause of freedom. As he points out, the same political intelligentsia, with its egalitarian-redistributionist philosophy, has played a prominent role in the decline of our country's position in the world.

Another refreshing aspect of this book is its defense of the competitive meritocracy that our Constitution brought into being; of the ideal of hard work, competitive achievement, and self-fulfillment in freedom. Yet the effect of the redistributionist philosophy is exactly the opposite. It punishes the hard-working and amibitious and rewards those who are not.

The capitalist miracle, which created the extraordinary wealth of our nation, occurred in the United States because this explosion of wealth is uniquely a result of individual liberty. That is the true defense of capitalism. Egalitarianism is a morbid assault on both ability and justice. An American who is hostile to individualism, to the work ethic, to free enterprise, who advocates an increasing government takeover of the economy or who advocates the coercive socialization of American life, is in some profound sense advocating that America cease to be America.

The viselike grip of government control—of an economic dictatorship which is expanding geometrically year after year—has had a frightful impact on the producers of America. Whether in the form of the preposterous energy bureaucracy, against which I fought vainly, or the incredible torrent of governmental edicts and rulings overall, or the ravenous devouring of investment capital by government borrowing—this death grip of government on our economy has inevitably caused a decline in productivity. This appropriately named book exposes much of the economic insanity that has damaged our economy to a tragic degree, and while there are areas that, in my view, deserve greater attention, nonetheless it provides overall a perceptive analysis of a shocking and dangerous situation.

As Mr. O'Shea points out, we have to contend not only with redistributionist zealots in Congress and the Executive Branch, and with the regulatory bureaucracies themselves, with their unmistakable mark of Big Brother, but also with a judiciary much of which is dominated by a coercive, redistributionist, and collectivist philosophy. The Constitution as "interpreted" by many of our judges resembles the Constitution of our Founding Fathers as little as the egalitarianism of our present system resembles the Constitutional vision of equality. Constitutional equality is equality of opportunity; egalitarianism seeks equality of results regardless of individual differences. The author's facts and logic make clear that it is a falsehood that the Constitution requires so many court rulings that punish the hard-working and law-abiding citizen. Those who believe this are being duped.

I am not sure I share Mr. O'Shea's optimism as to the significance of the "tax revolt" and all the current talk about people being "fed up" with big government. Americans continue to ask the government for "free" goods and services and to jockey for position beneath the federal faucet. Businessmen, who as a group, in particular, are incessantly victimized by the present situation, nevertheless run to the government in every crisis whining for handouts. All too often, too, the majority of Americans have failed to put their votes where their mouth was. Perhaps, however, before too much more time has passed, we will in fact see the beginning of a new era of understanding by the American people of the true nature of statism and collectivism. One must, of course, hope so, for we have reached the very crossroads between freedom and totalitarian rule.

We need books like *Tampering with the Machinery* to help alert and enlighten our citizens as to the danger we face. Through this book, I believe that many Americans will come to understand, or to understand better, the true causes of many government-engendered problems that overall threaten to destroy this nation, as we lose both economic and political freedom in the wake of the expanding state.

History is not a carpet rolling inexorably in the direction of collectivism. If enough Americans—inspired by this book, inspired by other books committed to the cause of human freedom, inspired by leaders with vision and by their own common sense and observation and their common belief in the liberty of man—become aroused to positive action, it is possible that we, and our children, will again enjoy the fruits of that brilliant interlocking of political liberty and economic liberty created by our Founding Fathers.

Acknowledgments

I wish to express my gratitude to several persons who have been of invaluable assistance in the preparation of this book: to my friend Kevin Starr, author and columnist, whose encouragement and comments played a significant part in my bringing the book to completion for publication; to Audrey Allison, whose accurate and efficient work with the manuscript was immensely helpful; to Robert Granucci, deputy attorney general of California (an example of the conscientious public servants of whom, we should not forget in an era of governmental waste, we have many), whose extensive knowledge of important court cases was of great help to me; to Ernest Scott, my editor at San Francisco Book Company/McGraw-Hill, to whose painstaking thoroughness and helpful suggestions this book owes a great deal indeed; and finally to my wife Barbara for her encouragement and her battle against procrastination, including finally sending me to the cabin with instructions not to return without a completed book.

L. O'S.

San Francisco
August 1980

Introduction

This is a time when, in the opinion of many, things have "gone to the dogs" all over. It is, of course, not uncommon, as believers in progress will tell you, for people to have this feeling; in the course of progress many things change, and inevitably some good things, or things that at least look good in retrospect, will outlive their time and go, but it hardly follows, etc.

And, it will be pointed out that in the golden days of long ago, say of early twentieth century America, infant (and maternal) mortality was high, and diphtheria common; and all kinds of diseases, like tuberculosis, rampant; and it took days to cross the country, whereas now the city-dweller, even of modest means, can be in the wilds in no time.

And, of course, in the graceful eighteenth century, all was not sunshine and roses; people died in filthy hospitals, anesthetics were relatively unknown, sanitary conditions were terrible.

All of this is absolutely true. And yet, it does seem that we might have a little less of the bitter with the sweet that progress has brought. Twenty years ago, say, all the terrible things that afflicted people in 1790 or 1910 had pretty much gone; and yet the quality of life had not yet undergone the rather radical deterioration of which most people are aware today.

What really has deteriorated? In terms of amenities, certainly, the case is not all that clear. To be sure, the fine old resort hotels of the past are even fewer now than they were then, with their stately columns and long verandahs looking across the lawns to the mountains or the lake; the glories of Pullman and ocean liner travel that once were enjoyed or aspired to are now all but a memory; enclosed rooms with humming air-conditioners have replaced breezes on tree-shaded porches; and the air and water are more polluted, and vacation areas more crowded.

But, on the other hand, good service is available today on jets, which get you where you want to go in less than no time; many more Americans are able to own or rent their own places in the country; air-conditioning is a tremendous boon to those not living and working in large old tree-shaded mansions with spacious gardens; and there are more and more facilities for recreation.

It is not in terms of those nostalgic amenities that one senses that things have gone to the dogs in the last two decades. Rather, it is in terms of what may be called the socio-economic dimension of life in the United States generally, and life in the large cities of the country, where the great majority of us live, particularly.

How has this come about? Are the basic causes things like the "depersonalization of modern life," "the technological revolution," and a variety of developments that, as far as can be seen, could not have been helped; or have we Americans, acting through our government or otherwise, played a prominent role in this going-to-the-dogs process?

By way of introduction to the territory, let us try a fictional day's encounter with today's problems, with an attempt, by means of running notes, to relate the problems encountered by a fictional homeowner to apparent causes in governmental action, where a connection is apparent but not entirely obvious.

The homeowner arises on some representative day in the middle to late 1970s, perhaps helped to do so by the noise of traffic outside. He lives on a hill, and motorcyclists like to race up it early in the morning.[1] Presumably, everything will be functioning in the house, although at great cost in terms of repair bills;[2] but the house may not be as clean as it might be, because in the first place, domestic help is hard to get, unreliable, and terribly expensive;[3] in the second place, if one could afford them, there would be the problem of where to house such employees since, with the spiraling cost of construction[2] and increasing real estate taxes,[4] it is hard to afford a house big enough;

---

[1]*It is against the law to operate motorcycles without adequate mufflers in the city, but the police have no time to enforce this (or many other formerly-enforced laws) any more. One reason is that court decisions have greatly increased their workload per major criminal violation.*

---

[2]*One reason many costs are high and there is so much difficulty with labor is that, under the protection of New Deal legislation, unions have grown so strong in these fields that their members constitute what amounts to a monopolistic guild; entry into fields such as plumbing is rigidly controlled and restricted by these guilds so that these craftsmen are very scarce and able to demand amazing levels of pay. The ability of unions to obtain what they demand has been greatly enhanced by authorities' unwillingness to deal with such things as picket-line violence.*

and, in the third place, help has been known to steal, and/or have friends and relatives who do.[5]

The morning paper may raise the homeowner's blood pressure. Here is a story about a former attorney general of the United States, Ramsey Clark, testifying before a committee of the state legislature. He has declared that it would "say something about us as a people" if we were to "put to death helpless people that we have in our power." He means executing convicted murderers, who perhaps were captured at the risk of the lives of those capturing them.* In another story

---

[3]*Domestic help is such a problem largely because various programs of help to the poor, for which taxpayers like Jones are paying, provide those who formerly furnished domestic help with an attractive alternate to doing such work. In a sense, Jones pays the government the money his father paid his help: also, in a very real sense, supporting a person of limited skills, but now in idleness at home rather than at work in an employer's home.*

---

[4]*Real estate taxes provide the local component of the total cost of welfare referred to in (3). Court decisions have broadened eligibility for welfare even beyond that prescribed by the legislative branch; e.g., new arrivals from other states are eligible immediately without any period of residency. Court rulings have repeatedly hamstrung efforts by state, federal, and local officials to curb welfare expenditures; they rise through prosperity and recession alike, and often federal bureaucrats veto local or state attempts to apply controls. Taxes also are high in order to do such things as pay city and county employees what it takes to keep them from striking, now that government no longer enforces the laws forbidding strikes by governmental employees, and hire buses to transport school children pursuant to a court order and the board of education's inclination.*

---

[5]*Hindering the ability of law enforcement to deal swiftly and effectively with criminals, as has been done by court decisions, can be assumed to play a part in the upsurge of crime that has occurred. Furthermore, with delays in the courts, a criminal, after being arraigned for an offense, is often free on bail and able to commit the same offense again before being tried on the first charge.*

*The passage of time will not alter Clark's remarkably inverted moral sense; from the June 2, 1980 *San Francisco Examiner*: "Iranian President Abol Hassan Bani-Sadr opened a "Crimes of America" conference today with a tirade against America. Former U.S. Attorney General Ramsey Clark, one of the participants, condemned the aborted U.S. mission to rescue the hostages as 'lawless and contrary to constitutional government.' "

another policeman has been killed. There is controversy about the large-scale busing of students that the financially-strapped school board is pushing ahead with, as it cuts back many programs. The stock market has had a sharp loss, attributed by analysts to the expected effect of an inflationary steel settlement on the balance of payments. There are rail and dock strikes again.[2]

If our friend heads for the office by bus, he had better have quarters in hand since the drivers no longer carry change, owing to a wave of robberies and murders.[5] If our friend walks any part of the way through commercial areas, he will see some interesting sights, including a string of establishments offering pornographic literature, newspaper racks with periodicals featuring articles on their covers like "Incest—Why Not?" and "Child Molesting for Women," movie marquees promising the "hardest core yet," or featuring homosexual or bestiality films, and "topless and bottomless" establishments.[6]

Posters and handbills and spray-painted slogans abound. "Off your boss." "Revolution now." In the financial district, young people beg for money or peddle assorted trinkets.[7] A pair of fierce-looking blacks in bizarre garb are coming the other way; our friend gives them wide berth, reflecting that they may be on dope, are very likely armed, at least with knives, and probably hate him fiercely for "four hundred years of oppression."

Once upon a time, say twenty years ago, the generally accepted view was that American blacks were making progress. They finally were getting a reasonably fair deal in most areas, although there was still much room for improvement, and some of them had succeeded greatly. They all ought to try by working hard. Now the gospel according to the press and television is that they are hopelessly oppressed, all of their problems are entirely the fault of whites and reflect not a whit on the Negro, and—how can you blame them if they hate all white people? Besides, there are no jobs for them.[8]

Our friend is liable to encounter frustrations and annoyances during his day. At lunch, in a very expensive restaurant, the waiter is

---

[6]*Supreme Court decisions have drastically reduced the ability of local authorities to restrict pornography and obscenity.*

---

[7]*In a case in a West Coast city, a court prevented the police from enforcing the law against peddling without a license for some time. Police also no longer enforce anti-panhandling laws, having more important things to do under current conditions.*

incompetent and the whipped-cream cake stale. At least the waiter is courteous; which is more than can be said for many.[2] The prices are incredibly high.[9]

Perhaps our friend will hasten homeward with trepidation if he has worked late. A lawyer was shot to death near his office downtown one evening not long ago. Here comes a cab. Jones hopes he has something smaller than a $20 bill, or he will have to hurry upstairs when he gets home and see if his wife does; cabs no longer carry much change, lest the cabbies be robbed and perhaps killed as well. There is a new breed of criminal afoot in the city, according to the police; members of this breed will, after robbing their victim, often kill him gratuitously. This phenomenon frequently is linked in the press to black hatred of whites.[10] Jones has friends who have been robbed, and he understands that it can be unpleasant.

The taxi driver has trouble getting to Jones's destination; apparently he is new. Cab drivers, Jones has heard, do not make all that much money, even though the fares in his city are among the highest in the country, and the drivers are paid enough in relation to the fares they collect to be driving the cab company, according to it anyway, out of business.[2] Perhaps not too many people ride cabs as a result of the high fares. In any case, the drivers have the alternative of welfare, which is handed out openhandedly by sympathetic welfare workers in the city. (A recent newspaper series in Jones's city described a reporter's success in milking the taxpayers without having been checked up on in the slightest; the welfare workers he dealt with, he wrote, gave him the impression that they would gladly give him "the

---

[8]*The absence of jobs for the unskilled is directly caused, in great measure, by minimum wage laws and (to a lesser and indirect extent) by the effects of strong unions, a product in turn of laws.*

---

[9]*Inflation is largely caused by deficit spending born of readiness on the part of politicians to cater to the demands of assorted special interest groups, in combination with expansion of the money supply. Union power is also a contributing cause.*

---

[10]*The courts have hamstrung the imposition of the death penalty as well as the administration of justice generally, which may have something to do with the incidence of murder.*

shirt off the taxpayer's back.") The taxi driver is unkempt; it was not that long ago that the cab company required its drivers to wear coats and ties. Times have changed.

Once home, Jones may well not go out again. Walks at night, even in "safe" neighborhoods, are not really safe.[5] There is a park near his home, but, even in the daytime, it is a good idea to stay out of it.

Jones' children are reaching school age. Public school will be completely out of the question, as children living in Jones' area will, according to the board of education's busing plan, be bused to a school in a slum area. Jones, it happens, can afford private school, but he feels sorry for those who cannot, those who worked and saved to buy a home in a nice neighborhood with good schools only to find that their children were to be sent across the city into the slums. When they objected, they were reviled as ignorant bigots by enlightened, prosperous people whose children attended exclusive private schools. So many families with children, including friends of the Joneses, have fled to the suburbs that middle-class children are becoming a rarity in the city. Jones has been informed that a majority of his city's public school children are from families on welfare.

Jones may reflect on how things have changed. He is not old, himself; hardly the age for sitting in front of a fire and bumbling about the "good old days." But he can, he is sure, remember things as being so different, so much better, just a short while ago. Bus drivers, for example, used to be polite. Perhaps such people are so rude now because the passengers are, but on the other hand, he knows it is almost impossible to fire a surly public employee now, and that certainly may have something to do with it. (If he is fired, of course, a bus driver will be able to rely on a variety of programs paid for by his employer and the other taxpayers designed to ease his problems.)[2] The phenomenon, of course, is not confined to the bus drivers. Everyone seems tenser, less friendly. Relations between those of different colors seem strained.

Of course, liberal writers will tell him that it is right that the black should at last recognize who his oppressor is and have gained the manhood to be no longer friendly to these sources of all his problems. But it seems somehow that the Negroes were happier before, as well as the whites, and somehow the "progress" that has occurred is not doing anybody much good, to judge from obvious outward appearances.

Jones's day is anything but an anomaly. The March 15, 1976, *Time* cover story, called "Americans on the Move," dealing with the phenomenon of movement from American large cities to smaller cities, towns, and rural areas, was replete with examples of the decline of the quality of, in particular, big-city life: crime, tension, and poor schools were cited repeatedly as the reasons for moving.

Jones has the distinct and unpleasant feeling that things are not right with the country in a much more general and broad sense. The once proud dollar has become a widely disdained currency, reflecting an apparent inability to compete effectively with foreign producers in area after area. Foreign cars are supplanting American; Japanese steelmen undersell American even in the environs of modern American plants (such as at Fortuna, California); Japanese television sets and cameras are everywhere; The American share of Near Eastern construction contracts has dropped from first to twelfth place: the list goes on and on.[2,11]

Our friend also feels a great deal of frustration at the way his country seems to get kicked around by foreign countries; he recognizes that he is not an expert in foreign affairs and assumes that his government is doing the best it can, but the flag-burnings and embassy-stormings that he reads about do not add to his general sense of well-being.

At first blush, it might have seemed that all the above problems, which may be called a representative, if cursory, sampling of the kind of thing that is meant by "deterioration in the quality of life," had little in common, and that they basically were things that, in an advanced, industrial society, just happen. But this is not the case, as reference to the running notes points out. The fact of the matter is that, almost without exception, Jones's problems are the product, not of inexorable natural forces, but rather of government—legislative, judicial, and executive—*interference* with the natural course of events.

There are some threads that run prominently through the impingements by government that we have noted: in terms of legislation, they are labor laws, welfare laws, minimum wage laws, and burgeoning regulation in general; in terms of judicial and administrative action, they are court decisions in a great number of areas: welfare, criminals and court procedure, racial composition of schools, pornography, obscenity, powers of government, etc., and a bureaucracy with a rampant desire to regulate. The long and short of the matter is that in an incredible variety of ways, in an incredible number

---

[11]*American industry has been hit with a series of government-originated body blows ranging from the preemption of productive resources to the creation of disincentives to work, as will be analyzed below.*

of areas, governmental action has come over the last couple of decades to impinge on the lives of Americans and to affect those lives in undesirable ways: undesirable, that is, as far as the feelings and wishes of the vast bulk of the population of this democratic country are concerned.

Given that this is a democratic country, the question naturally suggests itself how so much that is contrary to the wishes of the people could occur. The answer is twofold. In the first place, a great deal of what has been done has been done by the courts and the bureaucracy, who are not directly and immediately controllable by the popular will; in the second place, much has been done which, popular in and of itself, has had widely unforeseen, but nevertheless inevitable unpleasant consequences. No one is an advocate of having hillsides destroyed by erosion, or having fish killed by pollution in waterways, or having millions of people made unable to find work and turned into social dynamite; but there are advocates of unrestrained logging, unrestricted construction of polluting plants, and high minimum wage laws.

It is interesting that there has been so much publicity about the evils of tampering with the natural ecology and nothing to speak of about the socio-politico-economic ecology. The same people who take a militant Sierra Club-environmentalist approach to "tampering with nature" take a Corps of Engineers approach when it comes to society, politics, and economics. We must not dam this river, or build this pipeline, or cut this forest without first making an exhaustive, careful study of all possible consequences and ramifications of that action; in fact, a whole industry has grown up around "environmental impact reports." But if we see something in human society which we do not like, the only decent, enlightened and forward-looking thing is to immediately pass a law or hand down a court decision dealing with it, and those who object and talk about undesirable long-run effects are simply people who are blind or indifferent to human needs or with vested interests. The contrast is striking.

1

Political, Economic,

and Social Environments

T he basic concept behind the fad word *ecology* is unassailable: that a natural organism, such as an area of forest, functions efficiently through the continous interaction of its parts in the ways in which, through design or evolution, these parts of the whole have come to function. Kill the wolves and the elk and the deer multiply to the point where they starve. Pollute the waters with industrial wastes and the fish die and swimming as well as fishing becomes impossible. Cut down the forests and erosion sets in; and, deprived of their natural habitat, species die. It is a healthy thing that the current times are seeing so much recognition of the fact that man cannot tamper with the natural order of things without fouling things up in some way or other, unless the most extreme care is used.

Unfortunately, there is all too little recognition of the fact that human society, too, no less than a forest, is an organism, and that tampering with it can likewise foul things up. Under the leadership of a relatively small minority, the United States has been involved, particularly in the last couple of decades, in a far-reaching and devastating attack on its political, social, and economic ecology, and the widely-perceived deterioration in the quality of life in this country is not an unfortunate accident but rather the inevitable result of the tampering that has been done.

Pollution does not just happen; neither does a breakdown in respect for law and order. Erosion is not an act of God; neither is the spiraling of taxes and of prices and the increasing weakness of the dollar.

Human society is an organism, and it does not take well to engineering. It is based upon a natural and constant factor: human nature. *Plus ça change, plus c'est la même chose.* Those who have read literature and history know well that little has changed in human nature since the time of the Pharaohs. Ambition, greed, fear, laziness, courage, pride: they stay the same. It was not for no reason that for so long it was felt that an education in the Greek and Latin classics comprised the best possible liberal education. Reading even very ancient classics, we recognize ourselves and our contemporaries. We have our Robespierres today; and our Gracchi; and our Caesars, and our Senecas, and our Neros; and our Louis Philippes, our Bismarcks, our Pericleses; and all the rest.

Were human nature different today than ever before, the reading of authors of the past would be but an exercise in perplexity and in study of the incomprehensible. But human nature is basically the same. Every society requires order, and discipline; room for enjoying the benefits of labor and effectiveness, and for suffering the results of sloth and ineffectiveness; effective rewards and punishments.

Those to whom virtue is its own reward have never comprised a majority in any country at any time. Human societies work when they reward conduct that is beneficial to the society as a whole and punish that which is not; if they turn the other way, they rapidly deteriorate.

"Nature" is not sacrosanct or perfect in human terms. Weak animals are eaten by strong. Forest fires, started by lightning, burn millions of acres, killing wildlife. Predators prey. Yet we have today a healthy understanding of the valuable parts played by the various parts of nature. How ironic that the very people, educated, intelligent, aware, who are so sophisticated and wise about how risky a business it is to try to improve on or alter nature in the form of woods, are so ready to make improvements on socio-economic-political nature!

It is sad to see elk killed by wolves, but the wise ecologist knows that we must not kill the wolves, for they are part of "nature's plan" to keep the elk population within viable limits. But on the other hand, it is sad to see people suffer the pains of poverty, and we should avert that forthwith, and whatever effects the methods used may have on their willingness to work, and what effects this may have in turn on society as a whole, are not to be considered.

Unfortunately, good intentions alone, as has so often been said, are not enough, any more in the case of the economy than in the case of a forest, or a piece of machinery. Well-intentioned tampering is likely to do more harm than good.

2

The Economic Environment

Let us look first at the economic environment, for economics is at the root of so much. It is ironic that the same people who often proclaim the primacy of matters material and economic so often cannot be bothered to learn anything about economics. Even more than sociology, for example, economics is not an area where wishful thinking can substitute for facts. Learning the complex and by no means obvious-to-the-untrained-eye ways in which economic laws work is, itself, work; it is so much easier simply to cast about one, one's pure mind and soul unsullied by facts or understanding, denouncing what one's intuition and heart disapprove of, and also the system under which these affronts to one's values arise. Law after law has been passed posthaste in this spirit of indignant righteousness, and as a result the economic ecology of this country has been severely disrupted, and there is the devil to pay.

One thing should be remembered. No economic system has ever come close to competing with the free-enterprise capitalistic, private-property system, as a provider of the "greatest good of the greatest number." Whatever faults the system we now know has, whatever faults the system had before being tampered with, there is no satisfactory alternative as an engine of progress and prosperity. To paraphrase Winston Churchill, capitalism is the worst form of economy that there is, except for all other ones.*

The capitalist system is entirely natural. People own things, perhaps through inheritance, perhaps through paying for them with money earned by the work of their hands or minds. In order to earn more with what they have, they must utilize their human and material assets in a way that benefits others, so that the others will pay them; and the more efficiently they can use what they have to satisfy other humans' wants, the more profitable this application will be.

---

*To cite one example of the relative efficiency of public versus private enterprise, cited by a member of Parliament, in the British electric power system, 172,000 employees produce 211,000 kilowatt hours of electricity; in the private utilities of California, New York and Pennsylvania (which have the same population), 73,000 employees produce 268,000.

Thus all men and women, to the extent that they are motivated by desire for material gain, must constantly seek to apply their assets of time, money, machinery, etc., where they will get the best possible return; which means the most that anyone will pay for the use of those assets; which means in the way that most satisfies human wants as they are expressed through purchases.

The carping critic will proudly point to an example or two where businesses proceeded in one way even though their own interest would best have been served in another. That ineffective businesses lose their headway relative to those better able to use the resources at their disposal, and do so automatically and inevitably under the existing system, doesn't trouble these critics. All they require is to be able to prove that the system is not perfect, at least in the short run, and they consider their case for far-reaching governmental intervention proved.

In matters of natural ecology, this is the viewpoint commonly attributed to the Army Corps of Engineers. This river's water could better be used elsewhere—we will build a dam and a canal and divert it. But, ecologists will cry, how can you be sure that there will be no unfortunate side effects? And even if you could really, in a particular case, be absolutely sure that what is being done is for the best, it by no means follows that the whole of nature should be subject to the whims of the Corps of Engineers. On the whole, we do better to leave nature alone and keep a sharp eye on any tampering. Once we start interfering in one instance, no matter how desirable that particular instance may appear, we open the floodgates to a pattern of interference that on the whole will do more harm than good. Similarly, people who were "ecologists" ahead of their time, but working in the field of economics, and were denounced for their pains as lacking heart, used to argue.

It may in fact be argued that there is a great deal more persuasive case to be made for a general reworking of the map of the land by governmental action than for a general intervention by government in economic processes. By its nature, flood control and similar engineering *has* to be handled one specific case at a time. No one would think of proposing a law providing that all rivers of over a certain cubic feet of flow per day should be dammed exactly halfway between source and end and exactly 50 per cent of the excess flow be piped to one of a series of central reservoirs.* But with the economy sweeping, far-

*Considering the sweeping, nationwide requirements of the Clean Water Act (see page 45), one becomes less confident of this assumption.

reaching interventions affecting entire classes of people and industries are common.

Yet listen to the ecologists complain about the tampering that one particular case represents! "What right have they to ruin these people's river so that those others can have access to the ocean?" was the cry with respect to a proposed Florida waterway. Such considerations of equity as a matter of general principle are seldom obstacles to intervention in the economic sphere today.

3

The Assault on The

Economic Environment

Lhe list of assaults on the integrity of the economic environment, which may be called collectively the rape of that ecology, is a long one. The process really got under way in the 1930s, and parts of it are just now really starting to bear their noxious fruit. The body blows to the economic environment include government spending, runaway regulation, and three specific categories of legislation whose ill effects are so pronounced they deserve prominent mention: labor legislation, minimum wage laws, and welfare legislation.

LABOR LEGISLATION. In the decade of the 1920s, real wages rose to an unprecedented and hardly-equalled-since degree. At the same time, labor union membership fell by about one third. The wages rose, as they do in similar circumstances, not because of union pressure and strikes, but because with strong demand for the products of industry it was profitable to expand production; therefore, more workers were needed; therefore, to attract more workers, they had to be offered more.

In economic areas where there was no boom, in the area of buggy manufacture, say, workers were drawn away into areas where their talents could be more profitably utilized. (Nor did advanced buggy-making engineers proudly sit, unwilling to move or do work that was beneath them; in the absence of generous unemployment and welfare programs, they moved fast and took whatever was the best job they could find. Similarly, when gold and silver mining petered out, for example, in California's and Nevada's mountains, miners cleared out fast for places where they could make a living. Had today's well-intentioned programs been in effect then, we could read today about the hopeless cycle of poverty and dependence in the Mother Lode counties of the Sierra foothills.)

Thus do industries no longer in tune with the people's ever-changing needs gradually or, as the case may be, more rapidly, decline, as resources are shifted to more productive areas. No governmental decisions or deliberations are required; the profit motive takes care of the whole process. In fact, in the absence of interferences with the level of wages, it is rare in normal times that willing workers cannot find some work, even if it is in fields far removed from their experience.

Left-wing critics of the capitalist system will scream that the above is an oversimplification. It is interesting to see the liberal double standard come into play. It is considered reasonable discussion to say that the United States is fascist and imperialistic, or that American society is racist, or that the capitalist system is rotten, or that Congress fails to meet the needs of the people (this last means that it heeds the majority rather than self-anointed experts). These are not really oversimplifications, and only a nit-picker would carp and quibble. But when the over-simplification shoe is on the other foot, the forest cannot be seen for the carps and the quibbles.

The theory of the New Deal of the 1930s was that purchasing power was the key to economic recovery, and everything that enhanced that power was good. It was thought good for labor unions to be stronger. So laws were passed, starting with the Norris-LaGuardia Act, to enable unions to grow to an extent they never had been able to under free competition and an open contest. (It may be noted that this thinking—that strong unions drive up wages and prices—while at the root of New Deal plans for promoting economic recovery in a situation of falling demand and prices—has not been applied consistently; if under Depression conditions strong unions were therefore desirable and should be encouraged, then it should follow that under conditions of inflation it would be desirable to reduce union strength. But no such suggestions have been made in the current era of inflation.)

The Davis-Bacon Act of 1931 promoted the use of union labor on federal projects. Since then unemployment benefits have become more and more available to strikers, as have food stamps and welfare payments. In the case of railway employees, under the amended Railway Labor Act of 1934 striking employees or employees refusing to cross a picket line receive substantial benefits from a fund built up entirely out of employer contributions.

Employers trying to replace striking workers with workers willing to work find themselves in a state little short of civil war. We have come a long way from the 1920s, when a president of Harvard called the strikebreaker "the American hero." Nowadays, public authorities, often beholden to unions for campaign funds and election workers, are likely to take the position that the employer has no right to try to operate. Except in the South (which not by accident is one of the fastest-growing areas of the country), breaking a strike is not apt to even be attempted. (For a manufacturer to demand the right to reopen a struck plant is an outrageous "provocation," and if there is violence from the strikers that is understandable; but if an anti-Vietnam war demonstrator burns an American flag or a present-day draft registration opponent denounces his country, people's reaction is secondary to his constitutional rights—this is *not* a "provocation," and if people were to rough him up, they would deserve deep contempt and firm punishment.)

With strong unions, strong and fat strike chests, and a virtual exclusion of "strike-breaking" or "back-to-work movements," it is little wonder that today the typical major industry can be held up for just about any wage settlement, and thus little wonder that a succession of strikes and/or inflationary and industry-damaging settlements is seen. The situation is much worse in some industries than in others. The steel industry, perhaps partly because of repeated government involvement when there have been steel strikes, has seen a steady rise in wage costs (average hourly earnings were $11.30 in January 1980, versus $6.95 in all manufacturing) far beyond increases in productivity: between 1962 and 1978, earnings increased at a 7.3 per cent annual rate versus a 2 per cent increase in productivity. The sorry state of this industry, in terms of competitiveness and profitability, is no secret.

The ability of employers even to replace strikers has been progressively circumscribed. According to an article in the *Wall Street Journal* for November 8, 1972, "The Supreme Court reaffirmed earlier decisions holding that employers must rehire strikers unless permanent replacements are hired before strikers are told they are fired. . . . Under prior High Court rulings, an employer may refuse to reinstate economic strikers if in the interim he has hired permanent replacements. However, other High Court rulings add that strikers have an unconditional right to reinstatement with back pay, even if replacements have been hired, if employees continue a strike in protest to an employer's unfair labor practices."

More and more generous unemployment benefits, reaching the point where, according to a 1979 Congressional study, many recipients lack incentive to work, also have reduced an employer's ability to resist union demands.

This force—immensely powerful labor unions, created by federal intervention, has far-reaching effects on the economic ecology. Inflation is one result. Another is the decline of whole industries, where the industry's ability to compete, abroad or domestically, is affected. The railroad industry, sick unto death with highway and air competition, a few years ago faced a 42 per cent wage increase over forty-two months. It is no exaggeration to say that labor unions are at the heart of the industry's decline. When every train must carry perhaps twice the number of workers needed, when crews must be changed every hundred miles, when a whole network of restrictive rules hamstrings the roads' ability to give quick, efficient service, it becomes hard to compete. It is interesting to note that the ultimate corrective to excessive wage demands—the ruin of the employer and the total elimination of the jobs—is now being rendered inapplicable in many cases; if the railroad goes bankrupt, the government will step in and keep the paychecks coming from the limitless resources of the federal treasury and printing press.

It is also interesting to note that the once financially distressed Florida East Coast Railway, which successfully broke a strike about fifteen years ago, found that it could handle its business with less than half of its former work force; this year it paid the first cash dividends in its eighty-eight-year history. On a smaller scale, in 1979 the residents of Pend Oreille County, Washington, found that their branch line of the bankrupt Milwaukee Road could be operated on a self-sustaining basis by using local labor rather than railroad workers with costly union contracts.

Among the beneficiaries of union strength are the builders of labor-saving equipment. These also have been beneficiaries of coal industry unionization, but the number of coal miners has shrunk drastically. Other beneficiaries of the strength of American labor unions are foreign manufacturers and shipowners. The American Merchant Marine exists at all only as a result of government subsidies totalling in the billions, by which shipowners are paid the difference between foreign and ever-increasing American wages. (In the process one of the refuges of the marginal citizen, "going to sea," has been eliminated.) The steel industry, discussed above, is now finding itself less and less able to compete in its home market against foreign competition, to say nothing of competing abroad. It is the same story, although not yet on as dismal a scale, in the automobile industry.

These parts all add up. It is no accident that the United States' competitiveness has deteriorated to the point where even a 16.3 per cent devaluation of the dollar since June 1970,* involving formal devaluations and further devaluations through floating exchange rates, have failed to cure the balance of payments problem. So long as wages continue to grow in excess of productivity, this process will continue.

The ecological effects of powerful unions go much further. In the case of tightly-knit, closed-shop areas, such as the skilled trades in the construction area, the result has been to drive up the cost of shelter at a fantastic pace, all the while excluding from the ranks of these highly-paid workers men who are not related to union members. (Since few blacks are related to, say, union plumbers, this also works to keep minority members from skilled jobs.) Only recently has this situation begun to result in dramatic increases in the percentage of work done by non-union contractors.

The do-it-yourself movement has been spurred on apace by the astronomical wage levels unions have succeeded in achieving for such groups as plumbers and electricians. In many areas bricklayers have priced themselves out of the market, taxi use has declined drastically, and restaurants are ill-patronized and lose money with union help. When an executive spends time doing the work of a handyman, that time—which could be spent enhancing a company's planning for productivity—is being poorly utilized, with adverse consequences for American productivity overall.

MINIMUM WAGE LAWS. The legislatively-created power of labor unions, as noted in the foregoing, causes many jobs to be replaced by machines. If labor is reasonably cheap, one employs a person; if the person costs too much and a machine can be bought at the right price, it replaces workers. To be sure, other workers have jobs building the machines. But once they build the machine, its contribution to their

*Trade-weighted average, involving currencies of the U.S.'s fifteen principal trading partners, weighted according to our volume of trade with each. The figure, released by Morgan Guaranty Trust Company, is as of May 6, 1980.

employment is over, and ever after the jobs of the persons it replaced are gone.

Skilled workers are not so easy to replace by machines, but unskilled workers are another matter. Unions by themselves thus are one reason for the persistent plague of a lack of jobs for the unskilled. To really wipe out jobs, though, there is nothing like a minimum wage law. This just about guarantees that no one whose skills are not initially worth $3.10, or whatever the figure is raised to (it goes to $3.35 in 1981), will get a job. Frequently the only way an unskilled worker can obtain the skill that will make his or her time worth more than the "minimum" figure is by working, so unskilled workers are often dumped into a rubbish pile of "unemployable" persons, living on welfare and comprising what is commonly referred to as "social dynamite." As Temple University economist Walter Williams well puts it, according to a January 1980 *Time* article, "We have cut the bottom rungs off the economic ladder, and the consequence is that for the first time in U.S. history, we have developed a permanent welfare class."

This is no abstruse phenomenon; it exists all over. In 1966 minimum wage laws were extended to agricultural workers, effective February 1, 1967, and the *New York Times* carried a lengthy story, on February 13 of that year, about cotton pickers being reduced to total destitution as a result. The economics of the mechanical cotton picker had become too compelling. But in October 1972 the *Times* ran an outraged editorial entitled "Let Them Eat Cake" condemning Congress for failing to raise the minimum wage further.

The fact is that some people have very limited skills. Some will, with experience, acquire significant skills, but some are too limited to ever be capable of tasks beyond the very simple. They will either have relatively low-paying and unattractive jobs, which at least give them the opportunity to make a contribution to the economy's output and give them a feeling of dignity and worth, or none at all. The effects are similar whether minimum wage laws or the ill-advised engendering of militancy and demands, as with agricultural laborers, is directly responsible.

WELFARE. A third great cause of the staggering welfare burdens presently on taxpayers' backs, and growing heavier, is welfare laws themselves. Not only have payments become increasingly generous, being based on "need," which need of course increases with each additional child, but former restraints, such as residency requirements, have been eliminated by the courts. A welfare recipient can now get on the bus and head for whichever state is most generous. In fact, it may be some time before the state of former residence finds out he has moved; in the meantime, he can draw double pay, so to speak, or even triple or quadruple, if he doesn't mind traveling.

The task of the perennial welfare recipient is, of course, eased by the high percentage of welfare workers who have warm hearts and are inclined to be generous with the taxpayers' money. But, in fairness to the dolesters, it must be noted that often they have little choice, thanks to unions and minimum wage laws, between going on welfare and starving; and after all, since they have been told over and over that there is no stigma attached to living off the taxpayer, it is only human that they should believe this, at least to the extent of seeing little reason why they should work at a low-paying job, where one is available, when they can get nearly as much and lead a life of leisure. Thus welfare liberality keeps the marginal, those who could find jobs despite unions and minimum wage laws, unemployed also.

Another effect of welfare, touched on parenthetically above, is reduction in people's mobility: mobility in the useful sense, that is, in the sense of moving to where they are needed, rather than in the sense of readiness to travel to where welfare checks are highest. For example, Appalachia, while not as fashionable a concern now as a decade or so back, is still with us in the form of jobless inhabitants of the back country where the jobs departed long ago, with the mines. Still the people sit there on the porches, subsisting on welfare. In the latter part of the nineteenth century, silver and gold mining towns flourished in many corners of the West. Changes in precious metal prices, depletion of veins, etc., subsequently removed the economic justification of many of those towns. There was no welfare to speak of, and, having a strong aversion to starving, the people left. Presumably, they and their progeny have done useful work ever since, whereas had welfare been around then, we could read about their plight today. As another example of the same basic phenomenon, there seems to be a definite correlation between the duration of jobless benefits and when unemployed persons develop willingness to "pull up roots" to move to where jobs are available.

An interesting side effect of generous welfare payments is the current controversy, especially relevant in the states bordering Mexico, over illegal aliens. For at a time when many American citizens are to be found idle in the cities, towns, and countryside in states like California and Arizona, living on welfare after unemployment payments have run out, illegal entrants, generally with very limited or nonexistent skills or command of English, are able to find work. A recent article in the *Wall Street Journal* involved a visit to the Los Angeles area, where unskilled members of the American welfare culture were found grumbling and grousing with one breath about the aliens who were, they said, taking their jobs and, with the next, indignantly refusing to consider doing the kind of beneath-their-dignity work that was offered them and which aliens were gladly taking.

If aliens were taking, to a significant extent, the jobs that unemployed Americans are willing to do, one suspects that there would be less confusion as to whether or not to resume enforcement of the immigration laws. But many recent analyses have shown that the marginal income that welfare-ites could receive by doing the work for which they are qualified, even where the minimum wage hurdle would not be a problem, is generally worth less than the reduction in enjoyment represented by working rather than remaining idle, so that welfare at this point is straightforwardly subsidizing idleness and creating a real need for the illegal-immigrant worker.

UNPALATABLE RESULTS

These three governmental impingements on the economy—one-sided* labor legislation, minimum wage laws, and liberal welfare laws—are to the economic ecology more or less what a trio of polluting plants would be to a lake in our natural ecology. Taken together, the three impingements have helped to create galloping inflation and a more or less permanent underclass of unemployed welfare recipients, their numbers swelling relentlessly in good years and bad. This is an underclass constituting a tinderbox for riot and, day in and day out, the source of a majority of the violent crime against persons and property committed in this country. These impingements also, through their disastrous consequences, destroy in the minds of many the worth and validity of what is really the best possible system. But capitalism itself has not created this army of *lumpenproletariat:* interference with capitalism has.

The three factors above, especially the first, also have helped create a crisis for the dollar, decline in many industries and in many areas of the country, trouble in the profit area, and trouble in the securities markets. There are, of course, other factors that have come into play here, but the role of federally-created idleness cannot be overesti-

*If it wasn't one-sided, how could labor union power have grown subsequently to levels completely unprecedented in this country before, and how else explain the beginning of that growth coinciding with passage of the 1930s' pro-labor legislation?

mated; and in terms of that federally-created idleness, overly-strong unions must be seen clearly as major contributors to the problem.

This is not, really, a criticism of the unions; after all, their constituency *is* the bulk of *employed* workers, not those who might get jobs if excessive wage gains did not strangle the growth of industries. If labor in this country were a nationwide monopoly, one could fault the chief labor leader for not being sensible enough to avoid excessive demands that could only result in faster inflation and a threat to the value of the dollar. But the job of the heads of the unions is to do the best they can for their members: everybody else will be doing the same thing, prices will soar anyway, and their workers had better get their share or they will not be labor leaders long. It is rather short-sighted to drive companies to the wall financially, but if you are confident that government—that is, the taxpayers—will come to the rescue when that happens, then, "cry havoc and let slip the dogs of war." Maritime unions had about driven American-flag shipping from the seas, but a massive program of federal subsidization, passed by Congress during the Nixon Administration, revived jobs for their members. The Penn Central and rail passenger service have been rescued by Washington. Though the Chrysler Corporation debacle appears to involve primarily ineffective management rather than union unreasonableness, the prospect of governmental rescue conveys the same message.

Again it should be said that the above is *not* an indictment of American labor unions. The long run is one thing, but in the long run, as Lord Keynes pointed out, we are all dead. In the short run, more money and fringe benefits *now* are what union members want and their receiving them gets union leaders re-elected. When plants are leaving an area in droves and jobs are at stake *now*, unions often sing a different tune in terms of demands, as is appearing in a variety of interesting cases; but no such general connection is usually apparent between wage increases and loss of jobs. The jobs that might be created, and the promotion opportunities that thus might open up to union members where companies can earn better profits, are not all that tangible. A bird in the hand . . .

In recent years unions, especially those in areas (public service) where strikes are forbidden by local law, have been bombarded with proof that results are obtained by those who say to hell with the law and demand and demonstrate and demand. Did not the sainted Adlai Stevenson say that a jail sentence was becoming a mark of honor? It would indeed be a *rara avis* of a union leader who would forego seizing what his men wanted by any available means, when the lesson has been made so clear that "them as grabs, gits" in modern America.

The fault—as far as the economic problems of the United States go—lies not so much with the unions themselves as with the laws and the attitudes that have made them what they are. "Power corrupts, and absolute power corrupts absolutely." The power is basically a creature of the laws that have been passed. And who can fault labor union leaders for not taking a far-seeing and statesmanlike course going far beyond that expected of the leaders of government? Local budgets and tax rates have a way of staying under control until after the elections; the nation's policy abroad becomes noticeably less vigorous as presidential elections approach; the celebrated case of Stanley Baldwin, who later admitted that he had lied to the British people about the state of their defenses lest his party lose the election, is perhaps distinguished more for its candor than for its uniqueness.

THE FEDERAL SYSTEM AND THE ECONOMIC ECOLOGY

A discussion of what government has done to the economic ecology would not be complete without reference to a phenomenon which is taking on the characteristics of a torrent through a breached dike, namely the centralization of government in Washington. To sum up the indictment, this centralization has removed the most effective brake on misallocation of scarce productive resources by government spending, namely opposition by taxpayers to seeing their money wasted and their preference for keeping it and making their own decisions as to how it is to be spent.

There is a body of opinion in the country to the effect that the people do not know best how to spend their money and that if they are allowed to keep it they will spend it in ways that do not really maximize their long-run welfare. There is another school of thought, fast-growing and now more and more open, to the effect that even if people do know how to spend their money so as to effect their own betterment, it is nevertheless the right and duty of government to take the money and spend it on those who are more deserving than the taxpayers. Adherents of these schools of thought—and many adhere to both—are eager to take the people's money and have it spent at the discretion of those who, they feel, will do a better job.

This, of course, is socialism; socialism with greater or less emphasis on redistribution in addition to socialism, but socialism nevertheless. The basic principle of the capitalist free-enterprise system is that the market is the best allocator of resources. Apart from those areas such as police and fire protection, national defense, and a vigilantly controlled number of areas where government must do the job because the job is basic to the functioning of society and cannot be marketed in the normal manner or cannot be performed effectively by private enterprise, people are simply left the money that they have and earn and it is up to them to spend it on what they want. If there is demand for something, private enterprise, motivated by desire for profit, will provide it, as long as the economics of the situation are such that this can be provided profitably at a price people will pay.

We are talking about, fundamentally, rational resource allocation. If materials and labor costing $100 are required to produce an item or a service which people will only pay $50 for, there would be a net loss to society if resources were so applied. The entrepreneur would also lose his shirt, so this unfortunate development will not occur, or at least not very often, or for very long each time. If people will pay $150 for the item, then, if the scale of demand is great enough to justify the organizational talent required to make the item, it will be made available, and the net result will be that human wants are now better satisfied.

It is, of course, basic that only desires backed up by readiness and ability to spend money are considered here. If people want widgets badly but are not willing to pay enough to justify producing them, there will be no widgets. Similarly, if a group of people has a craving for them but not money to pay for them, the result will be the same: no widgets. Obviously, under this system, what is produced depends on *effective demand*—demand by people able and willing to spend their money to get what they want.

There is a system of free choice by people putting their money where their mouths are and spending their own money, usually earned by their labor and the fruits of their labor. Any other system places the power to make these decisions and allocate scarce resources into someone else's hands. Unless this someone is all-knowing, it is hard to see how the market mechanism could be improved on; and God has never indicated a willingness to take over the running of the American economy and making the innumerable decisions that are now made automatically through the market mechanism.

The problem with all government spending is that it is not accountable to the market mechanism. Generals in the Pentagon want a superior new tank; hundreds of millions of dollars get spent on it, perhaps unwisely. A group of people in a landlocked area, seeing what access to the sea could do for their property values, get a bill passed to build a canal, perhaps at a cost far exceeding the gain, to say nothing of the harm to people in nearby areas. The federal government spends $57,000,000 on a "new departure" in transportation—a "people mover" developed in West Virginia—and ends up considering ways to blow up the structures. In all cases, money—which means resources—has been wasted; the market mechanism has been bypassed.

But military procurement and people movers and canal-building are not in the same class, at least not in the minds of most people. The general consensus is that just as one tends to rely on one's doctor or dentist in health matters, so one tends to rely on the military experts in defense matters. There may be waste; one tries to cut it down; but the stakes are too great for penny-pinching. But it is otherwise with matters closer to home where people are, properly, more confident of their own instincts and judgment. The people of this country are not ready to accord to any person or group of persons the status of experts in how their money should be spent in domestic matters; there is no consensus that there are Olympian experts in Washington or the state capital or city hall or the county offices whose decisions are to be accepted as one would accept those of military professionals or medical specialists.

In an interesting article in the May 25, 1980, issue of *California Living* magazine entitled "Confessions of a City Planner," Lawrence Livingston, Jr., looking back over a thirty-year career involving many projects of great magnitude, notes that "in too many instances, planners' proposals have proved to be unjustifiably costly, ineffective, or, in some cases, actually harmful to the public interest." Referring to "public funds misspent," he concludes that "planners should seek and find an accurate way to gauge the gains and losses that will stem from their proposals. . . ."

Once government spending starts in the domestic sphere, the restraints and controls of the marketplace are no longer able to operate in the usual way. A group of people want widgets but are unable or unwilling to pay for them, or pay enough to make it worthwhile to make them? Organize the Better Living Foundation, whip up sentiment for a federal widget program, write your congressman, get exposure, and soon there indeed will be a federal widget program. You would like a paved county road through your ranch, at no expense to you? Your friend at the county courthouse can perhaps help. Your acreage would be worth much more with plenty of cheap water available? Organize your area, do some work in your state capital, and get the state to fund an aqueduct that will do the job. You like living on the coast, but are afraid a hurricane will wreck your house? Promote expanded "disaster assistance" and government-subsidized hurricane insurance.*

This sort of thing has always gone on on all levels of government, and the restraint has always been the opposition of taxpayers to footing someone else's bills. On the city and state levels, it has generally been possible to restrain government spending rather well for several principal reasons. First, the relatively limited taxing powers of these levels of government have often required projects and programs to be funded by bond issues, which voters can vote against. Second, local and state politics tends to involve bread-and-butter issues to a very large extent rather than broad ideological or international issues. Third, because these projects are close to home and can be understood and assessed on an individual basis by voters, they are more ready to form opinions and express them. Fourth, and very important, particularly on the local level, there is a direct and readily perceptible connection between government spending and taxes.

The local voter can see a project proposed, where local funds and control are involved, decide against it, and paying for it, and vote against the bond issue; or, if there is no bond issue, make clear to a county supervisor that the project isn't wanted. Since issues like Vietnam or Watergate or Iranian relations are not the chief issues in county elections, the supervisor may indeed listen if enough constituents make clear that they don't like it. And if there are cases of sloppy work and too free a hand in the welfare department, again local taxpayers, angry at the wasting of their money, may force changes. Even at the state level, while these forces do not operate quite as directly and as strongly, a great deal of what applies to the local government situation also applies.

Spending against the wishes of the people at the state, county, and

*The disaster-relief program is a fine example of how even the best-intentioned government interference can have undesirable economic effects for the country as a whole. There *are* areas of the country significantly more subject to natural disasters than others. Other things being equal, and absent government interference, people will choose to live elsewhere. With offsetting advantages, such as climate, access to beaches, opportunity to farm more acreage than would be possible given the higher price of land in safer areas, etc., these areas will be settled, but only to the point where the advantages and disadvantages, all being weighed by the individuals whom they affect, balance. "Private hurricane insurance is expensive, but all in all I'm willing to pay extra to live on the ocean, with the lot being cheap." This is reasonable, and productive resources are being used rationally in accordance with true costs and benefits. But bring in federal assistance, which is in effect a subsidy of those in dangerous areas at the expense of those in safe, and unwise location is encouraged and labor and materials are wasted. Now people are encouraged to move into hazardous areas even though the real costs outweigh the benefits. They receive the benefits but no longer have to pay the real costs.

local levels was, in fact, in the pre-revenue sharing era, very much restrained by local voters; as it still tends to be in the dwindling number of cases where the voters' own dollars are directly involved and no federal mandates are controlling. This is what "enlightened" and "progressive" people, who know better than the people what the people really should have, and assorted vested interests or "lobbies," meant when they said that "state and local governments were unresponsive to the needs of the people." *The catch-phrase is in fact a very impressive testimonial to the success of local and state government in being responsive to the wishes of the people.**

In fact, when examined closely, the often-heard statement that local and state government could not do things (so that the areas of responsibility involved therefore had to be taken over by Washington) because they "lacked the taxing power" also begs the question. "Lacked the taxing power" is nonsense. There are all sorts of taxes, including income taxes, that states can levy; and the same is true in counties and communities, with the exception, in some cases, of the income tax. The taxing power was there, but the people would not stand for its being used to finance the "programs" and "services" so dear to liberal hearts. Wholesale siphoning away of the middle-class citizen's money, to be spent partly on things that were "good for him," although unwanted, and (primarily) on the more-deserving poor folks and on special interests, could successfully be done only on the federal level.

On the phony grounds that the states, counties, and cities were not providing for the needs of the people, activists unwilling to let the allocation of resources be determined by the wishes of the people through the market mechanism have succeeded in getting the federal government into domestic spending in a previously undreamed of way. Since the first year of John F. Kennedy's administration, annual non-defense spending by the federal government has risen from $47 billion to $379 billion—a rise of over 700 per cent. Payments to individuals have risen 900 per cent: from $22.9 billion to $213.2 billion.**

*To take a current example, with studies indicating that mandatory automobile "safety inspections" basically benefit only the auto repair industry, there is sentiment in favor of their discontinuance, and five states have repealed their requirements (leaving twenty-seven with them); the mandatory-inspection enthusiasts have responded by seeking *federal* automobile inspections.

**Allowing for inflation, that is, in constant 1972 dollars, non-defense spending rose from $77 billion to $216 billion while defense spending *declined* from $73.8 billion to $68.3 billion.

This is a disastrous development in terms of proper resource utilization for two main reasons. The first is that the ability of the people to control spending on this level is far less than in the case of the other levels of government. The second is that their willingness to do so is less.

The change has occurred with devastating force because of the elimination of what had been at least something of a restraining hand on federal spending—the "balanced budget" principle. On the surface, as seen by the reasonably sophisticated observer, there did indeed appear little reason why the budget should be balanced year in and year out. Particularly at times when there was slack in the private economy, a little more spending than taxing would certainly have no disastrous consequences in and of itself. The government, after all, has generally not done anything as crude as simply printing money; spending more money than it took in has been (and is) financed through selling government bonds. To be sure, the dollars that bought these bonds could not also be used to buy bonds of private corporations; but just as those corporate bonds might have financed capital improvements, so one could point to federal projects of at least presumable actual value financed through *government* bonds.

Of course, the projects were seldom as productive, viewed as a long-run investment in human welfare, as private investments in productive facilities; but this was not the real problem with deficit spending. The real problem, far too little-stressed, was that *once the direct link between federal government spending and federal government taxation was broken, even that barrier to wholesale misallocation of resources via federal politics was removed.* Had Lyndon Johnson said, "This is our Great Society program designed to help the poor, and in order to pay for it I am simultaneously proposing a 30 per cent increase in federal income taxes," the outcry would have been enormous and effective. But by then only a few old-line fuddy-duddies made any noise about the once-worshipped "balanced budget," and Lo! the Great Society.

One need only look at the reasons why local spending can be reasonably well controlled by the people to see why under present conditions federal spending can hardly be: (1) The federal government has unlimited taxing power; (2) federal politics tends to involve broad ideological issues and international questions to such an extent that a Congressman is unlikely to be too worried about anger at his voting for a wasteful project, particularly since (3) voters scarcely can be said to scrutinize such projects on a nationwide basis, rather looking at only those that directly affect their areas, where in fact the general stress is on "getting their share"; (4) The voter typically sees little connection between a particular federal program and the payment of personal taxes, so far away is Washington and so huge the federal budget.

It is in terms of willingness to control government spending that probably the most insidious effects of shifting to Washington occur. For our money is going to Washington anyway; every other part of the country is hard at it, trying to get its share or more; the least we can do is try to get every federal dollar we can get our hands on, for *our* area. And if some is wasted here, it's not our money, really, and even the waste probably helps our economy, and the people building even a totally useless pyramid, say, spend their paychecks in our stores, restaurants, hotels and bars; so why worry? And, atrocious as these sentiments may sound, as a practical and factual matter, they are reasonable and sensible sentiments. It would be nice if all municipalities would try to save federal tax money as they would local tax money, just as it would be nice if all labor unions forewent wage increases to stop inflation and improve the country's balance of payments position. But this is the real world, and one had better get his share. We see this all the time. A commission in San Francisco in 1974 approved a new fountain for Market Street (offensive to most aesthetic senses) that would cost $1.5 million; the amount was brushed aside on the ground that 80 to 90 per cent would be federal funds. Only after some doubt was cast on the amount of federal money to be counted on were the opponents of the fountain able for a time to prevail. Over and over one sees one set of standards applied locally to projects that the local taxpayers must finance, and another, utterly lax, applied to programs which the federal taxpayers are to finance.

In a thoughtful article in the June 2, 1980, issue of *Business Week*, Bess Christensen, a concerned housewife in Lompoc, California (it was, by the way, at the bank there that W. C. Fields was the "bank dick" in the famous picture by that name), takes note of the success of her city manager in obtaining millions of federal dollars for such things as a new park, a new city hall, a new water storage tank and flood-control ditch that unfortunately will prevent winter rains from percolating into the soil to replenish the ground-water supply, a new senior citizens' center, and a new community center. All these are things, says Mrs. Christensen, "the citizens don't want enough to pay for directly." But, she writes, "when the question 'Do we need this?' is raised in city hall, the council members say, 'If we don't take it, someone else will.' "

This is the really disastrous thing, in terms of the economic ecology, that galloping federalization of domestic spending has done. It has put it largely beyond not only the power but also *the will* of the taxpayer to control it and has opened the floodgates to the misallocation of scarce productive resources—labor, capital, talent—on an unprecedented scale. No wonder a national public opinion survey, published in mid-December 1979, showed that Americans believe nearly half of federal revenues are wasted, versus much lower percentages for state and local governments!

A rough analogy to the situation we have now, and one that well points up the lunacy of it from the standpoint of the citizens and taxpayers, would involve a group of men in some town—let us say they are fifty members of a local lodge in upstate New York. Their incomes vary, but one thing they all have in common is that they cannot afford to buy everything they would like. They have to set priorities and decide, with the income they have, what they will buy and what they will do without.

A clever fellow among them, named Kallikak, comes up with the idea that they are, all of them, letting themselves and their families down by leaving many important human needs unfulfilled; they are not being responsive to the needs of their families. He has an idea: they should seek money from El Paso.

But how are they to get money from El Paso? The clever fellow has a brilliant plan: first, each of the men will set aside around 30 per cent of his earnings (the best-paid somewhat more, the poorest-off somewhat less); then, they will all, by some kind of majority vote, select someone in El Paso; then, they will send him the money. The man in El Paso will, of course, have to keep some for himself, and to pay for such secretarial help, etc., as he needs; for it will be his job to decide which of the fifty men gets what, of the remaining money. They will be entitled to present their proposals and requests to him; but it will be up to him who is to get what. He may also, to whatever extent he wishes, prescribe how the recipient is to spend it: for example, he may allocate $500 to Sam Zilch, but only on condition that Sam spend it for a new dining room table, and he may reserve the right to approve the style and construction of the table. And this way, each of the fifty will have a good shot at some money from El Paso, to help meet the needs of his family.

Unless the lodge is composed entirely of feeble-minded persons, the developer of this interesting scheme is likely to be lucky to escape without physical damage. Give *our* money to some guy in El Paso and then plead for part of it back, after the guy blows part of it on himself? Have this jerk tell me what to do with my own money, even what kind of dining room table to get? Are you crazy? Can't you see, you jackass, that this "money from El Paso" is all our own money, in the first place? This is the stupidest harebrained scheme I've ever heard of!

Of course, it is. But it is virtually an exact analogy of our current system of federal grants to local governments. The only real difference is that a certain amount of what is paid in is paid in through the "hidden tax" of inflation born of deficit spending rather than in taxes.

As a matter of fact, the situation in reality is worse than in the analogy. It is not only with respect to the funds sent to Washington and then offered back that federal bureaucrats and their fiats can override local judgment (presumably superior *because* local) as to how the money should be spent in the local community, i.e., how resources should be allocated. No, in a variety of ways, cities and states are made to do in their own sphere and with their own funds what the bureaucrat in Washington wants, on the threat of having their federal grants cut off or held up. The current threat by a federal official to cut off funds to communities whose zoning does not provide "satisfactory" lot sizes (see page 000) is a perfect case in point.

"CURIOUSER AND CURIOUSER"

The prognosis is rather iffy in terms of putting a stop to this, although hopeful signs are finally beginning to appear (see Chapter 16). Once it was a cardinal rule of government, because it was a cardinal principle of Republicans and most Democrats, that government had no business in business; and that a project would either be done by private enterprise or not done at all. Thus, President Coolidge vetoed a proposal for federal development of power from tidal action at the Bay of Fundy. Of course, there were exceptions even fifty or a hundred years ago. The land grants that accompanied the building of the transcontinental railroads are an obvious case in point. But in general, certainly on the federal level where the potential for really serious waste of resources exists, keeping the government out of business was the rule.

This rested on two factors, both of which have vastly weakened by now. One was belief in classical capitalistic economics, or perhaps better put, understanding of economics. It was generally understood that a capitalist economy, operating in response to market forces and enlightened self-interest, could not be improved on in satisfying effective demand, that is the real wants and desires of those with money to make those wants and desires, that demand, effective. The capacity of advanced capitalist systems to tackle projects of great magnitude and even novelty, where the potential for profit (resulting necessarily from the expected capacity of the projects to satisfy effective demand) was sufficient, has been immense. The Suez Canal is a case in point; so is the construction of toll roads and bridges; so is the automobile industry; the development of the banana industry in Central America; etc. Wherever the product or service to be provided can be sold to purchasers, but private enterprise is not doing so, it is a pretty safe bet that the endeavor is not economically justifiable.

Government mathematicians can, of course, prepare projections which will show that if the assumptions are correct, then such-and-such a return on capital will be received, so therefore the project is economically viable and taxpayers' money should be used to do it. But if private capital will not touch the project, it is a safe bet that the return shown is not adequate to compensate for the risk that the projections and assumptions will turn out to be overly optimistic, given available alternatives. It is too often forgotten that there is not an unlimited supply of capital, and there is not an unlimited supply of productive resources, which is even more to the point; if capital and men and materials and machines and machine tools, etc., are working on Project A, they cannot simultaneously be working on Project B, so the requirement is not that a return be envisioned from a project, but rather that the return be the best available with that degree of risk. Otherwise, we have misallocation of resources, as with the $57 million "people mover," or the spending of nearly $100 million to turn most of Washington's Union Station into an ill-conceived "Visitors Center," followed by the March 1980 appropriation of $36 million to turn it back into a railroad station, and the other thousand-and-one boondoggles that become known regularly.

The second key factor that in times past kept government out of business was the willingness of our citizens to accept *effective demand* as all that needed to be considered except in very limited humanitarian cases, such as providing a "poor farm" to avert actual starvation. What this ultimately boils down to is whether one believes in the capitalist system or not; whether one accepts its allocation of wealth and buying power among the members of society or does not, i.e., feels that it can be improved on, by mortals. Obviously, even if we understand that a project would be a poor use of resources in terms of satisfying effective demand (demand backed up by dollars to spend), we may feel that "great human needs" will be satisfied by it and go ahead anyway. But let it be well noted that when you start talking about satisfying "human needs" instead of effective demand, you are saying that you believe that the capitalist system has misallocated wealth, or has distributed it inequitably. There is no other basis for this "human needs" talk. We all have "needs" that we cannot afford to satisfy, ranging from a Rolls-Royce or a luxurious country estate to a larger apartment for a large, income-pinched family. When you talk about providing "decent housing" to the poor, you are saying that the poor have not been given a fair shake by the free enterprise system, and that they are more deserving, more worthy, of having their "needs" provided for at someone else's expense than someone else.

It has always been possible for individuals who wish to help the less fortunate (or, often, the less able and/or less willing) to do so and even get a tax break in connection with their charity. But it is a different matter when the immense authority and taxing power of the federal government are brought into play so that the members of Congress can be charitable at the expense of the taxpayers. In times past, it was felt that the free enterprise system's allocation of rewards was fair, and that it was up to the individual who felt that such was not the case in a particular situation to be charitable out of his own pocket, rather than its being government's place to favor some people at the expense of others.

Of course, it was also the case that, since only a very low level of income taxation was politically feasible for a long time after the ratification of the Income Tax Amendment to the U.S. Constitution in 1913, the ability of Congress to misallocate resources was in any case very limited, even had the two factors cited above not been present. But the fact that it was politically unfeasible reflects the other factors rather than being an independent one.

Now both of the two key factors are vastly weakened. Not surprisingly, the Depression shattered a great deal of faith in the working of the free enterprise system. The Depression not only revealed that there can be severe downs as well as severe ups in the economy (with some good lessons regarding money supply and the like), but also it caused many to forget entirely, or simply never to learn, that at any given point in time, given a condition of reasonable health and activity in the economy, all the assumptions about the "invisible hand," as Adam Smith called the free market mechanism, working more effectively than any alternative human hands are still valid. The second factor, willingness to accept the distribution of income and wealth made by the marketplace, has been eroded to a phenomenal extent.

Other factors have also come into play. The programs of the 1930s provided a precedent for government involvement in business and the economy; the experience of the war years conditioned the people to not being able to spend their income for goods of their own choice; Keynes's stress on deficit spending in time of recession snapped the essential link between government taxation and government spending. The truth is that Keynes advocated deficits in time of depression or recession and surpluses in time of reasonably full employment, but once the concept of deficit spending was accepted his fine distinction was lost. Now it is accepted that the federal government can properly involve itself in anything, the people are accustomed to having a huge percentage of their income taken from them in taxes, and the financing of government spending by borrowing—borrowing capital that otherwise would finance constructive, profitable private projects—has become almost entirely accepted.

The results, of course, are absolutely horrible. In the foreign area, of course, motivated by various considerations, some sound and some, like guilt over our prosperity, unsound, the United States has dissipated its resources on a phenomenal scale through various foreign assistance programs. At home, government programs of all sorts have proliferated, pouring billions of dollars down assorted ratholes such as the vast "War on Poverty" programs, so little of whose funds got beyond building a "poverty bureaucracy" to actually helping the poor in any lasting way; ill-planned public housing efforts, for example the famous Pruitt-Igoe high-rises in St. Louis that ended up being demolished; and the inevitable large-scale waste in general. It is difficult to read a newspaper without running across one or another example of such misuse of resources. Donald Lambro, in his book *Fat City* (Chicago: Regnery Gateway, 1980), estimates that over $100 billion of the federal budget goes for programs we would be better off without and lists a hundred such programs.

Two things that are inherently bad about government involvement in what had been the sphere of business are, first, there is no need to make a profit and no real incentive to do so; second, governmental entities do not go bankrupt. The first means that there is no real motivation for efficient use of scarce resources; the second, that there is literally no limit to what a government enterprise can waste.

Take the case of a public transportation system. It can be argued that its operation conveys benefits beyond those which can be measured at the fare box. The elderly are able to live in the city because of the transit system. If there were no system, the streets would be clogged with cars, etc. And yet, it seems odd that nowadays the value of a service cannot be measured in terms of profitability and return on capital as it was in the past. If this new approach is really valid, why should its application be limited to areas such as transportation? It would be as reasonable to apply it practically anywhere, effectively repealing the discipline of the market mechanism. After all, many industries confer benefits by their existence that "cannot be measured in terms of profit." A money-losing factory is still a fine thing for the town in which it is located, especially if it is at least partially owned by outside interests. Should it then be taken over and operated by the government rather than closed as unprofitable? This is no way to run a railroad.

Of course, the theory that a transit system should not be expected to be profitable, or even break even, is wonderful for those who run it. The Municipal Railway in San Francisco has shown an ability to lose larger and larger amounts of money, the losses growing geometrically, for once this idea gets accepted (and those responsible for running governmental enterprises accept it with wonderful alacrity), all pressure for efficiency disappears. During a transit strike a couple of years ago, the city continued to function; and, I dare say, if the whole thing had in a sense been begun again from scratch—selling off the streetcar and trolley bus lines and equipment in a unit, if possible, to the highest bidder, selling buses to the highest bidder, letting individual or corporate entrepreneurs make proposals to the city for routes to operate, and then letting them charge fares, set schedules, and select equipment as they wished—the result would have been a profitable system that would have met the real public transportation needs of the city. For years, so-called "jitney buses" have operated, privately-owned, along Mission Street in San Francisco, providing faster service at higher prices than the municipally-owned buses.

At any rate, the point—which applies to all government enterprises, not just transportation, and is borne out by experience throughout the world, from the steel and coal industry of Great Britain to the railways of Argentina—is that the absence of the profit motive is ruinous for efficiency.

In private industry, if management is not successful in terms of profitability, the board of directors is likely to make changes, and if the board is remiss, major stockholders are likely to take the lead in seeking changes in the board in order to improve the value of their holdings; or if that fails to occur, and there is indeed potential for profit if management were effective, there is likely to be a tender offer by outside interests interested in taking control, changing management, and building up profits and earnings per share so as to make a good capital gain once the price of the shares has risen to reflect the improved results. If the situation is beyond remedy, there will be liquidation, either by the company itself or by trustees appointed in bankruptcy proceedings.

None of this applies in public enterprises. Even if giant deficits were not part of the projections, and of course often they are not, there are no profit-conscious directors or shareholders or alert takeover specialists ready to move; and there will be subsidies from the taxpayers instead of bankruptcy. Thus, while an ill-conceived and/or ill-managed enterprise in the private sector will sooner or later either be shaped up or come to the end of the line so that no more money or other productive resources are wasted, a public enterprise can go on wasting them forever.

The case of the Bay Area Rapid Transit (BART) system is an illustrative case. Financed by taxes to the tune of over $1 billion after being presented to the public as a marvelous new departure in transportation, this system does indeed involve new technology, including highly sophisticated automated train control systems and a gauge of track not found anywhere else on earth. Unfortunately, the highly sophisticated automated train control systems do not function as well as standard 1902 railroad systems, so that service between San Francisco and the East Bay, the main point of the whole system, was delayed for years. But the general manager, a public relations man without prior operating experience, with a record of being arrested for drunken driving, was not replaced for years. The board, a collection appointed by local politicians, included such transportation experts as an officer of the local longshoremen's union. Losses spiraled astronomically, and while hope was finally at one point presented by the refusal of the state to make up more deficits until the general manager was replaced, which was done, in the private sector this enterprise would have been straightened out or have gone bankrupt long before those moves. It continues running up gigantic deficits.

As another instance of what government enterprises can do, we, of course, have the Postal Service; and now Amtrak, of which a May 1974 *Fortune* article said, "Seldom has a company been blessed with such an unexpected opportunity and seemed so determined to blow it." Several hundred million dollars later, in 1980, a government-commissioned study indicated that no real progress had been made in correcting a situation in which several dollars worth of labor and other resources were consumed for every dollar of service provided, as measured by fares paid.

Nor is there any sign that our average politician has learned anything from the myriad failures and notorious waste of government efforts; rather, he votes to involve Washington in one new area after another with heedless abandon. According to a May 19, 1980, Associated Press report, "The House voted today to use federal funds to promote a system of youth hostels in the United States. . . . The bill would set up a one-year National Hostel System Study Commission and give it $5.1 million to work with. . . . There are an estimated 200 youth hostels in the United States now, but sponsors of the legislation say there is no plan to tie them together and no system to make sure that hostels are built in areas where they would be the most useful." It can be pretty well relied on that, once the federal people get a chance to really do their work in this area, the cost of providing a bed for a night at a youth hostel will compare with that at the Waldorf.*

The ghastly pass to which we have come has, of course, the obvious dimension of the proliferation of government operations. Relatively new and less visible, but also most disturbing, is the transfer to the private sector of characteristics of public enterprise. As noted above, if no one straightens it out, a mismanaged or hopelessly uneconomic (perhaps because of changed technology) enterprise finally goes out of business and no further allocation of resources occurs. This is not true, however, if government steps in to rescue it. This is now what has started to happen. The Lockheed case was the first sizable instance of this; it was to some extent capable of being defended on grounds of national defense considerations. Then came the Penn Central case, followed by a government plan for reorganization of the northeastern railroads. In May 1974, the *Wall Street Journal* carried an article suggesting that the taxpayers might have to spend $1 billion to restore the Penn Central system. Now it has been decided by Congress that the federal government should provide Chrysler Corporation with $1.5 billion lest it go out of business. It is indeed ironic that, just as Britain has finally decided that artificially keeping losing enterprises afloat is a futile policy, the United States has taken a major step further into the swamp of that policy.

*This latest example of the mind-boggling readiness to involve the federal government in one new area after another reminds me that, a couple of years ago, my wife and I stopped at a service station on an interstate highway and were less than pleased with the rest rooms. Well, I said facetiously, the next thing you know someone like Teddy Kennedy will propose a Federal Rest Room Standards Act. We amused ourselves discussing how eventually thousands would be employed promulgating standards, devising forms for service station operators to fill out, and driving around the country inspecting facilities. This absurd scenario no longer seems so far-fetched. Nor is it really, in terms of our economic health, all that funny (see "Jobs vs. Jobs," Chapter 4).

If enterprises that are ready for bankruptcy and liquidation are kept alive by the federal government, the forces of the marketplace have been suspended. The Chrysler precedent is an ominous one.

Ominous too are recent developments in using federal funds, money that the federal government has gathered from all over the country—from municipalities and states which have practiced prudent, frugal fiscal management—to rescue cities that have spent profligately rather than practiced fiscal discipline. The New York City case in the mid-1970s set a very visible and large-scale precedent. Here was an immensely wealthy city whose excessive generosity toward its employees and nearly everybody else (it even operates a television station), coupled with a disastrous insistence on continuing a policy of rent controls that was destroying much of its real estate tax base, had brought it to the edge of bankruptcy. It was rescued by, first New York State, and then the federal government.*

Across the continent, the chickens started to come home to roost in San Francisco in 1979; its politicians, too, had bought the support of municipal employee and other unions by similar generosity; in fact, in city employees per capita of population, San Francisco was second only to New York among large American cities. All the while, capital spending, maintaining the city's physical plant, had been starved. The famous cable car system, for one thing, had been run into the ground, and in 1979 it had to be shut down. All it took, however, was a trip to Washington in January 1980 by the mayor, an early supporter of President Carter, and the federal government—the rest of the country, that is—promised a quick $30 million to repair the system.

What effects this openhandedness toward the imprudent, at the expense necessarily of the prudent, will ultimately have on prudence in state and local spending will depend on whether it gets stopped before the whole country gets the idea that in local-government financial affairs it's possible to eat the cake and have it too.

REGULATION IN GENERAL

Particular note was made above of specific governmental interferences whose significance, quite far-reaching, is often overlooked. Reference should also be made to a problem that is becoming increasingly recognized, but which nevertheless continues to grow—that of regulation in general.

*William E. Simon, in his excellent book *A Time for Truth* (New York: McGraw-Hill, 1978), pointed out the total speciousness of the claim by New York City officials that welfare payments to newcomers lay at the root of the city's woes.

One reason so many young people want to go into government or law these days is that they have the idea that the problems of society are to be solved by governmental and legal action. Not, alas, in the former case, by getting government off people's backs and out of their affairs, but rather by further ordering of human activities by laws and regulations; not, alas, in the latter case, by cutting away counter-productive legislation, or by using the law to obtain relief from hindrances and interferences, but rather by passing new laws and more imaginatively and doggedly using existing laws and the courts to more closely circumscribe what people can do in their daily lives.

This whole mentality evinces a mind-boggling degree of economic ignorance. Take, for example, the question of how to fuel power generators and furnaces, a many-faceted problem to which vast numbers of bureaucratic man-hours are being devoted. It is all so complex, as federal energy planners see it. What sort of tax or other incentive is appropriate to encourage conversion of existing equipment to burn cheaper fuels? Should it be different depending on the size, age, etc. of the furnace? What cost figures, now that fuel costs are regulated, should be used in determining what really is the cheaper fuel? Are they the same in different areas of the country? And so on and so on.

What idiocy! By simply allowing prices for different fuels to seek their natural levels, and leaving decisions as to conversion up to the individual furnace operators, the whole "problem" would solve itself, with complete allowance for regional cost differentials, remaining economic life of furnaces, etc. If there was a noticeable disparity between present availability and likely long-term availability of a particular fuel, the long-run price would rapidly approach the short-run price, as fuel suppliers with an eye on profit would hold fuel that was expected to become scarcer off the market in anticipation of higher prices later: and conversely with fuel expected to become more plentiful: they would want to unload it before the glut hit.

The most sophisticated mechanisms for handling price fluctuations have come into being without any government interference or "planning." Look at the system of commodity futures markets. This system makes it possible for a user of soybeans, for example, who needs a secure future supply, to contract now for delivery six months or nine months or a year from now at firm prices reflecting the best judgment of the market as to prices likely to be prevailing at the future times. That judgment is based on crop planting estimates, weather predictions, and a plethora of relevant facts obtained and analyzed by experts, the whole complex system requiring no "planning" by Washington bureaucrats.

In considering the conversion of a piece of equipment to burn a cheaper fuel, the owner of an old and soon-to-be-retired furnace in an area where the difference in cost was slight would decide not to convert it; a brand-new furnace would be dealt with differently (why, the owner would even differentiate based on the cost of the conversion, which obviously will vary with different pieces of equipment and even with the availability and cost of conversion know-how!)

All of this, which a gigantic bureaucracy can regulate and administer cumbersomely and inefficiently, would simply take care of itself in an un-hamstrung economy. Yet this is not the way federal bureaucrats, or President Jimmy Carter, think. One wonders whether Mr. Carter thinks the "invisible hand" is some particularly elusive branch of the Mafia.

One particularly egregious and current case of the folly of the regulatory mentality has been discussed, but such cases, of course, are legion. Consider the federal 55-mile-per-hour speed limit. It is indeed more economical to drive a given car at 55 than at 75 miles per hour; but (1) some cars use less gasoline at 75 than others do at 55, and (2) "time is money." Instead of leaving it to the individual to decide whether it is worthwhile to sacrifice his time for money in his own automobile transportation (as people certainly seem capable of doing, e.g., in choosing between full-fare and standby air transportation), government makes a blanket decision that is the same for everybody, and obviously involves a great deal of waste of the productive resource that is human time.* Much the same is true in the case of federal temperature regulation, which, according to an April 1980 Louis Harris poll, 57 per cent of executives surveyed believe has reduced office productivity.

By subjecting to law and to regulation vast areas of human conduct that should be a matter of free choice and free contract between individuals, government has worked great damage on the efficiency of our economy. Considering that the price mechanism is the most fundamental allocator of resources in a free economy, it is obvious what harm interference with it must be doing.

Even where it does not impinge on the pricing mechanism, the regulatory urge results in burdening business activity. A combination of the regulatory mentality and the natural bureaucratic tendency to expand activities and responsibilities works, at the state and local as

---

*At 50 m.p.h., it takes three hours to go 150 miles; at 75, two. If your car gets twenty miles to the gallon at 50 and fifteen at 75, it requires seven-and-one-half gallons at the slow speed and ten at the fast; you save two and one-half gallons. At $1.20 a gallon, this is $3.00, less than the minimum wage, and considerably less than what most Americans would consider attractive pay for spending an extra hour sitting in their cars.

well as at the federal level, toward the proliferation of regulation. To take another example, California bureaucrats decided, in 1978, that there was a great need to test all bottled water sold in the state. If the label said "mineral water," for example, there seemed to them a crying need first to define "mineral water" and then test all waters according to the standard. They levied a licensing fee on all bottlers selling in the state and decided that "mineral water" had to contain a certain amount of dissolved solids. Then they ordered eight of the twenty-five waters they tested to remove "mineral water" from their labels and ordered Canada Dry Corporation to call its club soda "mineral water." They also banned the sale of Vichy water (sold worldwide for centuries) on the grounds that it had fluoride in it and drinking vast quantities of it for a long time could discolor teeth.

This sort of nonsense, which, according to a June 11, 1979, *Business Week* article, several other states were planning to emulate, obviously accomplishes nothing worthwhile. When we reflect that we have cited only a couple of examples of a widespread phenomenon, and consider the costs, including loss of speed and efficiency involved in coping and complying with regulations (the economist Murray Weidenbaum estimates the overall annual cost at $121 billion), and then the waste of time and energy that their promulgation and administration represent (the Carter Administration budget proposed $3.6 billion for the *federal* regulatory network for fiscal 1980–81, a 33 per cent increase from the previous year), it is striking how massive is the assault on the economic environment caused by today's regulatory mania. According to a study by prominent economists released by the United States Chamber of Commerce in 1980, the regulatory boom of the 1970s has substantially reduced the economy's growth potential. And there appears absolutely no limit to the appetite of a certain mentality for imposing regulation, in order that human activity in the United States may be governed, not by the free decisions of individuals, all over, but by Big Brother. It is as though these people had some sort of rampant addiction, so that the more regulation they succeed in imposing the more they want.

A particularly zealous enemy of free choice is Ralph Nader. He and his movement have battled unceasingly for regulation of this, that, and the next thing, and have helped bring about the subjecting of one area after another to federal fiat. Hiring and promotion are subject to scrutiny by Big Brother for possible racial, sexual, or age bias, and many want to extend that to "sexual orientation" as well. The complexities of regulation of employment practices are so great that at least one enterprising firm mails businesses, nationwide, a brochure offering all-day seminars, at various locations, on "How To Conduct A Lawful Employment Interview" at a $150 per person fee. Federal drinking water inspectors, under new federal standards, are drinking and testing tap water all over the country and giving orders to waterworks operators. Department of Housing and Urban Development officials want adobe brick quality regulated and monitored, and prevent the use of this time-tested, low-cost material for housing Indians in the Southwest where government support is involved. In his latest offensive, Ralph Nader is demanding federal regulation of college admissions testing programs, just one step removed, as Stanford University admissions dean Fred Hargadon points out, from federal regulation of college admissions themselves. There are obviously those who have no understanding of the point of the free enterprise system or of a free society.

4

"Jobs" vs. Jobs

Among the unfortunate things that have happened to the United States over the last few decades is an obsession with "jobs" to the detriment of understanding what makes a job a job. Some people are receiving paychecks for doing their jobs, but others may be more meaningfully be said to be receiving "paychecks" for doing their "jobs." A job is a real job and its existence, and the doing of its work, represent a real addition to real output of goods and services, and make a positive contribution to the overall well-being of the country, when it is created to serve a real need. If I want my house painted and I hire you to paint it, you have a job and you get a paycheck and a positive contribution to the aggregate well-being of the country is made. If my house doesn't need painting but I hire you to do it in lieu of giving you charity, you have a "job" and get a "paycheck," but no positive contribution to the aggregate well-being of the country is made.

It is not going too far to say that a major reason we have a problem with inflation in this country and with our balance of payments vis-à-vis the rest of the world is that there are too many "jobs" and not enough jobs in this country.

To take an extreme case to illustrate the point, there can actually be more real output in the short run with 20 per cent unemployment than with full employment, as well as infinitely more in the long run. Let us say that we are in a deep depression, and 20 per cent of the potential work force is unemployed. All that is being produced is being produced by the remaining 80 per cent, *except* that, here and there, at least some of the 20 per cent are doing *something* that someone wants and is paying them for: odd jobs, part-time gardening or appliance repair, etc. Now let us say that we create a federal program to build useless monuments. We employ the entire 20 per cent, and achieve full employment. The only problem is that now real output is *less:* the useless monuments add nothing to anyone's standard of living, and the real output that the unemployed were doing part-time has been lost. And this is only the short-run damage. Next year, say, when the business cycle is on the upswing, and more people are needed to do productive work, some of the 20 per cent will stay on as before, building useless monuments.

One of the fundamental problems with the creation of "jobs" is that such a "job" generally puts an end to whatever useful activity the person involved was carrying on; another is that the holder of a "job," particularly a reasonably well-paid one, is less likely to be available for a real job when one comes along. The theory with government "job" programs, of course, is that otherwise wasted human time will be used to do something useful; the problem is that things that people really want done generally do not wait for such government programs to come along to get done.

What percentage of the people in the potential work force in the United States are performing real jobs vs. "jobs" or nothing? The question is a good one. The amount of an individual's earnings is not a good indication, although in a utopian free market a person's earnings would pretty well approximate his or her real contribution. In the real world, however, especially a government-regulated world, it does not. The extortionist who collects money for not smashing your windows has not made a contribution to the country's aggregate well-being corresponding to what you pay him.

A look at some of the categories of people who are either idle or with "jobs" (some of which might be called pseudo-jobs—those that perform for their employers a function that *in the circumstances* is useful, perhaps even vital, but which should not need to be performed at all*) gives an idea of the dimensions of the waste. We start with the obviously non-producing: welfare recipients and those on the unemployment rolls and presumed to be totally unemployed; and those "no longer actively seeking work," whether or not on welfare. Their numbers, clearly, are considerably greater than would be expected with less generous unemployment compensation provisions; according to an article in the August 29, 1979, *Wall Street Journal*, "a congressional watchdog agency says unemployment insurance benefits have become so generous that many recipients lack financial incentive to get a job." Hardly surprisingly, the study found "that the higher the proportion of income replaced by jobless benefits, the longer the recipient remained unemployed."

Next, we can look at the retirement rolls. While a retired person who wishes to be retired is generating, and enjoying, leisure, which certainly is equivalent to a good or service for that person, men and women who are compelled to retire when they are able to work and would rather be working represent a wasted human resource. We can add to the waste a substantial percentage of the federal bureaucracy. According to a mid-1979 report by The Joint Economic Committee of Congress, the average government worker wastes or mismanages 10 per cent or more of his share of federal expenditures, and growth in productivity lags far behind that in private business. This does not even consider the fact that many federal employees are engaged in altogether useless activity. Then we must consider a percentage of those in the state and local bureaucracies (smaller than the federal percentage, but substantial nonetheless); and then all the persons employed—as lawyers, accountants, compliance specialists, typists of forms, etc., whose "productivity" is in coping with the requirements of the bureaucracies. Also, to the extent that a person other than the best qualified is employed, to satisfy racial or sexual quotas, we are dealing with at least a partial non-producer; similarly with excessive employees required by "featherbedding" agreements with unions or kept on the payroll for other reasons. A case in point is the almost invariable effort by financially troubled municipalities and school districts, in difficulty largely because of excessive numbers of

---

*An example of this sort of thing is the Madison, Wisconsin, farm equipment dealer cited in the August 20, 1979, issue of *Washington Report*, who noticed that there were six projects on which he was working: "I was suddenly aware that each of these projects was government imposed," he said. "None would contribute in any way to the successful operation of our business." A person who spends all of his or her time on such work could be said to have a pseudo-job.

persons on the payroll, to "save jobs," as though putting people on the payroll is the objective rather than getting a job done.

Nor does it stop here: in the category of those whose labors, when all is said and done, really add nothing to the overall supply of desired goods and services—*real* output—must be included those involved in the production of things desired not in themselves, but required by government. Here we are talking about such things as new federal office buildings, vast sewage treatment and other pollution control equipment that goes beyond what is worthwhile on a cost versus benefit basis, school buses for forced busing, and much, much more.

The present situation in the anti-pollution and sewage treatment areas is a perfect example of the grievous waste of resources that federal "solutions" to problems (or "problems") can produce. Now, no one is in favor of polluted air or water, and if cost is not considered, everyone will favor clean air and water. But in fact the question posed in the consideration of far-reaching federal legislation in these areas in the 1970s seemed to many simply to be, were you or were you not in favor of pollution? It was somehow assumed that we could have very pure air and water as well as unhampered economic prosperity and progress (just as we could have "guns and butter" while engaged in Vietnam), or that any cost would just be paid by the nasty, polluting, super-profitable corporations, or that a real commitment to clean air and water made foolish any attempt to "count the cost."

This latter attitude seems definitely receding now that the costs are being felt and felt with pain.* According to a *Wall Street Journal* article in January 1980, Patrick Caddell, polling for President Carter, found that 49 per cent of Americans favored converting utilities from oil to coal even if it meant more air pollution versus 38 per cent opposed, as compared to 50 per cent against to 35 per cent in favor just a year before, with a similar shift in sentiment about strip mining.

One is inclined to suspect, from experience generally, that leaving pollution to be handled with more discretion at the state and local level, without such far-reaching federal requirements, would have offered better prospects of having reasonable decisions made on the basis of some kind of informal, if not formal, cost-benefit analysis on the part of the people directly involved.

A retired person with a choice of where to live is unlikely to select Gary, Indiana; or Pittsburgh; or South Amboy, N.J.; or Youngstown, Ohio. The *raison d'être* of these cities is, not as sites for good living, but

---

*According to the *Wall Street Journal* (June 4, 1980), American manufacturers spent an estimated $23 billion in 1979 to meet federal environmental standards.

as locations of industrial manufacturing; and in general those who are living there are doing so not so much on account of the amenities they provide as because of their opportunities for earning money. The general consensus in such localities might well be in favor of allowing a fairly high degree of pollution in the interest of economic health. (People downstream, with a different approach, might wish to require a stricter approach, at least to water pollution.)

On the other hand, where appreciation of the beauty of the natural environment is the major cause of an area's being settled, an entirely different attitude would be expected to prevail. Local, or state, or bi-state regulation of intrusion on a natural environment is manifestly not without its problems, as witness the long struggle between conservationists and commercial/casino interests at Lake Tahoe on the California-Nevada border, but at least it permits a degree of adaptation to local needs and conditions. That is sadly lacking in the current pollution control situation, where the requirement is not even that a body of water be left in at least a certain state of purity but rather that treatment of a certain level of effectiveness be utilized. The *process*, not the result, is what is mandated, resulting in ludicrous waste and misdirection of human and material resources. Former Environmental Protection Agency Administrator William D. Ruckelshaus spoke in 1977 of the experience of a company in the Northwest. Their plant, he said, discharged solids into a large river. Since there was little industry in the area and the river was wide and deep, the water continued to be very pure and fish throve in the river. But, under mandate to use the "best practical current treatment" to reduce what was put into the river, under the 1972 Clean Water Act amendments, the company had had to spend $52 million. Although with instruments a difference could be measured (27,000 pounds a day were discharged vs. 180,000 previously), no one could *notice* any difference otherwise. One would have to say that at least the major part of this large expenditure of human and material resources was wasted as far as producing any benefit for which those affected would be willing to pay. But this is only the beginning.

In 1983, Ruckelshaus went on, under the law, the requirement would become the use of the "best *available* treatment." This, he said, would cause a further cost of $50 million and result in an almost unmeasurable further decrease in solids (or in dissolved oxygen levels) in the water at that point in the river. Here, certainly, we are talking about total waste, and clearly not about an isolated instance. When no distinction is made between discharging waste into a huge river and into a small lake that is on the edge of developing serious water purity problems, massive waste is guaranteed.

Federal sewage treatment standards, applied to municipalities with, of course, "federal money" providing most of what must be spent, are another case in point. In the summer of 1978, on a cruise to Alaska, my wife and I disembarked at remote Skagway (population about 600) for a ride on the narrow-gauge White Pass & Yukon Railroad and some sightseeing. We noticed one of the familiar "Jobs for Your Community" signs: about $1.8 million, mostly in "federal funds," was to be spent to provide new sewage treatment facilities.* I sputtered to my wife about the absurdity of spending $3,000 for every man, woman and child in Skagway to improve sewage treatment miles form nowhere. Then, in 1979, a newspaper article caught my eye. The Skagway plant had actually ended up costing $3.5 million ($4,000 for each of the town's by then 870 inhabitants). But it had proved to cost so much in fuel to operate it that the city, claiming continued operation would bankrupt it, had shut it down; federal officials were suing.

The $3,500,000 or so in little Skagway, of course, is only a drop in the bucket. Nationwide, the federally-mandated sewer program represents an estimated $95 *billion*, all told. Much of this will do as little good, in terms of benefit for which any American would be willing to pay, as the Skagway absurdity. A new study by the federal government's own General Accounting Office indicates that for $12 million, Rochester, N.Y. could accomplish what is really worth accomplishing in this area; but what federal agencies are requiring will cost $300,000,000. Again, it is worth pointing out that the scarce resources wasted here—flushed down the sewer, so to speak— cannot provide the goods and services that Americans *do* want, and whose prices, they being in such short supply, are rising so rapidly.

It would also seem clear that the incredible volume of litigation spawned by our laws and their interpretation involves a vast amount of what is, in terms of ultimate results for the economy as a whole, useless work, much of it by very bright minds. Japan has fewer than one-quarter of the lawyers per capita than the United States, a further indication that litigation and lawyering are consuming far too much American talent and time that would be better utilized to meet real needs rather than artificially created ones. Of course, with an annual budget of $330 million for the federal Legal Services Corporation, which finances assorted legal activists, much of the litigation is being

*Those "jobs" can be great for a community that has the luck to be primarily on the receiving end of the "federal funds" pipeline. The voters/taxpayers are generally more averse to people being paid modest sums to sit around idle than to their being paid princely wages to do useless work.

brought about through Washington by the taxpayers, who often must also hire their own lawyers to defend themselves against the lawyers their tax dollars are paying for.

Another area in which much wasted activity is being carried on as a result of impingement by government is the medical, specifically through the open-handed funding of tests and treatment of various categories of poor persons. Case after case has been uncovered, the 1979 California "Medi-Cal" scandals being an example, indicating that this is going on on a massive scale, of blatant profiteering by enterprising and less than entirely scrupulous physicians and other medical entrepreneurs: a person whose medical expenses will be funded by the taxpayer represents a walking opportunity for profit, to be processed through as many tests as feasible—with the public paying. Here too, obviously, the work of processing the patient beyond what is reasonable, is work that involves "jobs" adding nothing in terms of satisfying real wants.

Still another area characterized by much waste is that involving the handicapped. Manifestly, those unable to walk and forced to rely on wheelchairs through no fault of their own are deserving of sympathy. In the current era, given that many of this group are so as a result of injuries sustained in Vietnam, whither their country sent them in a war that ultimately turned out to have been fought for nothing, a war whose uninjured deserters and draft evaders ended up amnestied and virtually pardoned and forgiven, it is quite understandable that there should be a widespread feeling of guilt with respect to these unfortunates, and it is commendable that there has been a general determination to "do right by them." But it is also clear that the rhetoric of "discrimination" has played a part in the policies that have been adopted vis-à-vis the handicapped. If you talk about "discrimination" to a fair-minded American, you get an indignant response. "Discrimination against the handicapped" sounds particularly vile: it suggests hateful people, with, for whatever reason, an animus toward the unfortunate. A one-legged man appears, seeking work as a ticket-seller, a job for which manifestly his crippled condition would not affect his qualifications; a villainous employer smirks and snarls, "We don't want no crips around here."

But of course that is not what "discrimination against the handicapped" is all about. What the phrase actually condemns in today's usage is the quite understandable and reasonable fact that institutions and facilities have been set up with the vast preponderance of the population, those who can walk normally, in mind. If Americans generally are guilty of "discrimination against the handicapped," why, then, so is God, for He created mountains that the handicapped cannot climb and lakes in which they cannot swim.*

It is decent and proper to seek to help the handicapped in every reasonable way, but requirements have been promulgated that impose costs on society out of all proportion to the benefits they provide the handicapped. Many intersections in my city have had four sidewalk corners converted to new slanted surfaces but, while I have seen many bicycle messengers speed up or down these slopes, often imperiling pedestrians, and one or two blind persons confused by the absence of a normal curb, I have never seen a person in a wheelchair taking advantage of the convenience, although I am sure some of the disabled do—somewhere. It has been said that every disabled person could have been provided with a device or an attendant to help with curbs for life for far less than this concrete work has cost. (And this concrete, and the concrete workers, are obviously not simultaneously able to work on housing, which is so high-priced and in such short supply.)

Again, federal guidelines are aimed at requiring public transit buses to be equipped with a kind of elevator to lift wheelchair users onto the bus. A recent study by SPUR (San Francisco Planning and Urban Research Association) demonstrated that free, specially-equipped taxi service could be provided for all handicapped persons for a fraction of what such transit equipment would cost; a similar conclusion was reached by the American Public Transit Association in Washington, which estimated the cost of what is presently required at $3 billion initially and $300 million annually.

While it is argued that the handicapped prefer being in the "mainstream" of life to being provided with special services, it is unquestionably true that, alas, they cannot altogether so be. The conservationists, for example, would never stand still for making the John Muir Trail in the High Sierra "wheelchair accessible," with

---

*The desire to repeal reality where handicaps are concerned has produced such an absurdity as the case of the would-be nurse who was unfortunately deaf. She sued for admission to nursing school on the grounds that the law said that no otherwise qualified person who was handicapped was to be rejected solely on account of the handicap. Except for the fact that she was deaf, she was qualified, reasoned her lawyers; so she could not be refused admittance. Lower courts accepted this reasoning (as presumably they would have accepted the argument of a would-be airline pilot that, except for being totally blind, he was qualified), but the U.S. Supreme Court did ultimately rule that the law meant what Congress obviously intended it to mean (on the assumption that Congress had not totally taken leave of its senses): only a person qualified *despite* a handicap, not one who *would* be qualified *if* it did not exist, was protected against rejection due to the handicap. Whew!

paving and underground power cables to provide battery-recharging facilities. "If wishes were horses, beggars would ride," but in the real world a severe physical handicap must inevitably substantially inconvenience its possessor.

Would it not, then, be more reasonable to provide services on a cost-effective basis to the handicapped rather than to mandate immense expenditures of labor and materials in a vain attempt to repeal disabilities? For what is being spent to rework the sidewalks and vehicles and buildings of this country, equivalent special services could be provided for the handicapped, with regular trips abroad, and enough left over to make a considerable investment in enhanced efficiency and productivity for American industry; the handicapped, one suspects, would themselves prefer such a use of resources.

(Fat people may be our next case of "discrimination": according to a January 1980 Associated Press story, "Fat people are discriminated against almost as much as blacks and other minorities, a Maryland State study concludes . . . fat people are victims of discrimination in almost every aspect of life, from their workplace to theaters and sports arenas." The latter references raise the specter of laws requiring the expense of jumbo seats and aisles in all public places; the former, of an army of federal fat rights enforcers, real heavyweights perhaps, descending on Americans. And if fat people, many of whom simply *do* eat too much, deserve the protection of the law, what about smelly people, many of whom simply *do* bathe too seldom, or ugly people, who obviously cannot be blamed for their condition at all? The person who rejects an ugly would-be spouse may find himself or herself in federal court.)

Those who are occupied in work that ultimately does no real good all have buying power, all right: but all of the real goods and services that they, like everybody else in the country, want have been produced by the rest: those with real jobs. And, as for those, while they are doing all the producing, they have to give up a large share of the fruits of their labor to those who, really, are non-producers.

We should not be unaware, either, of something like the "multiplier effect" we learned about in Economics I. What this means, here, is that where people are engaged in a fundamentally useless activity, there are others, too—those who provide their supplies and so forth—also uselessly engaged. Take a corps of bureaucrats who do nothing but shuffle each other's papers and promulgate troublesome regulations (obviously, while some such bureaucrats do exist, most do at least something part of the time that is of some value; for purposes of making this analysis simple, however, the assumption is worthwhile), and those in private industry whose time is, on the other side, completely absorbed in coping with the regulations. None of these people, by definition, is producing anything by way of a good or service that anyone wants: they all might as well be sitting at home watching television or playing poker.

But they cannot operate without support! They need typewriters, and paper and ink, and office space (which means structural steel, and glass, and concrete, and carpeting and air-conditioning equipment, and ultimately steel and plastics and iron ore), and automobiles (and *their* component parts), and gasoline for their traveling. Since all of these resources (including the human effort involved in the manufacture) ultimately are absorbed in an enterprise that produces nothing, they too, in the last analysis, accomplish, and amount to, the same thing: nothing. As far as the national *output* of *desired* goods and services is concerned, *all* these people and materials are irrelevant. But how much better off we would be had they been channeled into doing something worthwhile, something that produced what the market desired!

We are indeed a rich country, and our very richness, perhaps particularly as seen in contrast to the rest of the world immediately after World War II, has given many people the idea that there is no limit to what we can afford. But our productive resources are not the Biblical loaves and fishes. I remember an insurance man talking to me about insurance for my company. For only such-and-so, we could have protection against this-and-that. And then, we could add whatzis coverage for only a few more dollars. Perhaps I had begun to frown, or perhaps he was just an honest man, for suddenly he smiled and said, "You know, it's easy to get nickeled-and-dimed to death."

What he meant was, of course, that it all adds up. All the generous, hang-the-cost impulses, bringing the taxing, borrowing, and spending power of the federal government into play, end up, finally, with a huge cost in terms of shifting resources away from what the people really want as measured by their willingness to pay.

For all practical purposes, we have too large a part of our population occupied building useless monuments and too few providing the real goods and services that people want. If a way could be found to feed them into real jobs, we would find ourselves with more real goods and services, less inflation, and a healthier dollar.

The ill effects of bad economic policy and concomitant misallocation of resources go far beyond simply making the general standard of living in the short run lower than it would otherwise be. That is bad enough, but, because for political reasons so much of the absorption of resources by government decision has been financed through inflation rather than taxation, people's and companies' assets and income behave capriciously, depending on how they happen to be situated. Hardship is distributed on a rather haphazard basis, largely unrelated to the degree to which prudent planning (as appeared at the time) was done. This has been particularly cruel to our older citizens, who thus become among the chief victims of bad economic policies. The ability to plan ahead is reduced; and the pattern of investment is distorted. Instead of buying new machinery for a plant, which in a normal environment would, let us say, be the most productive use for a small factory-owner's capital, the money is put into leveraged real estate or gold, because the owner sees those alternatives as more profitable during rapid inflation. Such distortion of the capital-formation process will haunt us in future years.

Our situation is very serious; as Harvard economics professor Otto Eckstein told a conference on U.S. competitiveness in May 1980, "The forces of decline can be stemmed, but if we fail to come to grips with our problems, the U.S. will wind up taking a back seat to more disciplined countries such as West Germany [and] Japan." In addition to its other bad effects, inflation appears to be, understandably, diminishing the propensity of American individuals to save; in 1979, the average U.S. household saved around 3.5 per cent of disposable income, down from 8 per cent in 1975: these figures compare with 14 per cent in Germany (16 per cent in 1975) and even higher rates in Japan.

Tax policy, of course, is not irrelevant here; according to Malcolm Forbes, writing in the March 31, 1980, edition of *Forbes* magazine, Dr. Horst Schulmann, the head economist of the German government, told him that our low savings rate was due to our tendency to tax *income*, rather than *spending*, to such a great degree. In most industrialized countries, for example, interest income is exempt from taxation to a large extent (up to $5,000 a year in Japan); here, on the other hand, it is not, and, again opposite to what is typical elsewhere, the borrower can deduct his interest payments from his taxable income: which facts obviously, even apart from rapid inflation, would encourage borrowing more and saving less. (But it is not the purpose of this book to present what would necessarily be a lengthy and technical discussion of tax policy.)

As a further effect, the lessened productivity fostered by bad policy and the general adversary relationship of government toward business that is prevalent in the United States, with the concomitant relatively unwell economy and sick dollar, have in turn begun impinging on the country's will and ability to maintain the kind of military strength necessary to keep the world safe for American interests: one hates to see defense spending increased when we are already economically pinched. In turn, this is producing further adverse effects on American economic health. The matter of the United States' position in the world will be analyzed at some length in later chapters.

5

Arcadia Revisited

J ust as conservationists, or natural ecologists, are wont to paint a picture of untampered-with nature, in all its beauty and ecological/environmental integrity, functioning properly (clear streams, healthy fish and birds, rich humus, etc.), so it may be refreshing for a moment, before going on to examine what has happened to our socio-political environment, to pause and consider the pleasures of an unspoiled economic environment:

Business entities seek profits, filling human needs to do so. There is little government spending and most of what is spent is funded and controlled at local and state levels. The presumption therefore is that whatever resources government diverts from the market economy of the private sector are properly and efficiently used in accordance with the wishes of the people. Capital for expansion of industry and development of new products and industries and companies, and creation of jobs in a changing, dynamic economy, is relatively plentiful, as there is no constant deficit spending, funded by selling government securities to the capital markets in competition with private companies, to siphon off the savings of the people into financing wasteful government projects.

Where needs grow, industries grow, and geographically and in terms of industry, capital and workers flow toward growth areas. Capital and labor are compelled to move in response to changing needs, for long-term subsidies to inefficient operations and locations don't exist. It is a wrench at first, but thereafter people are glad they moved. It is somewhat like the man roasting uncomfortably in the sun but not able to screw up the courage to dive into the cold lake; if he is pushed in, he is done a favor: after a few seconds of discomfort, he is used to the water and able to swim with complete enjoyment.

Managers with vision are blessed with increased profits and greater ability to attract capital, while their opposites suffer diminutions. By a natural, continuing process control of productive resources is shifted to those most able to use them well in satisfying the needs of the consumers.

Ingenuity is constantly finding ways to improve productive processes and meet the demands of the marketplace; thus, particularly with an expanding population, workers' time becomes worth more and more to employers and real wages rise. Workers' pay also increases as businesses expand and they progress in their jobs and to more responsible ones; some, after saving their money, begin their own businesses.

If there is a substantial supply of unskilled workers, their wage may be depressed, but at the right price their services will be bought, and as they become more familiar with their work and acquire skills and good work habits, their services fetch more and more, just as Andrew Carnegie progressed upward from a bobbin boy in a textile mill. The unskilled will not stay idle rather than work because the available level of welfare is less attractive than any work (and welfare for able-bodied people is considered, except in the most unusual circumstances, a disgrace); as a result, they keep and increase their self-respect and the devil does not find work for their idle hands.

There are unions and there are strikes; but, as employers are not helpless against union power, union demands are relatively moderate, and industries are not ruined or made unable to compete on the world market by union demands, particularly as it is known that the government and taxpayers will not step in to foot the bill for an excessive settlement. This strengthens management's resolve even where a union is relatively unreasonable. American goods compete effectively at home and abroad, except, of course, in such areas as may contain inherent efficiencies abroad; resources, human and capital, shift out of those areas into more promising efforts.

With innovation, efficiency, mobility of resources, and the avoidance of the diversion of resources to unproductive uses by government decision, domestic industry competes so well in export markets in relation to that in countries suffering, like Great Britain, from the opposite conditions, that the currency gains increasing value against others in the world instead of being devalued, so that American citizens are able to buy other countries' products on more favorable terms, thus further enhancing their standards of living.

Not all these things, of course, happen instantly. There are delays; but the market mechanism inherently rewards efficiency, punishes inefficiency, and draws resources toward their most effective uses, all without any decision by government or any motivation being required of the persons interacting in the economic environment other than their own long-run self-interest. In fact, the process is probably well on its way, in particular cases, before bureaucrats could even become aware of a "problem" for their attention.

To those who say that this economic environment model is too far from current reality to serve a useful purpose in being considered, we can reply that an unspoiled natural environment is also far from the current reality in many places in this age of polluted rivers and beaches, erosion, junkyards, billboards, proliferating subdivisions, freeway congestion, and all the rest. Yet to the natural ecologist the contrast between what could be, at least to a much greater extent than now, and what is, is one of the most powerful goads to action. If only this river could be clear and clean again! The ecologist rises up in anger against those who have made it a sewer.

So has the economic ecologist the right to remind us of what might be and to feel anger at the damage that has been wrought. In fact, in terms of the desires and wishes of the people, the harm wrought by the fouling of the economic environment perhaps exceeds the harm done to the natural environment. The over-cutting of trees may at least have provided people with desired housing. The plants that pollute the rivers generally do so in the course of producing products desired by the people. But what has the creation of the tremendous human waste of idle millions accomplished? Again, many Americans are quite insensitive to natural beauty and would much rather have a new car and a polluted river than a clean river and no car, so that to them the concept of a damaged natural environment is meaningless; while considerably rarer, one suspects, are people indifferent to their own economic welfare, which is what suffers from damaged economic environment. When we consider things like crime on the streets and in people's homes, it becomes even harder to contend that the natural environment, though important indeed, is a matter of anywhere near as *much* importance, as far as the "greatest good of the greatest number" or the welfare and happiness of the American people as a whole are concerned, as the economic and socio-political environments.

6

The Socio-Political Environment

There are environments and environments. In nature there are desert environments, alpine environments, plains environments, and Arctic environments; in one large state, such as California, the total environment might be said to consist of a group of separate environments surrounded by ocean and mountain barriers. Some environments are, from a human point of view, far preferable to others. Looking at the economic environment a few pages back, we assumed that there is a general preference for the lush fruitfulness of the capitalist, free-enterprise environment over the desert of socialism. Furthermore, that environment is still basically the one this country is organized within, and there is no sign that there is a widespread desire to switch to the socialist environment.

This is important, for what is out of place in a temperate fertile environment may be appropriate and "ecological" in a desert, or in the harsh conditions of Siberia. It is relevant, as mentioned at the beginning of the preceding discussion of the economic environment, to remind ourselves of what basic economic environment—the capitalist system—we are living in, and why this is the best economic environment. What is "ecologically sound" initially depends on the nature of the environment. Which is to say that the social and political environments cannot be studied in isolation from the economic. Someone might be tempted to say that, even though something in the political area is unecological in terms of the economic environment, the lack of fit is of no concern because the existing economic environment is not the one he wants. But the economic environment cannot be so lightly dismissed. The determination of what is appropriate in the political and social environments cannot be made *in vacuo* as though the economic environment does not exist or is not, as in fact it is, a given. There is a basic commitment on the part of the country as a whole to the economic system that produces the most goods for the greatest number, or the greatest good of the greatest number, and the general view is, rightly also, that capitalistic free-enterprise is that system. The socio-political environment, then, should be one that fits with the economic environment and complements rather than works at cross-purposes with it. To take an extreme example, an economic system of industrialized worker collectives will not work well with a feudal social and political structure.

Similarly, if occupations crucial to the success of the country or of its economy are low in attractiveness, offering inadequate material and non-material rewards to attract the best people to those areas, the country will suffer. In terms of the economic health of the capitalist countries of the world today, there seems a definite correlation between economic health and the position of people in business. In Great Britain, the notable "sick man" of major industrial nations through the 1960s and 1970s, executive compensation, after taxes, is abysmally low; furthermore, the old prejudice against being "in trade," as opposed to holding a government position or being a barrister or gentleman farmer, say, still seems to carry weight: being a businessman is not a prestigious occupation.

In West Germany and Japan, which have notably buoyant economies in 1980, business people do well financially, and also are regarded generally as holding positions of prestige.

In the United States, which is not a basket case like Great Britain but certainly is not in the same economic category as Germany or Japan either, business owners and managers are financially well rewarded—this aspect of the economic environment is functioning quite well—but occupy positions of relatively little prestige in the eyes of the opinion-molding, "intellectual" group; one indication of this fact is the lack of appeal of business to bright young people. The Harvard Club of New York City sends its members brief descriptions of the young people who receive its scholarships each year. The descriptions include the career goals of the recipients. Some want to be doctors; almost all want to be lawyers* or government officials; hardly any intend to go into business. The "class notes" section of the *American Oxonian*, journal of the American Association of Rhodes Scholars, similarly shows that practically all this intellectually elite group have become professors, lawyers, or government officials. This is a sign of a poor mesh between the economic and socio-political environments.

---

*Lawyers, lawyers: at the rate people are becoming lawyers, one might fear massive unemployment for lawyers in the future. But no: behold the ever-growing flow of new government regulations and laws. We already have more lawyers per capita than any other country in the world, but we have a long way to go before a 1:1 ratio between lawyers and others is achieved and *everything*, from adding a shelf in the corner grocery store to pruning the hedge, requires legal advice.

When we were discussing the health of the economic environment, or, put another way, the functioning of the economic system, it was possible to discuss quite objectively what was and was not "ecological" in terms of its success or failure in conducing to the assumed, given, understood goal of an economic system: satisfying human wants—taken to mean, by general agreement in our economic system, satisfying effective demand. But when we talk about the "socio-political environment," meaning, in a way, the rest of the features of organized society that affect our lives and well-being, we have a different situation. To be sure, given the economic environment and, particularly, the premises on which our economic system is based, one can, in some cases, see clearly whether or not a given law of institution is consistent with the economic environment in terms of whether its underlying premises are or are not at odds with our system of capitalism. The popularity of lawyering, and the unpopularity of business, as careers for bright young people have already been noted. For another example, a court decision (part of our socio-political environment) to the effect that an employee may not be dismissed for bizarre garb or disrespect to his superior would seem to rest on a *Weltanschauung* at odds with the free enterprise idea that freedom of choice, including the freedom of employer and employee mutually to choose each other, is the best and fairest thing in the economic sphere, and that outside intervention is bad on principle; therefore, one would be justified in saying that this was unecological in terms of the overall environment, the socio-politico-economic whole.

But it is not always possible to judge a small piece of the socio-political environment, which in the aggregate plays such a large part in Americans' satisfaction or dissatisfaction, in terms of whether its underlying premises conflict with those underlying the capitalist system, our basic economic environment. It also makes sense to judge the health of our socio-political environment, and whether something is ecological, on the basis of correspondence to what Americans in general *want* in their socio-political environment, as expressed in various ways. One piece of legislation may be at odds with the economic environment although in line with what Americans want in their political environment; another may be "unecological" in terms of both.

Before setting out to analyze how today's socio-political environment fits what Americans as a whole desire, it might be well to review a few basic facts about human societies that are fundamental to what kind of environment makes sense to reasonable people and why. In the first place, no society can function without leaders and led; fortunately, in the light of this fact, the breadth of human abilities is such that some lead and others naturally follow. While all persons may be "equal in the eyes of God," this is a theological concept. "Equal before the law" is a legal concept, and also a fine and just one. But "equal," in terms of this life and its needs, people most assuredly are not. Some are very short, others very tall; some strong, others weak; some stupid, others brilliant; some evil, others virtuous; some honest, others not; some industrious, others lazy; etc.

Yet so pervasive has the idea of "equality" become that one almost hesitates to enunciate these truisms, anticipating a cry that this "oversimplifies" (what a common refrain whenever an accurate generalization is made!); that it overlooks the role environment plays in molding the individual; that with proper work, like perhaps a ratio of two full-time college-trained social workers per "lazy" person (nothing less has worked yet), the characteristics of natural inequalities can be effectively combated. Well, in the first place, even when the areas where individuals can be remolded are removed, plenty of ineradicable inequality remains; and in the second place, this society does not consider it a profitable use of human and material resources to sacrifice, say, the full time of one highly talented individual to obtain a marginal improvement in one or two or five shiftless persons. The input is excessive in relation to the output. Thus in the real world the inevitable existence, the continuing existence, of fundamental inequality among persons in character traits as well as in physical and mental characteristics is a fact of life.

If all humans have immortal souls, we all may look forward to an eternity in which we all receive our just deserts, based, presumably, on virtue; compared to which eternity our brief span on earth counts for a mere moment. The capacity of persons of the humblest abilities and position to distinguish themselves in bravery, selflessness, etc., presumably relates thus to future eternal rewards. But it does not relate to ability to run a business. Here and now, position cannot be apportioned based on a determination of how good, in the moral sense, a person is (for one thing, how would this be determined, and by whom?). Nor can the fact that all, or nearly all, human beings have two legs permit each to have an equal position and income in life. Utopias have been tried; they all have failed, and even in utopias there is generally a leader. As far as normal human society is concerned, there always have been and always will be leaders and led, or, if not, then soon rulers and ruled. Whether the country is China under Maoism or Russia under state socialism or Germany under Nazism, or Uruguay under liberal democracy; whether we deal with a country or with a garden club or a work gang, there are leaders and led.

A sound socio-political environment is one in which people accept their positions on at least a temporary basis and plan to move upward in the system. That is, a man who is a janitor does not attribute his position to a malevolent system and think that he has as much right to run the company as the board of directors. Rather, he may tell himself that he will do better when he finishes his night school courses; or that he will start a little store when he has a bit more money saved up; or, he should have stayed in school; or even that he likes the job because it is not demanding, or it is just the best job he is capable of getting (which is very likely near to the truth, or he'd probably be doing something else).

Inheritance is a hard thing for some people to swallow, since what you inherit has nothing to do with your own deserts; but then, neither does the brain you are born with, and, looking at the matter from the other end, one would be pretty angry if he were told that he might not give his property to his children; that the state would take it instead. In a society where property has meaning, where property is property, it can be disposed of freely, and the rights of inheritance or giving are inherent. Constructively, people should accept this as the breaks of the game. Naturally, if one is on the bottom it can be very comforting to think in terms of having had bad breaks, and, human nature being what it is, a high percentage of those on the bottom will at least half believe this. What gets dangerous, though, is when they not only feel they have been dealt bad cards, but also feel that the whole deal is crooked. If people are being *told* that by "opinion molders," and if laws are passed that make no sense except on that assumption, then we not only have things being done with the socio-political environment that are unecological with respect to our economic environment, but also we have a bad ecology on the socio-political environment's own terms, unless a majority of the American people share such ideas.

For a society to flourish, rewards and punishments need to work in a coherent way to encourage behavior that is generally approved as constructive and to discourage the contrary. We have come a long way from this in this country today.

7

The Rape of The
Socio-Political Environment

We discussed in earlier chapters the far-reaching negative effects, in terms of waste of material and human resources, of governmental tampering with the economic environment. The waste of human resources is more than just an economic matter. The idleness and despair that it represents have created a tremendous threat to the peace of our cities and the safety of the people and their property. Unfortunately, the socio-political environment has been more of less simultaneously subjected to changes which make this threat even worse, while being amply undesirable otherwise.

EXPANSION OF CRIMINALS' RIGHTS

Having created a Frankenstein's monster through meddling with the economic environment, the social engineers proceed to take off its chains and chain, instead, its keepers. To an extent unheard of before in this country and unknown anywhere else in the world, court rulings have made the apprehension, conviction, and safe keeping or disposal of the criminal incredibly difficult.

If all the rulings on procedure with suspected criminals that were made under the Warren Court (1953–1969) bore in an apparent way on the goal of preventing the innocent from suffering unjustly, matters would not be so bad. But, rather, these generally can only work to help a guilty person escape. The "third degree" obviously is not to be defended; a weak person may indeed confess to avoid a beating. But will he confess to a crime he did not commit merely because he was not told that he had the right to remain silent? Or because he was not told that he had the right to see a lawyer? Or because he was not told that, if he couldn't afford a lawyer, one would be provided for him free? This strikes one as rather far-fetched.

The respected Commonwealth Club of California, a *pro bono publico* fact-finding organization, a few years ago completed a two-year study of the effects of court decisions on law enforcement, listening to experts of all shades of opinion. Here are some of that study's conclusions:

There can be no question but that delay in the courts and the exclusion of evidence caused by court decisions have resulted in the acquittal of guilty persons and in the avoidance by criminals of conviction for the actual crime committed, with resulting sentences also not commensurate with the crime.

No case has come to the Section's attention . . . involving conviction of an innocent person pre-*Miranda* under circumstances giving reason to believe that under *Miranda* this would have been avoided. [The reference is to *Miranda vs. Illinois*, where the warnings about the right to remain silent, to consult a lawyer, and to have one provided free were required.]

In terms of compensating beneficial effects upon society as a whole, there has been no perceptible improvement in police-community relations, or in public confidence in the administration of justice: on the contrary, that confidence has generally declined with the view becoming widespread that the safety of law-abiding citizens has been sacrificed to legal quibbles and concern for the criminal. These areas involved hoped-for beneficial effects, but the Section has been unable to find evidence of such effects.

. . . recent court decisions have had a significant adverse effect on the efficiency of law enforcement. This has been particularly pronounced in the case of the exclusionary rule decisions and less pronounced as far as the *Miranda* decision is concerned. The exclusionary rule decision must be regarded as a significant hindrance to justice. . . .

The authority of the trial judge to require civility in the trial court has also been eroded by appellate decisions.

Matters have gone so far into the dream world of strange and complicated little games that many people seem altogether to have lost sight of the most basic purpose of a court trial: to determine whether a person is guilty or innocent of the crime charged. Instead, the emphasis is on successfully navigating the treacherous passages, where the slightest error may well mean that an appellate court will set a vicious criminal free on a technicality.*

On January 13, 1980, the *Los Angeles Times* syndicated a fascinating article dealing with a young Illinois man who had been arguing with his mother for years over division of his late father's sizable estate.

*At times I cannot help shaking my head in bewilderment over the question of what rational motivation can be governing the courts in such cases. For example, in the Braeseke case in late 1979, the Supreme Court of California overturned the conviction of a young man who had, after the full Miranda rigamarole, confessed *twice* to cold-bloodedly murdering his parents and grandparents for their money. As a dissenting justice saw it, the majority were apparently adopting the position that *no* voluntary confession could be used in evidence.

One day, he got his mother to come up to a twelfth floor hotel room he had rented, supposedly for a party to celebrate his engagement, knocked her unconscious with a baseball bat, and threw her out the window, with predictable results.

This is all rather clear, not just from the blood-splattered hotel room and such evidence as was provided by persons who saw the mother's body slowly lifted out the window after a sufficiently large opening in the glass was smashed out, but also because when the son was being treated at the hospital for his cut wrist, a neatly written reminder list covering the preparation and execution of the murder was found.

The thing that struck me in reading the article was not so much that the filial son's attorneys had high hopes that his conviction could be reversed on appeal (he was convicted even though the money arguments, the motive, were kept from the jury) on the grounds that finding his murder reminder list constituted an "illegal search and seizure" (that sort of thing has become commonplace), but rather that the writer of the article, while focusing at length on the propriety of the prosecutor's theorizing that the murderer's failure to allow for bleeding, rather than proving that the bright young student surely could not have committed the crime, stemmed from exposure to television's oversimplified versions of murders, nowhere displayed the slightest perception of concern that, if an obviously guilty monster of this sort could hope to be freed on such a technicality, the criminal justice system had completely lost sight of its reason for being.

It is well to bear in mind, first, that the exclusionary rule was unheard of in this country until quite recently, and obviously its absence did not, over the centuries, bring about a descent into some sort of "police state"; second, that no other country has the rule; and third, that *by definition* it results in keeping truth, facts, away from a jury to the benefit only of the guilty. This rule, the product entirely of judicial creativity, is absolutely senseless.

In the early 1970's (how swift is American criminal justice!) there was a particularly horrible series of crimes in Texas; no fewer than twenty-seven young men had been murdered. The chief culprit, apparently, was a homosexual sadist. One of his helpers, who was found guilty of involvement in six of the murders and who murdered the chief sadist in August 1973, was found guilty the following year in the case of the six and sentenced, reasonably appropriately (not to death, for at the time the Texas death penalty, thanks to the kindly U.S. Supreme Court, had been rendered invalid), to six consecutive life sentences. Then, four years later, in June 1978, came news that a higher Texas court had overturned the sentence: no mention was made of any question as to the man's guilt; rather, the presiding judge had apparently not been receptive enough to the motion that the site of the trial be changed, on the grounds that too many people in the area had become familiar with the facts.

Another facet of the form-over-substance trend of recent court decisions, given the objective of determining guilt or innocence, is that, instead of an open-and-shut case simplifying and accelerating the trial, such now represents a tremendous challenge to the judicial authorities. To look at another case, it seemed fairly clear to all that former San Francisco County supervisor Dan White shot Mayor George Moscone and Supervisor Harvey Milk; he had the motive, he had the gun that did the job, he was there, and he confessed to committing the crimes. Given all this, which should have facilitated the trial in terms of the objective of determining White's guilt or innocence, it boggled the mind, before the trial, to read that legal authorities were seriously shaking their heads about the problems of assuring White a fair trial in the light of, in effect, the widespread knowledge of his guilt. (Ultimately, under hot-off-the-press California Supreme Court insanity rules, White's lawyers successfully used a "diminished capacity" defense: we may shortly get to the point where everyone who commits a heinous crime is presumed, *ipso facto*, insane and hence immune from conviction and punishment.)

One might joke about the man who murdered a referee on the field at the Harvard-Yale game, in front of 70,000 fans, and then was released scot free on the grounds that he couldn't get a fair trial; but it is dangerous to do so: today's *reductio ad absurdum* is tomorrow's *fait accompli*. In fact, a Des Moines judge recently dismissed a drunk driving charge against a man whose "breathalizer" test proved him inebriated, on the grounds that he had been too drunk to "knowingly render his consent or refusal to the . . . test."

Coming, as noted above, at a time when the disrupted economic environment has yielded an underclass of idle and discontented persons, this disruption of the socio-political environment—in the form of rendering the conviction of criminals vastly more difficult—has seriously compounded the problem as far as its effects on liveability in the country and city are concerned.

POLLUTED RIVERS

In a free-enterprise economy, the lesson each person should be taught is: work hard, study hard, see what those who are well off do, and learn from them; seek to improve yourself. Obviously, the rewards people get should then be proportional to their progress.

But look at the current scene. Obviously, one principle people have been told to operate on is, "work hard, save, better yourself, and achieve better things for your children." In the newspapers a while back 'there was a report by Congresswoman Edith Green of Oregon based on reports from her constituents and others. It appears, the gist of the report indicated, that if you are rich, you will of course have no trouble getting your children a good education. If you are poor, or, better still, a poor Negro, your children will not only be actively sought by the best universities, but assistance will be available to an impressive extent. But if you are a member of the hard-working middle class, very likely having worked your way up from poverty yourself, you are out of luck: you cannot afford to pay the tuition, there is no government aid available, and anyway, the best universities are not particularly interested in your children. They are not fashionable right now.

This is no exaggeration. Just about all of the most prestigious private universities in the country have adopted programs designed to attract poor blacks, including those not, by usual standards, qualified for admission, and to make their path at the university easier, even to the extent of eliminating grading and offering "black studies" majors (which presumably qualify a person to teach "black studies" to others knowing no better). But for every less-qualified Negro admitted, a more-qualified student—white or black or brown—must be turned away. The steelworker's son is not in vogue at Harvard, and he will not in any case be offered a major in Polish studies if he is lucky enough to get in.

What is true in education is also true in housing. If you are poor, the government will help you rent or even buy "decent housing," and if you are well off you can buy that house in Greenwich, Connecticut; but in between, you are on your own with limited resources.

Again, take busing. The precept was, work hard and save and move to a better neighborhood, and your children will be able to go to good schools. Not so fast, fella. Your children will be put on a bus and shipped into the heart of the black slums, while people who, if they do have school-age children, are unlikely to have them in public schools themselves, tell you that it is culturally enriching for your children to have this opportunity. There are more likely to be a few poor Negro youngsters at the expensive private schools, recruited and provided with scholarships, than white truckdrivers' children.

Busing, of course, in terms of sheer idiocy, has to be considered as in a class by itself. Whatever might be accomplished by busing slum blacks in limited numbers into a middle-class white school where the former standards, both intellectual and behavioral, were maintained, is irrelevant to the real world, where the busing of large numbers of blacks and a collapse of standards are involved, in turn producing an exodus of white pupils and, in reasonably short order, a citywide duplication, in reasonable approximation, of the former black slum school, with the poor of other races thrown in, and with all of busing's logistical and parent-teacher communication difficulties. And then people begin wailing about "resegregation," and complaining that the schools are not adequately integrated, overlooking the fact that you can't have integration without whites.

Any attempt to maintain standards so that a school remains one that middle class parents will consider suitable for their children is an uphill battle. If standards of behavior are maintained, the immediate result, given the undenied conditions and behavior patterns of the Negro slum school, will be a disproportionate incidence of suspensions and other disciplinings of the Negro students, which liberals will denounce as "racism." As spokesman Peter Holmes of the Department of Health, Education and Welfare warned a few years ago, taking note of this (to him) very sinister phenomenon, "as the worst offenders are identified statistically, they will become the subject of a full scale investigation that will lead either to satisfactory corrective action or legal proceedings." In liberal San Francisco, the school board took the bull by the horns and courageously eliminated suspensions, with predictable results in terms of safety in the schools.

Attempts to maintain academic standards are no easier. If for no other reason than relatively poor socio-economic background and previous education in the presumed-inferior slum schools, it would be surprising if Negro youngsters were *not* disproportionally represented in the various types of "slow track." Big deal! So what else is new? And yet this is a state of affairs with whose existence the liberal mind has great difficulty coping. Newspapers run front-page stories about the amazing discovery that black students in the "fast track" are fewer proportionally than their overall numbers in the New York public school system and devote great attention (this is big in California as this is written) to the "excessive" representation of black children in "EMR" ("educable mentally retarded") classes. For an integrated-by-busing school to maintain the same academic standards as it had, and to treat its pupils in a color-blind manner, is to be forced to be constantly on the defensive against charges of "racism," and it is a rare educator who will choose all the harassment and annoyance rather than quietly give way.

Studies of what has actually happened with busing tell the same sad story, whether the locale be Pasadena or Dayton: no improvement in black learning, dramatic declines in achievement levels in the formerly predominantly white schools, exodus of white pupils from public schools and of white families from the city—"resegregation." It happens over and over and, as can be seen in the light of the foregoing analysis, virtually inevitably. Busing means the ruin of a city's public schools and a severe dislocation of the city's ethnic balance. Furthermore, it costs great sums of money, wastes pupils' time and much scarce fuel, makes cooperation between parent and teacher much more difficult and virtually impossible in many cases (it is, ironically, in the case of the poorest families, where active cooperation by the parent is most likely to be urgently needed, that inability of the parent to afford transportation to the faraway school is most likely to prevent parent-teacher conferences), and is fraught with dangers to children from missed buses, traffic accidents, inability to walk home in the case of an emergency, etc.

And yet it goes on, ordered by judges of, it would seem necessary, incredible obtuseness. Yet, in July 1979 the United States House of Representatives narrowly failed to muster a majority for a constitutional amendment to ban school busing for racial balance. Some who voted against it claimed that they did so because, while they were against busing, they did not want to "tamper with the Constitution." It is, of course, possible that they really are that stupid, but that is a fairly tall order. After all, it is obviously the judiciary who are *presently* tampering with the Constitution, as it was written and intended to be and understood to be throughout our history. Furthermore, there are many constitutional amendments on many subjects, from the number of terms a president may serve to the presidential succession, involving far less urgent need in terms of harm to the country in their absence. Nor, with the recent great enlargement of the federal judiciary and President Carter's pattern of naming liberal, activist judges, is it rational to expect the problem to go away through more judicial restraint.

Mark Twain once wrote, "He was a Congressman. He was a fool. But I repeat myself." Still, in the case of most of the Congressmen who explained their vote on the busing issue in terms of tampering with the Constitution, it is safe to assume, not that they were really so stupid, but rather that they were terribly afraid of being called racists. While the principle has not, so far as I know, been openly enunciated, a basic sign of being a racist, as many see it, is to be against something that a large percentage of blacks are for, and, while perhaps not a majority of their race, very many blacks, including National Association for the Advancement of Colored People leaders, are strongly in favor of busing.

The same is true of white liberals. Now, I ask, shaking my head, how can any sane person, unless perhaps he is a very cynical bus-company owner, be in favor of busing, in the light of the obvious facts about what it does and does not do (such as in an important Pasadena, California, study) to improve the education of the black students? That is a difficult question, and answering it is not essential to the thrust of this chapter; yet one hates to leave such an intriguing question unanswered.

There are people who, through ignorance of the facts or sheer stupidity, or some combination, honestly believe that busing is a good thing. But what about those who know the facts and are not stupid? Here the real answer, one suspects, is subconscious rather than conscious. In the absence of busing, most Negro children, because of housing patterns, go to predominantly Negro schools, which on the whole are very bad, certainly noticeably worse than the average predominantly white public school. This disparity in school quality gives many Negroes, as well as white liberals, a feeling of indignation and outrage. While busing may not help the black kids, it sure will wreck the white kids' schools and eliminate that intolerable disparity. Shameful though this motivation is, so much so that those so motivated—who may not realize it or be willing to admit it even to themselves—would never acknowledge it publicly, it is human enough, and one strongly suspects that it is a major element in the pressure for busing. (In the case of some very cynical left-wing politicians, there is also the fact that white exodus from the city, caused by school busing, offers them the prospect of increased political power.)

Or, going back to the ways in which people in our country today are being given the anti-work message, take Small Business Administration loans. The SBA was set up (here again, an interference with the economic environment) to assist small businessmen who, although deserving of loans, somehow were unable to obtain them through the usual channels (the question obviously arises, if profit-motivated bankers allocate loans to the best-qualified borrowers, how it was that it made sense for government to divert funds from the private sector to lend to those not considered to qualify; after all, a point often overlooked, capital resources are not unlimited, and what is spent one place is not spent somewhere else). In the past decade, however, the program took a very different turn. If you were a struggling small businessman, black or white, SBA funds were harder to get than if you were a Negro without business experience who thought you wanted to go into business. (After this practice had been tried for years, an August 1979 *Fortune* article reported that the percentage of those receiving SBA help in this last category who ever became self-sufficient was abysmally low—7 per cent.) Similarly, the proliferation of projects, some supported by government and some by well-meaning big businessmen, to finance blacks in starting businesses ignores the non-black whose qualifications may be better. Well, the feeling seems to be, he can just make it on his own; these other fellows *need* help.

The whole recent fashion of being obsessed with the problems of the poor is another case in point. "Work hard and pull yourself out of poverty." This implies that it is possible (and who can really say it wasn't and isn't?); and, if we reflect a minute, it must follow that if struggle will do it, then if someone is lying on the bottom, though indeed he or she may have had "bad breaks," it *does*, to some extent, reflect on the person.

But who is the darling of the press, the media, the pulpit, the liberal politician? Is it the struggling middle-class man, perhaps black, born into a slum tenement in the era of a far fewer "programs for the poor," who has achieved a home and is burdened by heavy taxes and all kinds of problems, including crime, not of his making? Is the stress on easing his burdens, including the crushing burden of welfare and swollen property taxes? Ha. No, it is the impoverished slum-dweller, especially the black one, especially if he whines bitterly about all his problems being someone else's fault. This impoverished slum-dweller can, it seems at times, do no wrong. If he commits crime, it is because of his poverty and despair. If he drops out of school, it is not because he is perhaps a bit lazy or stupid; he has to drop out to find work. But if he has no job, that is because he is a forced dropout. Of course we cannot fault him for not going back to school or taking part in a program to learn a trade, because we have failed to reach him and he feels alienated from a racist society. If he is violent, what can we expect, cooped up as he is in the despair of a filthy, garbage-strewn tenement? If he throws his garbage out the window and makes a mess of his home, it is because he understandably resents having to live in old, deteriorated housing. If he is violent even though he lives in what was initially a neighborhood of detached one-family homes with lawns (or space for them) like Watts, you have to understand that there still is despair and bitterness in his heart. William Sloane Coffin, the well-known Yale University chaplain, has made another step forward and uses the term "Violence No. 1" to refer to poverty:

thus violence by the poor becomes "Violence No. 2," a reaction we are supposed to understand.

If our example makes a shambles out of his brand-new, taxpayer-provided public housing, it is because (a) it is still not good enough, and he resents second-class housing, or (b) you cannot blame him or attempt to impose middle-class values on him, or (c) he lacks pride of ownership, so the solution is to give him homes that will be his own property. If he is given title to a home and still makes a mess of it, either (a) or (b) apply or (d) his payments were too high in relation to his income and so he felt cheated.

Thanks to what has been done to the economic environment, it *is* hard for the unskilled to find work. But most do find it; the unemployed are a minority even in Harlem; which proves that it is possible to do more than sit around wallowing in misery and casts doubt on the qualifications for martyr's status of those who do.

If our friend the slum-dweller squanders his earnings or his welfare check on liquor or "sharp clothes," instead of saving for the future, it is the only way the poor man can escape from the drab misery of his existence. If he preaches violence and hatred of all white people, it is what one must expect from centuries of oppressive white racism. Every time there is a black riot, the newspapers soon after carry extensive analyses of why it happened, and the reasons always are (no matter how surprising they may seem at first in the light, say, of the fact that the affected area always seemed a rather pleasant neighborhood) that the police were racists and there was "smoldering resentment"; and that there was despair and alienation and a feeling of hopelessness and some incident triggered it off. The rioters are always understood, and the solution is always more programs to help them and an attack on white racism.

The middle-class white, on the other hand, is in a different category. If he resents Negroes moving into his neighborhood, it is not that he has an understandable fear of seeing what he worked hard for deteriorate into a slum such as he was born in and in which he feels most Negroes live; no, he is a vicious bigot motivated by fear, ignorance and hate. If he is against busing, it is not out of natural concern for the welfare of his children, but because he is a racist. He is either "waspish" or, more likely, an "ethnic"; a "Middle American." Instead of being the backbone of the country that he once was told he was, he seems to have become an undesirable element, an obstruction in the way of the plans his betters have for the improvement of the poor. It must be bewildering.

Even more bewildering, in the light of what he had been taught, must be the situation of the middle-class Negro. "Work hard, save money, respect those above you and learn from them, and you too can enjoy the good life." A good life marred, granted, by discrimination, but still, compared with black slum life or life in Africa or Haiti, the good life indeed. But who from the black community is it who is adored by the media, who is it who is listened to with rapt attention by white intellectuals and highly educated people? Whose faces appear on the television screens and the magazine covers? Is it prosperous Negro lawyers and businessmen who have come from the slums and shown what hard work and ability can do? No, it is the hate-preaching firebrands in African garb, young boys or girls on trial for murder, ex-convicts calling themselves ministers of this or that, and the like. The middle-class black finds that he is now an Uncle Tom, beneath the contempt of enlightened people. He was told to think of himself as an American, not as a Negro; now he is condemned for having "abandoned his people in their struggle."

Dr. Thomas Sowell, a black economics professor, has well described in his book *Black Education: Myths and Tragedies* (New York: David McKay, 1972) some of the scandalous excesses perpetrated in this area, with some college recruiting programs deliberately seeking out black students at the bottom of the eligible range while passing over capable blacks eager for education who have readied themselves for college by their own hard work. For example, Cornell denied admission to a black girl with college board scores in the top 1 per cent, saying "her cultural and educational background does not indicate deprivation to the extent necessary for qualification as a disadvantaged . . . student. In spite of the fact that both of her parents are laundry workers, she has been adequately motivated by them to a point where she has achieved academic success and some degree of cultural sophistication."

Not too long ago it was contended that all people must be treated equally regardless of race. But first came court orders requiring busing of students purely on the basis of their race, to "correct racial imbalance," and now we have out-and-out discrimination against whites, as in the case of Marco DeFunis, who was only admitted to the University of Washington law school after getting a lower court order. The Supreme Court in April 1974, in the *DeFunis vs. Odegaard* case, sidestepped the question whether discrimination against white people was constitutional on the ground that since DeFunis by then had been admitted and graduated the question was moot. Carl Rowan, former United States ambassador to Finland and a Negro, subsequently wrote in his syndicated column to the effect that, if a university administration felt that the presence of a certain percentage of blacks, Chicanos, Indians, etc. in an educational institution made for better education, why then, surely that was within their discretion—an interesting foreshadowing of the Supreme Court's *Bakke* decision. One can imagine what the reaction would have been at the Supreme Court and with Rowan had the contention been that, if a state university administration felt that their students would get a better education with no blacks in the school, or only a very small number, *that* was within their discretion!

We may indeed be reaching the point where the white people of the country, who do comprise the overwhelming majority of the population, will have, and will acquiesce in, second-class status.* For that is the meaning of "affirmative action" quotas; there is no reasoning, no matter how sophistic, that can obscure the fact that a positive quota for one group is a negative quota for the remaining group. Racial discrimination in the United States apparently is constitutional and proper, provided it is directed against white people; just as sex discrimination is right and proper provided it is discrimination against men.

Perhaps it will soon be contended that, in order to make up for past oppression and escape the tyranny of the majority, and to stop it from being politically profitable to cater to the baser instincts of (white) mankind, all certified members of minority groups should have five votes in all elections. I hesitate to put this idea down, as this year's *reductio ad absurdum* has in recent years had a way of being fulfilled within a couple of years.

Things have gotten rather hilariously absurd where race is concerned. In the late 1970s, a New York judge got around to ruling that employers could not question prospective employees as to whether they had criminal records on the grounds that, since blacks were statistically more likely than whites to have such records, the question was racist in nature. Along a similar line, when, in September 1979, police in National City, California, south of San Diego, began to crack down on juvenile delinquent "lowriders" (who drive cars altered so the bodies are closer to the ground), the head of the Committee on

---

*The 1978 *Bakke* decision of the U.S. Supreme Court, in fact, sanctions the idea of second-class status for "non-minority" Americans; they may properly be discriminated against in admission to educational institutions, so long as the discrimination is not excessive: while there must not be spaces set aside for which a white applicant cannot *possibly* qualify, it is all right to hold his color against him to *some* extent in the admissions process; the *Weber* case (1979) sanctions the establishment of second-class citizenship for whites by private employers.

Chicano Rights, one Herman Baca, "said the anti-lowrider campaign
. . . is 'racist in nature' because most of the 170 arrests . . . involved
Chicano youths. 'They are doing this just because the majority of
young people cruising the streets have a mode of dress and drive a
certain type of vehicle and because they are Chicano,' Baca said,"
according to the *Los Angeles Times*.

The idea that if a certain type of antisocial behavior is especially
prevalent among a particular ethnic group it can no longer be combated without one's being guilty of racism is mind-boggling in its
absurdity. This was, of course, the basis for John Lindsay's attack on
his New York mayoral opponents in the 1960s (they were against
"crime in the streets," most of such was committed by blacks and
Puerto Ricans, so his opponents were racists), but one didn't realize
that this sort of idiocy traveled well.

This principle also appears to apply to the quirks of favored minority groups, as witness the 1979 Detroit court decision that speech
patterns of slum blacks, such as in "He go to the store," were not just
bad English but rather represented a new "language system" (Black
English).

A variant of the foregoing concept is that customs, practices, and
procedures carried on with complete legality from time immemorial
can be attacked as somehow illegal or unconstitutional if they seem to
affect the average minority group member adversely relative to the
average white, whether or not any such motivation was present and
regardless of the reasonableness and sufficiency of non-racial considerations. In 1980, according to a United Press dispatch early in the
year, "The Justice Department is studying suburban zoning laws . . .
civil rights chief Drew Days said yesterday. Laws requiring lots to be
minimum sizes . . . may be discriminatory by pushing housing costs
too high for most minorities to afford new homes, the assistant
attorney general said. He suggested that lawsuits threatening to cut
off federal Community Development Act funds could be filed. . . ."
In other words, if residents seek to preserve the character of a desirable suburb by preventing, through zoning, the dividing up of a given
lot into little lots, each with a mini-house on it, they are going to be
accused of racial discrimination, the tortured reasoning being that
since the average "minority" is poorer than the average white, anything that precludes the construction of cheap housing units consti-
tutes racial discrimination. Taken to its logical conclusion, this would
preclude any zoning or housing standards, since obviously the
cheaper it is to build housing, the more likely it will be that the poor, a
disproportionate percentage of whom are "minorities," can afford it.

In 1975, the New Jersey Supreme Court had eliminated one step from the reasoning process by simply holding, in effect, that no municipality had the right to be zoned so that there was not "an appropriate variety and choice of housing for all categories of people who may desire to live there."

It has also become very difficult for employers to use standardized tests to select employees. The·*Duke Power Co.* case,* decided by the U.S. Supreme Court in 1971, hit that utility hard for using tests in hiring for menial jobs which measured skills far beyond those required to do the job for which the people were being initially employed as well as requiring high school diplomas. No blacks had qualified for the menial jobs on the basis of these requirements, and the Court concluded, perhaps correctly in the light of the fact that prior to the 1964 Civil Rights Act, subsequent to which the utility had instituted the requirements, it had had a policy of hiring only whites for the jobs in question, that the real purpose of the tests was to prevent blacks from being hired rather than to select menial workers with potential for eventual promotion.

Even so, with the burden of proof on the employer to show that any test is "job-related," as rather narrowly interpreted, a considerable burden is placed on the most completely "color-blind" employer who merely wishes to select the best employees, with *some* consideration—certainly not unreasonable—of their growth potential. There is reason to hope that employers will be permitted some reasonable degree of discretion in this area; in 1978, the U.S. Supreme Court affirmed a decision allowing South Carolina to use teacher competency tests even though they disqualified 83 per cent of black applicants versus 17.5 per cent of white.

Another new idea is the no-Negro-ever-deserves-to-be-fired-and-anyone-who-does-so-is-a-racist principle implicit in black rage at Andrew Young's eventual but long overdue separation from the Carter administration. This principle intervened in politics across the continent in San Francisco in late summer 1979: a black woman was fired by the city's Commission on the Status of Women, a commission consisting entirely of appointees of the ultra-liberal Mayor George Moscone, who had been murdered less than a year earlier. According to the commissioners, she would have been fired earlier had she not been black. But the two blacks on the commission immediately resigned in protest; an opponent of the current mayor charged that the firing was a "step backward into the 19th century"; black leaders said

*Willie S. Griggs et al. v. Duke Power Company, 91 S.Ct. 849 (1971).

they would oppose the mayor unless she got the woman reinstated; the mayor, Dianne Feinstein, declared that she would replace the commissioners if they did not reinstate the fired woman; and, lo and behold, she was in fact speedily reinstated.

A year earlier, when it was found that San Francisco's parking meter collectors had typically been working something like half-time and personally retaining a major share of their collections, and the Negro city and county tax collector, under whose jurisdiction the collectors worked, was suspended from his duties, a prominent local minister of the same race, the Reverend Amos C. Brown, thundered, "Again the sinister forces of institutionalized racism have sought to destroy recent political gains of the black community."

Obviously, if members of one ethnic group are to be immune from being held to normal standards because their forebears were poorly treated, the same logic should apply to others similarly situated; and also in reverse where appropriate: thus, Irish, Armenians, German and Polish Jews, and Chinese, to name a few, would have virtual lifetime tenure, while Turks, Germans, and descendants of the Russian and English ruling classes would be fired capriciously from one job after another. Complications will arise where, for example, a person is of mixed Armenian and German ancestry: would one cancel out the other? But such problems will be well within the capability of a vast new federal bureaucracy to handle.

Or take youth. Not too long ago, young people were told, "Study hard, learn from your professors and from the body of accumulated knowledge; learn too from those older and more experienced than you, so that when your turn to run things comes, you will be ready." People have done this, only to find that the principle has apparently shifted; knowledge and experience are not needed and youthful good intentions, unsullied by experience or knowledge, are the most important thing. "Listen to our young people!" And if the rest of the country does not do their bidding, why, they will lose faith in the system, and then they will turn to violence, and it will all be our fault, so hurry up and do what they say. During the Nixon Admimistration, a delegation of college presidents called on the President of the United States to tell him that he must make quick and drastic changes in a vital area of foreign policy and war because their students demanded it and would become violent on their campuses otherwise.

Even in the case of immigrants to this country, things seem to have become topsy-turvy. "Learn English, so you can become a citizen and become a real part of your new country," was fundamental advice for generations. But now all sorts of little "bilingual education" fiefdoms have developed in the public schools, in many cases encouraging students to remain in a predominantly non-English-speaking culture. As far as exercising the right to vote is concerned, it would have seemed fundamental that a person unable to cope with ballots or other forms in English ought not to be encouraged to vote; how could he make an intelligent choice if the only input he had came from contact with foreign-language persons and publications? You certainly do not get a ballot in English if you become a citizen of Mexico, or of any other non-English-speaking country.

Yet, under the provisions of a little-noticed portion of the recent Voting Rights Act, the absurdity of which *San Francisco Examiner* columnist Guy Wright has well exposed in a series of columns, this is now required in the United States. Federal bureaucrats, with their typical zeal, in fact are threatening San Francisco with a lawsuit if it does not embark on a massive program including an "outreach plan" to find and register Chinese- and Spanish-speaking voters, and large-scale hiring of polling-place officials who speak those languages, through "community groups." Great opportunities for patronage and getting more Democratic votes; but isn't knowing English a requirement for citizenship?

The response of public and private authorities to violence, to law-breaking, to unruly conduct and uncouth demands, also conveys messages that are not conducive to the smooth and orderly functioning of our society. Particularly in the 1960s and 1970s, students, minority members, civil servants, municipal employees, to name only a few groups, all learned, not that obedience to the law and courteous requests work best, but rather that rioting, threats, destruction of property, violence to individuals, and striking in violation of the law are what get results. They may—as may all—get the impression that, in general, those in authority, private and public, have lost confidence in their right to sit where they sit and to enforce the laws and rules.

There was a particularly striking instance of this phenomenon in Washington, D.C., according to an Associated Press story on November 8, 1972:

After seizing three truckloads of government documents, militant Indians today began leaving the Bureau of Indian Affairs building which they occupied almost a week ago.

White House aides have agreed to set up a task force to review Indian needs.

"We have destroyed the BIA," said Dennis Banks, national field director of the American Indian Movement. . . .

Banks made his comment as the Indians began dribbling out of the building in twos and threes. Many were seen carrying off native American artwork and Indian artifacts that were on display in the four-story structure. . . .

The Indians . . . lately have tightened their security around the building.

White house aides Leonard Garment and Frank Carlucci and Indian negotiator Hank Adams signed the agreement last night after about six hours of negotiations. . . .

Yesterday's negotiating session was scheduled after a U.S. District Court ordered the federal government to oust the Indians.

Paralysis of the federal government in the face of seizure of its property is, of course, nothing new; in 1971 a group of war protesters seized the Statute of Liberty and held it for days, we recall; and the 1969 occupation of Alcatraz Island, which left the island thoroughly vandalized, lasted for months. Vandalism, by the way, was the order of the day at the BIA, too; halls were defaced with paint, garbage was strewn, and bathroom fixtures were smashed. Just as in the other two incidents noted, there is no sign that the trespassing vandals in the BIA caper had any punishment to fear.

Obviously, what people are in effect being told now is not constructive in terms of the effective functioning of the social, political and economic system, to say the least. Something is radically wrong with the socio-political environment. The new precepts seem to be, "Don't work, for if you do the fruits will be taken from you and given to those who do not; and it is no disgrace, no disgrace at all, to be on welfare (the *New York Times* reported in August 1971 that a federal official informed the State of New York that requiring able-bodied welfare recipients to pick up their checks personally constituted "harassment"); remember, this is a fundamentally unjust society, and those who have do not deserve what they have, just as those who have not are the really deserving.

"Don't study, for that is a waste of time and intuition is the real source of solutions to problems; Don't obey the law, unless you feel like it, for the laws, like the whole socio-economic system of the country, are unjust; Don't respect or emulate those above you, for they probably got theirs undeservingly and dishonestly, and we respect rebels, not toadies (a black person may get the idea that he is a traitor to his race if he works for a white person); Demand, don't ask; Yell, don't speak; Threaten and riot, for this is the way to get what you want."

These precepts are not conducive to the constructive progress of the society. What they are conducive to, particularly combined with the economic dislocations noted earlier, is a general breakdown of

76   TAMPERING WITH THE MACHINERY

civil society, or movement in that direction, such as has been witnessed in this country in recent years.

What has been happening is that the politico-social environment has been moving toward a state quite out of tune with the still basically capitalist structure of the economic environment. People who live by the "new precepts" discussed above are not likely to be of much use to themselves or others within the basic framework of the country; and even partial infection with these ideas will have its deleterious effects.

Many young people in recent years (although this phenomenon appeared to be receding as the 1970s ended) went in for "dropping out" of society altogether, via the drug or revolution route, others devoting themselves to a variety of "meaningful" and "do-good" activities: legal aid for the poor, harassing reports, via "task forces," on companies and industries and sections of the government; social work, especially in the plethora of new programs spawned under the Great Society. Others, who take jobs, nevertheless feel alienated from the profit-oriented business world but need to eat. Among the blacks, already suffering from excessive unemployment thanks to the disruption of the economic environment, the malaise is proportionately greater. The way to get attention, for some blacks, as well as other minorities, appears to be to scream and to burn, and to threaten; for many of our young of all races, the way to make money appears to be in crime, drugs, pimping, or latching onto a spot in a federal "anti-poverty" program.

While it would be an exaggeration to say that such new precepts of life are taking over, or are shared by a large percentage of the population, they have certainly made significant inroads upon American life. In fact, a great deal of what at first glance may appear isolated instances of deterioration in the quality of life actually are directly related to this force:

- Crime, both in the individual cases and in the mass case of mob violence;
- The belligerent, unfriendly attitude of so many people in subordinate occupations, and of so many young people and minority group members;
- The polluting of the streets and countryside with hippie "lifestyles"; which many of the alienated find so congenial;
- Failure of authorities to enforce the laws;
- Soaring welfare rolls;
- Soaring taxes;

- Unwillingness of unemployed people to accept service-type and other entry-level jobs;
- Disruption of the peace and quiet of the citizenry through a constant news diet of crime, demonstrations, demands, and threats;
- Disruption of the school system, through busing, lack of discipline, orientation toward the slowest, and the resulting cuts in taxpayer support;
- Tension and hostility between and among the races; and, very important,
- A growing feeling of anger and frustration among a large percentage of the population—both those who are convinced that the system is rotten and desire to bring it down and those who still believe in it but see it deteriorating.

In keeping with today's predominant glorification of the poor, the federal government (and to a lesser extent many state and local governments as well) has become the vehicle for the redistribution of wealth and income. I have already discussed the phenomenon of resource misallocation in connection with the economic environment. Taking effective demand, that is, demand backed up by persons willing and able to pay for a good or a service as the determinant of how resources *should* be allocated, the government's intrusion into the economic life of the country can be viewed as a misallocative of scarce resources. Looking at the socio-political dimension, however, the same intrusion in many cases takes on the character of a Robin Hood operation, which is one reason for the presently emerging vehemence of middle-class Americans' reaction against government spending.

While favored groups, including industries with "clout," have been major beneficiaries of government intervention in the economy, much that has been done has basically been done with the idea of shifting purchasing power from the presumed less-deserving better-off to the presumed more-deserving poorer-off segments of society. Thus, in tangible as well as intangible ways, a message that militates against thrift and industriousness is being communicated. Those who sit around and wallow in poverty will become eligible for this, that, and the other program—all distributing buying power to them at the expense of the productive citizens.

More and more, the concept has been spread that (and this necessarily rests on the belief that the free working of the marketplace does not fairly allocate rewards *and* that government can improve on its fairness) people are entitled to all sorts of things—first one, then another, and so on—that they cannot afford. Food stamps, from small beginnings, have become a major form of income redistribution. Cheap gas and electricity for poor people—"lifeline rates"—have become widely accepted. Government-supported cheap medical care—another shift from haves to have-nots—is already widespread and there is strong support in Congress for a federal system of national health insurance. We are starting to hear about "energy stamps" and "gas stamps" and "heating stamps," the principle apparently being widely accepted that the ability to go driving around the countryside in one's own automobile is some sort of inherent human right. (While planners agonize today about the failure of Americans to utilize public transportation, they shy away from letting the market mechanism force people to use it based on their income level. In the 1920s and 1930s, the heyday of transit, relatively few could afford regular use of private automobiles, so that the use of public transportation was widespread and providing the service by private enterprise comparatively profitable.)

Similarly, having to keep warm clothes on indoors in the winter is an indignity that the poor should no longer suffer. Perhaps we shall next have clothing stamps (which, of course, will be good at Brooks Brothers), furniture stamps (perhaps not good, at least initially, toward purchases of period Chippendale settees), and dining stamps. These things are generally presented in terms of whether one is or is not indifferent to the unhappiness of the poor, which makes legislators easy prey for one such proposal after another. What is forgotten is that the funds required are not made available from heaven. Each such "stamp" program means taking from those who have more to make the particular subsidy available to those who have less, and each is based on a presupposition that those who have earned more do not deserve part of what they have earned while those who have earned less deserve more: it is an imputation of unfairness to our free market economy.

Most private charities, which must convince their contributors that they are worthy causes, do a more efficient job than government in assisting the truly deserving, even where the basic necessities of life are involved, but a conviction that government ought to engage in redistribution in real life-and-death areas is not unreasonable: it is hard to argue that anyone deserves to die of starvation, even if that is what the free play of market forces would assign him. However, when people start to advocate redistribution in areas where comforts, and even luxuries, are involved, they are forgetting what the free enterprise system is all about. If government can take my property away so that someone will not starve, that is one thing; if it can take my property away so that someone can go for drives in the country, someone is operating with a very limited concept of private property and a very exaggerated concept of the proper role of the state.

The lamentable effects on rational resource allocation of galloping federalization of nearly every area of government have been discussed in relation to the economic environment. But they have another dimension, the political. Instead of being responsible for their own affairs, in the tradition of individual freedom and home rule that had so much to do with the founding of this country, all Americans, with respect to their city, county, and state governments, have become, with lightning speed, something close to wards of the federal government in Washington.

It is sad to see frugal and self-reliant townspeople decide to go along with a useless project that Washington bureaucrats think their town should have on the principle that the money might as well be wasted locally rather than somewhere else in the country. It is sad to see those who took care to live within their means presented with the example of profligate New York City rescued by the federal government, the ants' reserves raided to provide for the grasshopper.

It is even worse when federal money—the people's own money— is used as a lever to destroy the autonomy and independence of state and local government, going far beyond questions of how the "federal money" itself is to be spent. Do what we say *here* or we hold up your money *there*.

This virtual blackmail is going on all the time. A group of black policemen sues a city, alleging discrimination in promotion and demanding a monetary settlement for each of them. Discussion by the city fathers (and mothers) on settling the suit has to do less with whether it has merit than with the fact that the federal government is holding up millions of dollars of grants (in areas not involving the police department at all) pending resolution of the suit.

The activist federal bureaucracy is on the march across the country, with its guidelines and standards and rules and regulations. Not only governmental entities but educational institutions, business firms, indeed every entity involved with federal funds and federal contracts, faces being told to carry on its activities satisfactorily to Big Brother or be penalized financially.

An article in the February 1980 Stanford University alumni newspaper, entitled "Med School Fails to Meet Minority Goals," stated that "Stanford failed to meet its own affirmative action goals for hiring Medical School faculty, a federal report charges. Other schools within the University met faculty hiring goals, but failed to meet their targets for retention and promotion . . . according to an amended "show cause" notice from the San Jose Regional Office of Federal Contract Compliance Programs.

"Based on a three-month review by two compliance officers on campus, the University was cited for 15 deficiencies. Stanford Affirmative Action Officer Santiago Rodriguez . . . expressed confidence that satisfactory remedies can be developed for the deficiencies cited."

Early in 1980, until reversed by President Carter, a deputy secretary of energy, John Sawhill, had directed Department of Energy. personnel to avoid scheduling meetings and events, wherever possible, in states that had not ratified the Equal Rights Amendment, intending to punish economically those states of the Union which, exercising their Constitutional right, had voted against ratifying that amendment.

What such things are doing to the self-reliance and independence of the American people can only be speculated on. It is alarming that we seem so willing to acquiesce in our own money being used to take away our feedom of action and having our lives regulated from afar in area after area. And no detail is too small for Washington's attention: according to an April 12, 1980, article in the *Honolulu Advertiser*, "the state Board of Education has voted to allow only fruit juices, fruit nectar or fruit drinks to be sold in school vending machines. The Board's action . . . follows a federal rule, effective July 1, that prohibits the sale of sodas at schools until the end of the last lunch period."

JUDICIAL USURPATION

Nothing has served more to turn the socio-political environment of the United States upside down than the judiciary, in particular the federal judiciary. Many good books have been written from a lawyer's standpoint discussing one "bad law" case after another—Professor Raoul Berger's *Government by Judiciary*, for example. Here we can only sketch in broad outline what has happened.

We have all heard, probably, that the word is not the thing, appearance is not reality, and things are not always as they seem. For example, a student of comparative government could, by working from the Soviet constitution and documents relating to the legislative bodies of the U.S.S.R., discuss such things as the guarantees of free speech, religion, etc., that each Soviet citizen possesses, the democratic method of selection of the legislature, whence power flows, etc.

But few care to trouble themselves with forms that lack all real substance.

So let us, looking at substance rather than form, describe our American system of government today, in the words of a fictional foreign observer of high perception. His analysis might run as follows.

The United States of America—which is rather a misnomer, the country being for all intents and purposes a unitary state—enjoys a monarchical form of government of somewhat unique characteristics. Supreme power in all domestic matters is vested in a supreme junta (called the "Supreme Court" because its function was once judicial and it still retains some judicial functions; compare the "General Court" of Massachusetts, the official name for that state's legislative body); its nine members hold their offices for life once appointed by the president of the country. Their appointment is subject to confirmation by a senate elected two from each state, but such confirmation is automatic except in the case of known conservatives (persons lacking respect for the supreme authority of the junta).

Under the supreme authority of the Supreme Court, the country is divided into eleven "judicial districts," each with its own three-person minor junta, also holding office for life, once appointed by the president; and, each such district is further divided into districts under the rule of persons known as federal judges. These also, once enthroned, hold office for life.

A considerable degree of autonomy is possessed by the three-person juntas and by the individual judges within their respective fiefs, since the process by which an order (often called, in an archaic term reflecting the originally judicial origin of these offices, a "decision") is submitted for concurrence or reversal by the higher authority (an "appeal") is extremely lengthy; thus, even if one of the subordinate rulers decrees in a manner contrary to the views of those higher up, it may be years before the decree is overturned.

With respect to certain local matters, each of the fifty "states" (hence the name, United States of America) is subject to its own rule. In each state, the authority is in the hands of the local "supreme court," which functions similarly to the "Supreme Court" (junta) in Washington. However, the federal "judges" can overrule anything done by a state supreme court by pronouncing an ancient formula to the effect that a "federal constitutional question is involved," and then proceeding to order whatever they see fit.

The authority of judges is absolute. They can do anything from prescribing the details of the operation of a local school system to having prisoners freed, halting executions, setting hiring policies for fire departments and banks, changing the system of taxation, etc., etc. They can summarily imprison individuals or subordinate public officials they deem inadequately responsive to their orders or lacking in proper respect for their high office.

There are a variety of legislative bodies in the United States, both nationally and in the individual states, but they have no real authority, as the sovereign courts can, at will, repeal or "throw out" any legislation they pass of which they, for any reason, disapprove. Again, the ancient formulas require that they do this "in the name of the constitution": that is, they must pretend that whatever they veto is contrary to the nation's constitution, a document written in the eighteenth century, the true meaning of which the judges decide as they go along, not being bound by prior interpretations or the clear intent of those who wrote it or those who subsequently amended it (in the case of the state supreme courts, they may refer either to the same national constitution or to the constitution of the particular state); similarly, they must pretend that whatever they order is required by the national constitution. (This is sometimes difficult for them to do with straight faces, as when they purport to find something required that no one had ever for two hundred years dreamed was required, and things totally contrary to which had been done for two hundred years, but those "in the know" are not disturbed by the seeming inconsistency, as they are aware that it is only a ritual, a formula, that is being followed.)

In some states, the people have in theory the right to enact legislation directly, but this is no more meaningful than the apparent right of legislatures to pass laws, as the courts are free to "throw out" anything displeasing to them as the sovereign power. *Non placet.*

The right to present requests directly to the sovereigns is reserved to a special caste known as lawyers. In each state, lawyers are members of what is called a bar, which is not a saloon or a drinking club but the organization of all the lawyers in that state, who must belong in order to be able to deal directly with the sovereigns ("admitted to practice" is the term). Needless to say, these lawyers greatly value their special relationship with their sovereigns, and, in the case of any criticism directed at them, tend to rally to their defense, accusing any critics of *lèse-majesté* ("an attack on the judiciary," or "bringing the judiciary into politics").

Under this system, important decisions of public policy are excellently shielded from influence by the people. While initially a popularly elected president or governor does make the appointment, and there is a certain amount of influence by senators in the case of federal judicial appointments, and sometimes there is the need to be kept in office by popular yes-or-no vote, perhaps at twelve-year intervals, in the case of state judges, the popularly elected administrative officials are generally so preoccupied with other matters that no extensive analysis of how their appointees are likely to rule is made, particularly since many, especially among those who are not lawyers, actually believe that the judges only administer the laws in the light of the constitution. Furthermore, in any case, once appointed, the judges are sovereign, and as an additional factor, a president's or a governor's judicial appointments are almost never made an election campaign issue.

One reason they are not is probably the immense respect Americans feel toward their rulers. In a society of hail-fellow-well-met egalitarianism, the rulers occupy a very special place. Not being subject to election, as are ordinary officials such as governors and legislators, sets them apart to begin with. Then, too, there are the trappings of their high sovereign office. They wear robes; when they enter their majestic audience chambers to hold court, a functionary calls on all present to rise in deference. Their orders are always referred to as being "handed down," as from a lofty height; when one of the superior caste entitled to speak to the judge directly wishes to do so, he says something like, "May I approach the bench, Your Honor?" Judges do not have offices; they have chambers. A judge does not say, "I'll think it over and let you know later"; he says, "I'll take it under advisement," or, better still, "The court will take it under advisement," using the third person. Indeed, even a single judge is generally referred to as "the Court."

Thus, indeed, might an observant visitor from a faraway land write. In a very real sense, most of the significant decisions for major change in the government of the United States and its states have been made, over the last twenty-five years, not by legislators and state and federal chief executives, but by the courts; and they have basically been, while couched in the language of constitutional law, purely political decisions.

Does anyone really believe that the United States Constitution, all the way along, precluded the imposition of the death penalty on murderers, forbade non-denominational prayer in the public schools, forbade the states to regulate the performance of abortions, rendered illegitimate the system of basing one house of state legislatures (like the United States Senate) on geographical districts rather than population, required the freeing of unquestionably guilty and dangerous criminals because of minor flaws in their trials which had no effect on the verdict, precluded the setting of residency requirements for voting (or receiving welfare payments), required that woman reporters be admitted to the locker rooms of men athletes, and forbade making appointments on a political basis to non-Civil Service positions*; and that no court was sufficiently perceptive to grasp those things until the last couple of decades? Whether one is pleased or displeased with the result of one or another of the decisions involved, it is awfully difficult to argue seriously that they were the fruit of improved constitutional scholarship rather than the political preferences of members of the judiciary.

Earl Warren's liberal majority took a deep breath in the 1950s and set forth on the path of reshaping the institutions of the country to suit their liberal politics, and they found that they could get away with it, and thus it has been going ever since, with some degree of relief from the present U.S. Supreme Court—perhaps Richard Nixon's most worthwhile accomplishment as president. What a piece

*The last-mentioned discovery is contained in the March 31, 1980, *Branti vs. Finkel* decision of the U.S. Supreme Court.

of luck for the liberals! Instead of facing the probably hopeless task of fighting to reshape America in the legislatures and halls of Congress against overwhelming public opinion and odds, they had only the challenge (not inconsiderable, it is true), the Supreme Court having done their work for them, of keeping a straight face as they valiantly defended our ancient judicial institutions against those who would engender disrespect for them and bring politics into the judiciary.

The California Supreme Court in recent years has contributed two striking examples of just how unrestrained by law or precedent a court can be. In one case, *People v. Anderson*, argued in 1971 and decided in 1972, the court took up the constitutionality of capital punishment. In this area, it was obvious that the actual carrying out of executions while the capital punishment law was on the books, its constitutionality unquestioned, had for years been almost totally hamstrung by anti-capital punishment judges with a deep revulsion to the taking of guilty human life (in the form of convicted murderers).* This is an important tool of the activist judiciary: even without issuing a ruling against a given law, to delay endlessly its application on one pretext after another, in the hope that those seeking to carry out the law (which reflects legislative vote and presumably the popular will) will tire of the struggle and in the knowledge that enough delay will in and of itself render a law, for all practical purposes, non-existent, even though it is neither repealed nor ruled "unconstitutional."

(When subsequently, California voters in 1978, by a three-to-one vote, passed a new capital-punishment initiative painstakingly designed to meet all judicially-propounded requirements, the state's supreme court was to use this same tactic: nearly two years later, in mid-1980, as an exasperated dissenting justice noted earlier in that year, the court had yet to uphold a *single* death sentence under the 1978 law. Willie Level's conviction was overturned in May 1980 on the brand-new ground that, since at one point in his questioning he had expressed a desire to talk to his mother, his subsequent confession to beating someone to death with a chair-leg could not be used in evidence.)

*It is interesting that some who oppose capital punishment say they do so because of their belief in "the sanctity of human life." This would be a reasonable position if we were talking about hanging a man for stealing a refrigerator, but since what we are almost invariably talking about is executing someone for viciously depriving another human being of his life, it makes no sense at all. What stronger affirmation of the sanctity of human life can there be than the declaration that we value human life so highly that anyone who wrongfully takes another's life, with malice aforethought, loses his right to continue living among us?

But now, in 1971–72 the justices were dealing, at last, directly with capital punishment's constitutionality. It was on the books; juries had been sentencing accordingly; polls showed that an overwhelming majority of Californians favored it. On what ground to rule it "cruel and unusual"? The reasoning behind the decision was tortured. "Cruel and unusual" had to be considered in the light of the attitudes of the people of California. Now, had people actually been executed lately? No: well, then, the reason must be, not, of course, that the courts had hamstrung the process—but that the people did not *really* approve of capital punishment, thereby indicating their feeling that it was cruel and unusual! Q.E.D. The court, with a straight face, totally ignored the obvious fact that it was precisely the judiciary, not the people, who had been responsible for the absence of executions in the first place!

Another remarkable California Supreme Court decision, this one more recent, is the much publicized *Tanner* decision. The notoriety of this decision arises partly from the fact that, while the majority opinion was written in March 1978, it was not until December, conveniently after the November election in which four of the seven justices, including Chief Justice Rose Bird, were before the voters for confirmation, that it was released, although in the *Los Angeles Times* it was reported the day of the election that the case had been decided and the release of the decision was being delayed until after the election for political reasons; the rest of its notoriety arises from the decision itself.

Under the law in California prior to 1975, a judge had the discretion to grant probation instead of imprisonment even in cases where a gun was used in the commission of a crime. By overwhelming votes, the two houses of the California legislature passed a bill removing such discretion in such cases, and it was signed by Governor Jerry Brown in 1975. No one had the slightest doubt that what had been done was, indeed, to require the imprisonment of persons using a gun in committing a crime, and billboards with the message "Use a Gun—Go to Jail" were put up all over California.

In the case of a convicted felon named Tanner, the trial judge defied the law and granted probation anyway, contending basically that no law could take away his right to grant probation as he saw fit. An appellate court of three seasoned justices unanimously overruled this nonsense, recognizing the obvious fact that the legislature had the right to prescribe mandatory prison sentences. The California Supreme Court then overruled the appellate court and overturned the law, by a bare 4-3 majority.

That four justices found mandatory prison sentences for gun-using criminals offensive is, of course, incredible in the first place. But the reasoning, to call it that, that they employed was really astounding. Three contended that, in fact, the legislature had not really done what everyone knew it had done, because while the language of the law forbade the granting of probation in the cases covered, it did not specifically and explicitly make reference to the exact section of the criminal code under which such probation had previously been permissible and declare that it did not apply any more in the cases referred to; a requirement that no one had ever thought existed before, since even a beginning law student understood as law what would be self-evident to anyone with common sense, namely, that the new law obviously did, as it was intended to do, supersede any earlier law that conflicted with it.

Chief Justice Bird went further and contended that, in any case, the legislature had no power to prescribe mandatory prison sentences, on the apparent ground that its so doing would conflict with judges' God-given, or constitutionally given, right to parole anyone they saw fit regardless; this being an entirely new right, never before seen or claimed and in no wise traceable to any constitutional provision whatsoever.

So there we have what is really an altogether capricious overturning of a law obviously based on nothing at all, really, but four judges' personal prejudices; and yet, in California, as a result of the decision, the use-a-gun-go-to-prison law, passed by the people's representatives, stood repealed in effect (in this case, however, public outrage was so great and the determination of the legislature to have implemented what it had enacted so manifest that one of the original court majority saw fit to change his mind on a reexamination and the law was reinstated).

For the nation as a whole, it is the United States Supreme Court that has been the wholesale overturner of customs and institutions. One far-reaching case, *Reynolds v. Sims* in 1964, involved the election of state legislatures. Throughout American history, bicameral legislatures had typically consisted of a lower house elected from roughly equal (in terms of population) districts and an upper house elected by geographical areas often defined more by such things as county boundaries than by population. This, after all, is exactly analogous to the United States Congress: the House seats being apportioned on the basis of population and every state, no matter how populous or the contrary, having two senators.

But the Supreme Court ruled that both houses of state legislatures had to be apportioned on the basis of population, period. Why? The court used the phrase, "one person, one vote," quoting from one of their own recent decisions.* They might just as well have said "fair's fair" in support of their decision, since neither phrase appears in the Constitution or has any standing in constitutional law. Entirely apart from the analogy with the Congress, the fact is that the Constitution nowhere provides for universal suffrage at all, let alone some kind of universal suffrage wherein every vote has the same mathematical significance in terms of the election of legislators, federal, state, or local. Justice John Marshall Harlan, in his extensive dissent, pointed out that the "equal protection of the laws" language of the Fourteenth Amendment, on which the Court's majority relied, had nothing to do with voting rights, as indicated by that very Amendment's second section, which recognized the right of states to withhold the right to vote from adult males altogether!

What happened was that liberal justices, feeling that the power of conservative rural areas under *state* constitutions was a hindrance to the sort of "social progress" that was near and dear to their hearts, simply threw out those features of the *state* constitutions, deciding, without any real basis, to call them "unconstitutional." In this modern age, if the justices went up to a mountaintop to talk to the "gods of the Constitution" and then came down and announced what the gods had told them to do, and there was no rhyme or reason in relation to previous messages from the gods, there might be quite an outcry; but somehow purported legal reasoning, no matter how specious, seems to satisfy a high percentage of Americans today.

Another interesting example of creative court decisions forbade prayer, even non-denominational prayer, in public schools, based on the "Congress shall make no law respecting an establishment of religion" provision in the Constitution. Now, when the Constitution was written, more than one state in fact had an established religion (the Episcopal church in Virginia, for example), and it is quite clear that this provision, meaning exactly what it says, was designed to restrict *Congress*, not the states, even as to "the establishment of religion." No one ever dreamed that it was supposed to require official atheism at the federal level, let alone at state or local levels. The right of the vast majority of Americans who believed in God to enrich, as they saw it, their public institutions with religion was never questioned. "In God We Trust" appeared on currency and then on

*"The conception of political equality from the Declaration of Independence, to Lincoln's Gettysburg Address . . . can mean only one thing—one person, one vote." *Gray v. Sanders*, 372 U.S. 368.

coins; legislative sessions and school days alike opened with prayers; Christmas carols were sung at Christmas time.

After all these years, the courts now find that in fact the prohibition on the establishment of a religion by Congress means that, for all practical purposes, all references to a Supreme Being in any organ of government at any level is forbidden by the Constitution. What an absurdity!

The courts have also been discovering, belatedly, that all sorts of legitimate responses by civil authorities in accord with the will of the people are null and void because they conflict with newly-discovered rights on the part of offenders against public order—rights which no one had realized existed. The courts were not, for perhaps 150 years, inclined to second guess the states and their political subdivisions as to the exercise of their police power in accordance with duly arrived-at policies and laws. The citizenry wished to enjoy the public streets and parks without having their senses and sensibilities affronted by derelicts, drunks, beggars, drifters, persons of unsavory or frightening appearance or objectionable sexual orientation, and the like; and, under vagrancy and similar statutes, the police saw to it that the wishes of the citizenry were respected. It was not felt that a group of drunken bums had a constitutional right to congregate in a downtown square and make respectable strollers uncomfortable by their presence, let alone yell obscenities at them. Yet the intrepid judicial explorers of recent decades have discovered such constitutional rights, to the great discomfiture of the ordinary citizen.

Again, until fairly recently, it was a rare bird indeed who thought purveyors of pornographic literature had a constitutional right in terms of constitutional freedoms of speech or of the press to display their wares in sidewalk newsracks and in other places where the children of the community, as well as their elders, would be confronted with them; yet this, too, has come to pass. While in theory it might be possible to prove in court that this material violated community standards (considering a community in a statewide sense) and that it had "no serious, scientific, literary, or artistic purposes," the practical realities are another matter.

A May 1980 case in Providence, Rhode Island, provides an example of both the absurd distortion of the Constitution and the unrestrained intrusion into the lives of the American people that all too often are characteristic of today's judiciary. According to a United Press International dispatch, "A federal judge today granted a high school student's request to bring a male date to his senior prom. . . . 'The school's attempt to prohibit Aaron Fricke's expressive conduct is unconstitutional,' ruled U.S. District Chief Judge Raymond Pettine." Dancing, as the judge apparently saw it, is a form of speech; homosexual dancing at school functions is a fundamental federal constitutional right, which principals have no power to forbid. One does wonder whether the framers of the Bill of Rights would have agreed, and in fact whether in their most imaginative moments they could have conceived of any way in which a sane person could possibly find such a meaning in the First Amendment, but Judge Pettine's reasoning was apparently fine with the federal appellate court, which speedily affirmed his ruling.

We have also reached the point, thanks to court rulings, where the ability of the authorities to preserve an environment free from civil disorder has been sharply curtailed. If a mob, assembled from throughout the country with careful planning and the open aim of paralyzing Washington, D.C., sets about to do just that, virtually all end up going scot free. If a thousand Iranians attack a private home in Beverly Hills, only three or four are arrested.

The agents of law enforcement were formerly quite free to take a fair amount of preventive action when in their judgment lawbreaking was about to occur, although it had not yet happened; as well as to exercise a good deal of discretion in endeavoring to capture wrongdoers. Suspicious persons would be stopped, asked to give an account of themselves, and searched; motorists who were stopped for speeding would have their license and driver's license numbers radioed to a central bureau for checking as to possible past offenses. It was generally understood and accepted that the modest inconvenience involved, on the part of law-abiding citizens, was a small price to pay for the enhancement of law enforcement's ability to apprehend lawbreakers. But now even such brief inconveniences have been held to be unconstitutional violations of the questioned person's rights. In 1978, the California Supreme Court held that motorists stopped for speeding may no longer be required to wait a few minutes while their license numbers are radioed in for checks.

In these and so many other cases, the effect of judicial usurpation on the socio-political environment has been in one direction: toward reducing the ability of the conventional, law-abiding, majority to maintain the sort of environment that it wants and feels comfortable with.

8

Digression on Capital Punishment

The discontinuance or moratorium, for all practical purposes, on capital punishment in the United States in the last decade is an impressive demonstration of the power of the judiciary to thwart the public will. With perhaps 80 per cent of the American people in favor of the use of the death penalty, according to national polls, and with murder rates soaring, only one person has been executed against his will in the United States since 1967. The judiciary, in effect, has taken the position that, come hell or high water, criminals are not going to be executed in the United States, no matter what the people may say. It is as though judges were being asked to countenance something so horrible, so repugnant to their better-developed sense of right and wrong, that they cannot bring themselves—because of some "higher allegiance," no doubt—to remember the Constitution and the laws and their oath to uphold them and to stand back and allow convicted murderers to be executed.

Does their violent aversion really amount to anything? Are there such compelling arguments against capital punishment, albeit comprehensible only to a select few, as must weaken the confidence of the 80 per cent who favor it by instinct and judgment? Let us devote a little effort to examining the matter.

There are two basic reasons for a system of justice which includes capital punishment, just as there are two basic reasons for any system of justice: protection of society and punishment of wrongdoing; in the argument over the death penalty, the latter reason has largely dropped from explicit notice, the proponents of capital punishment having confined themselves largely to argument on the grounds of deterrence of capital crimes. It is true that the most tangible, the least controversial, reason for a particular practice, like capital punishment, is the protection of society. The question of punishment *qua* punishment is a far more abstract subject, fraught with religious and philosophical implications. With the protection of society, however, no one openly quarrels. The reasonable course, therefore appears to be to examine the protection argument for capital punishment first.

Taking the most important case of the penalty's application—murder—the relevant question is: are fewer innocent lives lost with capital punishment than would be lost with its abolition?

As far as I know, no one's argument runs, "Although capital punishment *does* protect society, it nevertheless is wrong and must be abolished." Such a position, which would deny the morality of society's defending itself against those who place themselves violently outside its pale, would be ill received, to say the least. Western civilization has traditionally placed a very high value on innocent lives. Thus it becomes necessary for the zealous opponent of capital punishment to argue that society is *not* protected by it. That statement is often made, in terms of the flattest certainty, as if it were a well-known fact among all thoughtful and educated people, that capital punishment affords society no protection against serious or violent crime: only the ignorant or the fanatical would think otherwise, it seems. A state governor who wishes to appearl enlightened and gain the plaudits of a high percentage of social workers, clergymen, and professors need only declare solemnly, "Killing does not deter murderers."

Deterring *potential* murderers, however, is only part of protecting society. What about the person who has already killed? It will be seen, I think, that the weight of evidence and reasoning is to the effect that capital punishment does deter; but it may be pointed out at the outset, without any possible contradiction, that further depredations by convicted murderers are definitely prevented by imposition of the death penalty.

Not everyone is willing to commit murder, and the man who has killed someone in the past is obviously somewhat riskier than the average person to associate with. But how can such association be avoided, if the man lives? Even if he were placed in absolutely solitary confinement for the rest of his days (and this is not generally advocated as a replacement for capital punishment), a danger of escape would remain. If, again, the man is released, he may kill again, as a fair number of paroled murderers have. It can be argued that potential future killers "should not be released"; but how are they to be detected with infallibility? Anti-capital punishment sentiments are heavy with hopes of rehabilitation, the evils of depriving criminals of hope, etc. It seems quite implausible that those who hold such sentiments, if in control of the administration of justice for severe crimes, would be so much stricter about granting paroles than the present administrators that *no* potentially repeating murderers would be released.

If parole is eliminated, the problem of innocent lives continuing to be endangered is not eliminated but only moved inside prison walls. The longer the sentence, the less a criminal can hope—or lose from bad behavior. In riots and other violence within prisons, those convicted of violent crimes play a leading role. The lives of other prisoners and guards are at stake. The danger is increased in that the ability to detect persons responsible for crime inside prisons is diminished when convicts fear reprisals; in such fears, the known presence of men whose willingness to kill has been demonstrated plays an obvious part. (The grisly torture-killings of suspected informers during the 1980 New Mexico prison seizure by inmates are a particularly gruesome reminder of the perils of inmate cooperation with prison authorities.) The result must inevitably be a prison atmosphere in which murder and other violence are prominent. British prison officials, according to the 1953 report of a special royal commission on the death penalty (probably the most recent intensive study of the matter), "contended that in the case of a violent prisoner undergoing a life sentence, the death penalty may be the only effective deterrent against his making a murderous assault on a fellow prisoner or a member of the prison staff."

There are, indeed, those who seek to get around this potent objection by advocating the retention of the death penalty for such crimes: let it be retained, they say, only in the case of murder by prisoners already convicted of murder. Those who argue thus indeed are hoist by their own petard: *for their own position admits that the death penalty has a uniquely deterrent effect:* and, if this is the case, why should it be allowed to operate only *within* prison walls?

Another striking demonstration of the weakness beneath the abolitionist's easy "there is no deterrence" may be had by examining the proposition that *all* punishment should be abolished, on the ground that it does not deter crime. For the abolitionist will say that the threat of death does not deter, because the criminal thinks he will not be caught; or believes a good lawyer can "get him off"; or is in such an extraordinary frame of mind that no rational consideration of possible consequences ever enters in: *and may not the same be said of any crime?*

At this point, the capital punishment abolitionist, unless proposing to defend the proposition that *no* punishment *ever* deters crime, will be forced to argue that a capital crime is, somehow, entirely *sui generis*. This argument is very weak indeed, however, since capital punishment covers crimes involving both action in the heat of the moment (e.g., killing during a kidnapping) and coolly-thought-out crime (e.g., in the Rosenberg espionage case, or in cold-blooded murder). What can it be about these crimes that makes them uniquely non-susceptible to normal deterrence? Nothing, is the answer, unless it is supposed to be severity *per se*, since, indeed, these crimes' only other common denominator is the external fact of their involving capital punishment. The principles of punishment and deterrence which apply to non-capital crimes apply also where the penalty happens to be death.

If all murders were committed in the heat of violent emotion and violent emotion precluded deterrence, the question would then arise, why punish aggravated assault and battery under such circumstances? As a matter of fact however, in the first place most murders are *not* so committed (the British royal commission found that, even in the case of murders of wives, the majority were *not* "heat of passion" crimes, but rather were committed coolly); and in the second place, as penalties for assault and battery and mayhem recognize, the angry man is by no means beyond rational considerations.

Is there anyone who argues that punishment deters no crime? When severe penalties for drunken driving or speeding are in effect, I have yet to see voices raised crying, "Such vindictiveness will deter no drunk driving or speeding!" As a matter of fact, there is considerable evidence to the contrary, as one might suspect from introspection alone.

So punishment deters crime, and severe punishment deters more: a fact no motorist nearing a known speed trap is unaware of. *Why won't this work with capital punishment?* "Look at the statistics, look at the statistics," the abolitionist may at this point begin to plead. I have every intention of paying respects to "the statistics." First, however, we must inquire how, in terms of human nature the abolitionists can explain the supposed existence of this strange state of affairs that is the basis of their position. "No deterrence." *No* deterrence. That is what they say, and they must say precisely that, for even the saving of a handful of innocent lives each year would, in most minds, clearly justify capital punishment; so they *must* say no deterrence, and must also ignore entirely the matters of repeat murders and of intra-prison murders and violence. *No* deterrence. How is this? The abolitionist, we are presuming, is not against all punishment nor in favor of punishing all crimes equally. Thirty days to one year, then, more deterrence; one year to five, more deterrence; five years to twenty, more deterrence; twenty years to life, more deterrence; but life to death, no more deterrence?

"For the professional criminal imprisonment is a normal professional risk," the royal commission found, "of which the idea is familiar . . . and which for him carries no stigma. The death penalty comes into an entirely different category." Sir Harold Scott, former London police commissioner, told of a gang he had dealt with: "Heavy prison sentences did not deter these men but the death penalty did, and we have not had organized trouble from this quarter since." Sir James Fitzjames Stevens, prominent in the criminal justice area in the nineteenth century, put the matter rather well:

No other punishment deters men so effectually from committing crimes as the punishment of death. This is one of those propositions which are in themselves more obvious than any proof can make them. It is possible to display ingenuity in arguing against them, but that is all. The whole experience of mankind is in the other direction. The threat of . . . death is the one to. which resort has always been made when there was an absolute necessity for some result. . . . All that a man has will he give for his life."

Human nature has not changed. Yet, *no* deterrence, none at all (above that of, say, life imprisonment), say today's abolitionists.

"Look at the statistics, look at the statistics." The chant is insistent. It is, I have always felt, a sign of weakness when a person is unable to meet logical arguments with reasoning but must rather place sole reliance, against reasoning, on an appeal to "statistics." If there is significant evidence in statistics, one would expect those who rely on it to be able to muster some reasonable explanation of *why* something is the case. When our reasoning powers tell us that something *must be* the case—and in fact there are specific factual instances of it—yet certain collections of numbers do not clearly indicate that it is the case, must we, in looking objectively for the truth, simply leap blindly to the position that all our reasoning is worthless? Often, in fact, to those who take their stand solely on "statistics" the figures are merely an excuse for a belief, not a reason for logical conviction.

But, anyway, let us look at the statistics, first asking what it is that we expect to find in them. If the effect of abolishing capital punishment were supposed to be, automatically, an immediate doubling of the murder rate, that result, or its absence, could indeed be detected. But what about a small increase in the number of murders (after all, a rather small number of innocent lives are all that would be needed)—would this show up clearly in the statistics? We at once begin to have doubts, considering that a great variety of factors bear on the question of the crime rate. But, thinking in terms of columns of figures, we might expect, for example, that it would be a profitable and meaningful thing to compare the number of murders in Holland, which does not have a death penalty, with the number in Belgium, which does. We might indeed expect that, and perhaps find in the comparison an argument against deterrence, if we are sufficiently naive about statistics in general and these statistics in particular. The fact is, however, that, though Belgium does indeed have a death penalty for murder in its legal code, that penalty has not been imposed since 1863. As the British royal commission noted, "in most countries where capital punishment has been abolished, statutory abolition has come after a long period when the death penalty was in abeyance." The lag between the last execution and formal abolition was 1892 to 1933 in Denmark, 1876 to 1905 in Norway, 1860 to 1870 in Holland, 1876 to 1890 in Italy, and 1924 to 1942 in Switzerland. And in the United States, as noted earlier, thirteen years have passed—with basically one exception—since capital punishment was last imposed.

So what would we *expect* statistics from these countries to show, or to prove? We might try to find an *abrupt* shift—difficult to find of course, for a state or nation on the verge of formally abolishing the death penalty would be unlikely to employ it assiduously up to the last. Further, when capital punishment is restored after a repeal, that restoration more likely than not will reflect a response to conditions of war or disorder, or a crime wave; which means that, in a country's experience, the death penalty may tend to be associated, on balance, with unsettled times, introducing a statistical bias.

It is virtually hopeless to look in year to year statistics for evidence of the long-run effect referred to by the royal commission in its report: "The deterrent force of capital punishment operates not only by affecting the conscious thoughts of individuals tempted to commit murder, but also by building up in the community, over a long period of time, a deep feeling of peculiar abhorrence for the crime of murder." (This concept of a long-run effect fits nicely with the fact that, though nothing much happened in Great Britain right after its 1960 elimination of what we might call its straightforward "kill a person—go to the gallows" capital punishment law, the British murder rate now, twenty years later, is much higher than it was prior to 1960. But in twenty years many other factors also can come into play.)

When "statistics" tell us nothing, we are forced to think. Is it true that the prevailing values which impinge on a person affect what he or she does with respect to society's laws? Yes, obviously; the effects of childhood influences are well known. Children who grow up in an environment in which theft is condoned or encouraged yield a higher proportion of thieves than children raised otherwise; certainly this is a reasonable thing to expect. Likewise, the role of relative rewards and punishments in communicating feelings of good and bad is one that can be readily understood. Is it reasonable to call for "statistics" here?

Statistics were studied in detail by the Royal Commission, made up of experts in the field, and that body reported that an absence of correlation between capital punishment and crime rates, where found, "cannot properly be used as an argument against the view that the death penalty is a unique deterrent . . . The figures afford no reliable evidence one way or the other . . . too many other factors come into the question."

This, of course, is *not* the same as saying that the statistics indicate that there is no deterrent. Unfortunately, the logical point escapes many people. I remember a debate on capital punishment at the Oxford Union years ago; our side, which consisted of John Sparrow, the Warden of All Souls, myself, and an English undergraduate, endeavored over and over to make our opponents grasp the difference between indicating that X does not exist and indicating nothing one way or the other. They either could not or would not see the difference. Sidney Silverman, a fiery Socialist member of Parliament, I remember, thundered, "They say there is a deterrent. Here are the statistics! Show it to us!" He might have as properly asked us to show him proof, in those statistics, that he was in Oxford, and refused to believe it otherwise.

If a rational person is interested in factual evidence to combine with his or her own reasoning and *aggrégate* statistics do not satisfy the purpose, there are several places to look, such as into specific cases, or into the testimony of persons intimately acquainted with the subject. In terms of specific cases, some rather clear instances of the deterrent effect of capital punishment are recorded. New Zealand abolished the death penalty in 1941 and restored it in 1948 after a sharp rise in murders. Of special interest is the case, cited in 1950 by New Zealand's minister of justice, of a man who set out to kill seven people. "He spoke openly about it and declared that the years he would have to serve in prison was a small price to pay for that pleasure . . . I am certain that if he had known that he would have had to forfeit his life . . . three persons would have been alive today."

Washington, Oregon, Tennessee, Missouri, South Dakota, and Arizona are among the states which have abolished capital punishment and later restored it. "After the repeal," according to Tennessee's attorney general, "we had a reign of crime of the most heinous nature in this state which brought about a complete reversal of public sentiment on the subject."

There is, too, the case of the English criminal who had, the royal commission was told by police officials, "left his 'jenny' behind. 'I had the stick ready for you [he said] but . . . at the last moment I changed my mind as I thought there would be plenty of your fellows about and I should get caught and have to swing for it if I did you in.' " Again, a sharp decline in crime in Glasgow was noted after three men were hanged in one year after seventeen years in which the death penalty was in abeyance.

Rather bizarre is the 1930 case, told of by Judge Marcus Kavanagh, of a Pole who brought his wife from Pittsburgh to Detroit and did her in, explaining that the reason he had moved was that Michigan had no capital punishment. In Washington, in another interesting case, during the capital punishment abolition of 1919 a man killed a state insurance commissioner, declaring that the state could do nothing to him but board him for the rest of his life.

And of course there are other cases. Exactly how many are recorded is not important; what is important is that this is the sort of thing that abolitionists say *never happens. Never.* Abolition would cost *no* innocent lives, they say, because *no* one is *ever* deterred from crime by capital punishment.

So much for the testimony of some specific cases. In terms of experts' views, what do people intimately associated with criminals believe? According to the British royal commission report,

From [the representatives of the police and prison service] we received virtually unanimous evidence, in both England and Scotland . . . that they were convinced of the uniquely deterrent value of capital punishment. . . . [They] had no doubt that the existence of the death penalty was the main reason why lethal violence was not more often used and why criminals in this country do not usually carry firearms. . . ."

With these "considered and unanimous views of these experienced witnesses, who have had many years of contact with criminals," noted the report, many others agreed. "The Lord Chief Justice Mr. Justice Humphreys, and the Lord Justice General felt no doubt that they were right." According to J. Edgar Hoover, "capital punishment, wisely administered, is a necessary deterrent to wanton criminal activity."

Different people may disagree, of course, and various statements may conflict; social workers, for example, were generally dubious as to the deterrent effect of capital punishment, the commission's report noted. One thing, however, stands out: no one claims and no evidence has ever been adduced to the effect that the death penalty deters *less* than some other penalty. (In part, of course, this is due to the obvious fact that any criminal who preferred death to a prison sentence could, if not deterred by religious scruples, kill himself.) But that point should be well grasped: some say there is X effect, some say there is X-1 effect, some say there is no effect; but none say there is a negative effect: where then is the "consensus" or the "average"? Can a reasonable person, given the observations of experts and specific cases, and his or her own reasoning powers, really deny that capital punishment has a deterrent effect, or that, since the death penalty additionally protects society from further depredations by convicted criminals, the inevitable result of abolishing it must be an increased toll in innocent lives?

As to the specious sanctimoniousness of the opponents of capital punishment on "moral" grounds, will anyone openly and seriously suggest that it is morally better that an innocent citizen should be murdered than a murderer put to death? From the standpoint of society as a whole, entirely apart from particular moral questions, the matter is crystal-clear: it is better that any number of outlaws who see fit to violate the laws on which the common order and good are based, threaten the basis of orderly society, and murder law-abiding citizens be put to death, than that one such innocent, law-abiding citizen should be killed. That the outlaw's wishes and desires cannot weigh against the interests of law-abiding citizens is a principle quite universally recognized; it has never been suggested that thieves' dislike of imprisonment is a factor which should be taken into account in drawing up laws designed to protect the community from theft.

"Society," of course, tempers the imposition of the death penalty, and of all penalties, with the knowledge that a parking violation, for example, does not threaten society and that more than such an offense is involved in being an outlaw from society. Thus, if double-parkers were hanged, society would lose rather than benefit: its own members in good standing would be losing their lives. This is also why innocent people are not called guilty and executed as a deterrent to wrongdoing: *society*, consisting of those who obey its basic laws, would be suffering.

To introduce further "moral aspects" is obviously to assume, implicitly or explicitly, a certain moral scheme. Now, private revelation and private moral schemes may impress their individual possessors, but they can carry no weight with others. The person who says, "it would be better to let these men live, even if some innocent persons must die," must, if his comments are meaningful for others, mean "better" in terms of common moral principles. Do Judeo-Christian moral principles encourage sacrificing innocent lives in order that murderers may live? Quite the contrary. Sin and injustice are primary evils: for an innocent man to be murdered involves a grave sin, a grave offense to justice; for a murderer to lose his own life involves justice, in the common view. "Whoso sheddeth the blood of man, by man shall his blood be shed."

Occasionally, the specter of the innocent man executed by mistake is raised by abolitionists. This specter tends to disappear again when it is realized that the total number of known innocent persons executed for murder in Western Europe and the United States in over a century (a century in which the penalty was in regular use in many countries) can virtually be counted on the fingers of one hand: the merest drop in the bucket compared to the number of known victims of repeat murderers, let alone the total number of murder victims.

Which brings us to a further matter, the matter of *punishment* not in order to deter others or protect society from an individual criminal, but rather in order to redress an upset balance of justice. "In case after case," declared the late Cardinal Godfrey some years ago, "[the criminal] has sinned with complete free will. Punishment is not merely a deterrent; it is meant also to redress an order of broken relationship between a man and his god."

Cardinal Godfrey expressed a principle of long standing in the Judeo-Christian world. Father Roland Potter, O.P., cites St. Thomas Aquinas's classical expression of the theology of punishment: "A man who has erroneously and perversely followed his will is made to suffer something against his will."

"We certainly find elements of deterrence, and bettering the delinquent," writes Father Potter; "yet the more basic element . . . is that of getting justice done, ultimately to the glory of God." Those who claim that punishment is moral only to deter or rehabilitate are not talking about punishment as such. They also apparently overlook the fact that Hell is hardly a rehabilitation center.

Even if capital punishment did not deter a single crime, there would still be a strong justification for it in terms of punishment *qua* punishment; and also in terms of society's claim to be able to determine, to some extent, the minimum standards of conduct for continued participation in a civilized community. As Lord Justice Denning put it, in testimony to the royal commission on capital punishment, in a view which the then Archbishop of Canterbury supported: "The punishment inflicted for grave crimes should adequately reflect the revulsion felt by the great majority of citizens for them. . . . The ultimate justification of any punishment is not that it is a deterrent, but that it is the emphatic denunciation by the community of a crime; and from this point of view, there are some murders which, in the present state of public opinion, demand . . . the death penalty."

9

Some Are More Equal Than Others:
Quotas, Race, and
Related Touchy Subjects

Scene: The admissions office of a state university medical school. On the glass door is lettered, "State University Medical School—Admissions Office." Posted next to this is a hand-lettered notice: "No Whites Need Apply." Inside, an official is seen seated behind a counter.

Enter a white man and a Negro. They go through the doors and approach the counter.

Official: (to white man): What are you doing here? There is no room in the class for you.
White: But I heard there were spaces . . .
Official: Those spaces are reserved for blacks, Chicanos, and Native Americans. Didn't you see the sign?
White: Yes, but . . .
Official: Can't you read?
White: I thought it was a joke. This is the United States, in 1978; I fought in Vietnam . . .
Official: The sign means what it says. Your skin is the wrong color. You're wasting my time.
White: But my recommendations, and my scores on the aptitude test, are outstanding! Surely . . .
Official: There are *no* exceptions. We are helping the disadvantaged.
White: But I've had a lot of disadvantages myself! My parents were poor, I was orphaned at six, I put myself through college while supporting my aged grandmother . . .
Official: There are *no* exceptions! Now please leave.

Exit *White.*

Official (turning to Negro): Sorry about that. Are you interested in a
    space in the entering class?
Black: Yes, but there might be a slight problem. You see, my grades
    haven't been very good—I spend a lot of time in Vegas and in
    Europe—my Dad's publishing business throws off a lot of
    money . . .
Official: No problem, as long as you meet our minimum standards;
    your skin's the right color.

That little scenario, it seems clear from the U.S. Supreme Court's
long-awaited *Bakke* decision in 1978, would *not* pass constitutional
muster with that august body. Absolute, inflexible quotas for minority applicants at public institutions, involving spaces from which
those who are not members of certain defined minority groups are
automatically excluded, are a no-no, by a bare 5-4 vote of the Court.

On the other hand, also by a 5-4 vote, with Justice Powell joining
with the four dissenters in the first vote, the Court held that, while
race as such could not be the *sole* factor in determining whether an
applicant could receive a space, it could, indeed, contrary to what the
California Supreme Court had ruled, be *a* factor. That is, white
applicant A, otherwise better-qualified than black applicant B, could
nevertheless be passed over in favor of B, if this were done in some
acceptable but not precisely defined way. Certain other things, therefore, are also clear:

1. The Supreme Court has constituted itself the Supreme Admissions
   Committee: and probably the Supreme Board of Employment
   Grievances as well, as what's sauce for the medical-school appli-
   cant goose is probably sauce for the business world gander;

2. There will be a lot of additional business for lawyers over the next
   decade or so, as the question of defining the constitutionally
   acceptable bounds of racial discrimination is endlessly litigated
   and adjudicated;

3. On this issue, the Supreme Court staked out a position far to the
   left of the California court, which has generally been regarded as
   one of the nation's most liberal, but which ruled 6-1 that overt
   racial discrimination against non-minorities could not be constitutionally countenanced;

4. The Supreme Court has, when all is said and done, given its stamp

of approval to "reverse discrimination," with, in effect, two racially-based classes of citizenship, with the one, to some degree, "more equal" than the other.

This is a momentous and disturbing development. In decision after decision, over the years, the rights of minorities to be free from being discriminated against by public authorities because of their skin color has been established and re-emphasized, based on the principle contained in the Constitution that all Americans are entitled to the same rights, regardless of race, color, previous condition of servitude, etc.

Even *Plessy*, in 1896, which ruled racial segregation constitutional and was the governing case in its field until *Brown* in 1954, was based on the assumption that, while black and white facilities were *separate*, they were also *equal*. There has never been a suggestion that unequal treatment based solely on race could be other than repugnant to the Constitution.

A five-man majority of the Court has now changed all that. A certain degree of racial discrimination against those not included in some definition or other of racial-groups-deserving-special-treatment (the very matter of definition being obviously also an area subject to endless litigation), meaning, basically, white people (and racial minorities not singled out for special treatment, such as Japanese-Americans), *can*, the Court is saying, be practiced constitutionally by public authorities. While in theory, or logically, the decision could be interpreted as permitting discrimination against blacks in some cases, this hardly seems the thrust of the decision: no, the Supreme Court, for all intents and purposes, has sanctioned discrimination against whites only.

Things could, of course, be worse. It is a sobering thought that if four members of the Court—William J. Brennan, Byron R. White, Harry A. Blackmun, and Thurgood Marshall—had had their way, they would be: they would have approved the Davis policies that excluded Alan Bakke, that is to say, my little scenario of a few pages back. Their reasoning, at least in the case of Thurgood Marshall, appeared to be that after hundreds of years of oppression, no favoritism toward Negroes can possibly be unconstitutional.

Had Lewis F. Powell, Jr. sided with the anti-Bakke four, we would have a situation in which blatant racial discrimination against whites would be countenanced by the courts. Institutions of learning and businesses would—a small silver lining—know where they stood, and no white would bother to go to court to seek relief from any discrimination short of, perhaps, a reserving of three-quarters (or half?) of the spaces in an entering class for members of approved minority groups—which perhaps even the anti-Bakke four would regard as excessive. But what a price to pay for minimizing litigation!

Had Powell sided with the remaining four members of the Court and upheld the California court, at last we would have had enunciated on the highest judicial authority what many Americans were sure went without saying—that there is no room under the United States Constitution for racial discrimination, no matter how well-intentioned, by public authorities and institutions. That way, too, the country would have been spared endless years of litigation and uncertainty—but spared it in a reasonable, rather than an unreasonable, situation.

What happens now? Obviously, with the green light flashed by the Supreme Court, reverse-discrimination enthusiasts will go to work with speed and determination to fine-tune their racially discriminatory policies so as to put them into compliance with what they conceive to be the Court's requirements.

The Court, be it noted, did not say that public educational institutions were constitutionally obligated to discriminate against white people, only that they were not constitutionally *prohibited* from it, so long as they didn't do it too blatantly. But what about the right of a governmental agency—the Department of Justice or the Department of Health and Human Services, say—to *require* such discrimination as the price for federal funding, or, in the case of a private employer, as the price for avoiding a lawsuit? Had the decision gone the right way, this would have been clearly precluded; as it is, it might very well be argued that, just as it is now the prerogative of the officials of a public institution to discriminate against whites if they choose, so, by the same token, it is the prerogative of federal bureaucrats to *require* such discrimination as a condition of receiving funds or avoiding a lawsuit. The lid on the Pandora's box of "reverse" discrimination has been opened up wider than it formerly appeared to be.

The *Weber* case of June 1979 was the next step in establishing two classes of citizenship; looking at the crystal-clear language of the Civil Rights Act of 1964, which forbids racial discrimination in employment, a five-man majority of the court simply declared that it didn't mean what it said at all; since it was adopted to help black people, it must be that the "spirit" of the Act, to which the Court appealed in ignoring the letter, sanctioned discrimination against white people. And while the decision only said such "affirmative action" was permissible, the immediate response of the Labor Department, according to its chief enforcer of affirmative action by federal contractors,

Weldon Rougeau, quoted in the *Wall Street Journal*, was, "there's just no question they have to do it. . . . we're going to see much more enforcement than we've ever seen in this area."

Intimately associated with the matter of quotas is the widespread assumption that, if a minority—a "disadvantaged" minority, that is—is underrepresented in some desirable occupation in proportion to its percentage of the relevant population, some sort of foul play is involved: that there is strong *prima facie* evidence that something is going on for which the proper remedy is government-ordered preference for that group, whether in the form of rigid quotas or in the form of preference for the group which, while not absolute, nevertheless puts it at a comparative advantage.

Examples are limitless: a federal judge finds that there are not enough Mexican-Americans and Negroes on a police force, especially at the higher levels, and considers that fact in and of itself sufficient to order that one minority member be hired, and one promoted to sergeant, for every white hired or promoted to sergeant; a lawsuit against a bank is settled by the bank's promising a one-to-one man-woman promotion ratio to higher positions; with its rigid quota system thrown out by the U.S. Supreme Court, the University of California-Davis Medical School develops a new system whereby in effect being black is worth five points, and being poor another five, so that a poor black gets ten and a poor white five points in the preliminary screening; Foreign Service qualification procedures treat members of different races differently.

FCC STIFFENS QUOTAS ON MINORITY HIRING BY BROADCAST FIRMS

WASHINGTON—The Federal Communications Commission voted to tighten its guidelines for hiring of minorities and women by broadcasting.

Broadcasters that don't meet the new standards will have their hiring practices automatically reviewed when their licenses are up for renewal.

The guidelines call for stations with staff of 11 to 50 people to have a percentage of minority and female workers . . . that is at least half the percentage of them in the local work force. The representation . . . in the top four job categories . . . must meet the same standard.

Wall Street Journal
February 14, 1980

If minority preference truly is utilized to compensate for some hindrance suffered by members of the minority group unrelated to their qualifications, so that in effect it makes a corrective adjustment to what had been a faulty scale which weighed the competitors of different races, then not only is justice served, but so is intelligent utilization of human resources: a plus for the economic as well as the socio-political environment. But if, on the other hand, minority preference is being imposed without rational basis, resulting in the hiring and promotion of less-qualified applicants, then exactly the opposite is the case.

What can be said about this touchy subject? Let us try very dispassionately to walk over the territory and analyze it. In fact, let us try to get away from the current areas of heated controversy into another area—sports. The general counsel for the University of California regents, Donald L. Reidhaar, subsequent to the *Bakke* decision of the California Supreme Court, said, "If it weren't for quotas it would be almost impossible to get minorities into schools and trained for such professions as medicine and law." This is a rather incredible statement, on the surface suggesting the attitude of an old-fashioned Southern racist as to minorities' inherent abilities to cope with difficult intellectual tasks, but which more likely, considering its source, reflected a conviction that in twenty or so years of life and education, virtually all minority group members' abilities to compete effectively with whites in terms of grades and scores on examinations have been crippled by an all-pervasive racism in our society. In order to facilitate calm analysis of the subject, let us instead consider the analogous statement. "If it weren't for quotas it would be almost impossible to get a proper number of whites onto college football teams and trained for professional football."

For indeed, although "majority" persons—principally whites—constitute nearly 90 per cent of the U.S. population as a whole, anyone who follows professional football—or basketball—knows that in fact whites are represented on professional football teams in nowhere near the numbers that their percentage of the population would indicate was appropriate, and, conversely, that blacks are overrepresented, on that basis, many times over.

Being a professional football player is generally considered an attractive occupation. Playing enjoyable games for a living is, for those who enjoy those games, anything but onerous; considerable publicity and prestige attend being a professional athlete; and not only is direct remuneration very high indeed, typically over $100,000 a year, but endorsement of this or that product, and investment of earnings, typically make a good professional athlete rich for life.

Yet whites have been able to secure these excellent jobs only in pathetically small numbers considering their percentage of the general population. How can this be? There are only a limited number of possible explanations; let us examine them one by one.

1. Team managers are deliberately hiring less-qualified blacks instead of better-qualified whites for racial reasons.

This, of course, is the answer most likely to occur to a federal bureaucrat or a federal judge. Considering the gross disparity, there is, they would say, a strong *prima facie* case for this explanation. The obvious solution, accepting this explanation, would be court orders requiring affirmative action programs and the hiring of only whites until they made up their proper percentage of each team; the only question would be whether different percentages would apply to, for example, the Green Bay Packers and the San Francisco '49ers, reflecting the differing percentages of whites in those two cities, or whether one percentage would be applied nationwide.

But it seems bizarre to think that team managers and owners, almost all of whom, especially the latter, are white, and who are interested in winning games for a variety of reasons, should deliberately reduce their chances for having winning teams by discriminating against members of their own race; so let us consider other possibilities.

2. Although no deliberate discrimination is involved, the criteria used in the selection of players are such as to lead to the selection of less-qualified blacks instead of better-qualified whites because the criteria fail to properly measure the true qualifications of players for professional football, and furthermore fail in such a way as systematically to penalize white players.

This, it must be said, seems implausible. Coaches watch prospective players play in college games; presumably, they also have them show what they can do by way of running, passing, and receiving, and systematically do all they can to select the best players they can get. While obviously different coaches' opinions of players differ, no one has ever established that players turned down for professional football, whether white or Negro, are in fact on the whole better football players than those selected; nor has anyone ever suggested why it should be that selection methods should *systematically* show whites in a poorer light, in relation to their true abilities, than blacks.

3. A far smaller percentage of whites than of blacks possess the very high qualifications required to play in this league.

a. Because, in terms of ability to play professional football, the white race as a whole, or on the average, is inferior to the black.

(1) Inherently: God gave the black race better football-playing aptitude.

This is a pretty shocking hypothesis, but it does fit the facts we have reasonably well. Physical size, strength, stamina, and agility are certainly not what one would expect fostered by growing up in relative poverty, with relatively poor medical care and diet; and yet see how many top professional football players are black! And, while the average white grows up under better physical conditions than the average black, with more advantages, see how few measure up! There *are* physical characteristics that seem entirely innate: for example, there *are* such things as pygmies; and, again, as regards degree of curliness of hair, shape of lips and buttocks, etc., there really *are* differences between members of the Negro and white races. They also are of different colors. May not blacks also be, on balance, better athletes?

(2) Not quite inherently, but almost, and for practical purposes the same thing.

This approach recognizes the obvious, that there are physical differences among races, and takes that as making plausible the explanation that Negroes are simply better athletes than whites, but attributes this condition to evolution over the millennia in different habitats rather than to God's original plans. As to there being differences, the proponent of this point of view can point out that Orientals do have less facial and body hair than whites or Negroes, and that they are also, on average, shorter (which has nothing to do with the well-known fact that, on average, Americans, for example, of all races, are getting taller generation by generation, representing not a Lamarckian inheritance of acquired characteristics, long ago refuted, but the effects of better diet, better living conditions, etc.); or one could refer to pygmies, again, noting that a pygmy baby raised by a Wisconsin family of Swedish ancestry on the same diet as their youngsters will still be a pygmy.

It is not, against a background of proven, definite physical differences among races, totally implausible that these might include differing distributions of the talents required for a top-flight professional football player.

As a hypothesis, given the very different climatic conditions of tropical Africa vis-à-vis Mesopotamia or Northern Europe, involving, in the case of Africa, readily available food and water and an absence of cold winters, it does not seem altogether unbelievable that with the Darwinian process of natural selection, whereby, with genetic mutations continually occurring over the millennia, the survival and reproduction of those most suited to their environment is furthered and those of the ill-suited hampered, survival of those with physical strength, stamina, and speed might have been fostered to a greater relative degree in Africa than in less gentle climes. If you were big and strong and fast in Scandinavia but let your fire go out in the winter, you and your children didn't make it, and your genes died out. Put another way, nature may have developed a brawnier race in Africa than in Europe.

There are certainly folklore elements—"strong back, weak mind," and the legendary sexual prowess of blacks, to name two—that also tie in with the idea that blacks possess physical superiority over whites. In fact, a recent article in *Time* magazine, touching on the over-representation of blacks in professional athletics, quoted at least one prominent Negro athlete as attributing the phenomenon to Negro superiority.

Given the standard bell-shaped curve of normal distribution, this condition would not need to be very pronounced overall for it to have a very pronounced effect at the extremes of competence. If everyone to the right of B is acceptable, the slight difference in qualifications

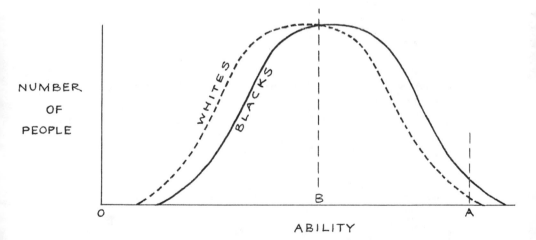

represented by the two curves will lead only to a small imbalance in the group's representation in a given area. But if only those to the right of A are acceptable, the disproportion is extreme. Since only the *crème de la crème,* so to speak, of athletes qualify for pro football, the phenomenon observed—severe under-representation of whites on these teams—could be explained with the positing of even a very moderate overall qualification differential between the black and white races.

> (3) *Whether or not (1) or (2), in fact, in the case of this generation, at this point in time, whether due to poor diet, lack of physical exercise, or whatever.*

While in some cases young blacks certainly may be required to perform more hard physical labor than young whites, representing better preparation for the rigors of football, nevertheless, in view of the overall inferiority in health, diet, living conditions, and medical care among Negroes in this country, on average relative to whites, this explanation is implausible.

> *b. Whether or not a. is true, the different distribution of this ability in the two races is such that a disproportionately small number of whites possess the exceptional ability required.*

This, also, is not ridiculous on its face. There could, in theory at least, on the average, be equal physical aptitude for football between the two races, so that the average Negro would have precisely the ability of the average white, and yet, for whatever reason, there might be a disproportionate number of blacks at the high end of the distribution curve.

> *4. Whether or not 3. is the case, of those who are available for, or apply for, positions on professional football teams, a disproportionately small percentage of qualified persons are white.*

> *a. Because, due to the notorious past anti-white policies of football team operators, a high percentage of qualified whites are discouraged from applying.*

This is too obviously silly to require analysis.

> *b. For other reasons.*

Under this assumption, while the average white may be as good a potential professional football player as the average Negro, whites on an overall basis are just not as attracted to football careers and/or to the kind of college football (USC instead of Harvard or Yale) likely to lead to a pro career.

Could this be, if it is the case, because the high degree of relative dominance of the game by blacks discourages whites from thinking of pro football careers, even though racism is not a factor? Unlikely, because there are many white pro footballers (Joe Namath, for one, comes to mind), and, even if the large number of playing blacks might discourage a white from considering pro football *today*, this would not explain how football came to be so heavily black in the first place.

The explanation may, rather, lie in the alternatives to a sports career, as they are perceived by the average black and the average white youngster possessing athletic talent.

This is not just a matter of successful black athletes being more visible to the young black than successful black doctors, lawyers, or businessmen. No, for if that were the whole story, it would hardly explain the phenomenon, for not too long ago there were no Negroes on professional football teams. It was the success of white football players that blacks sought to emulate, initially.

Perhaps the best way to put it is in terms of a weaker pull from other occupations in the black case than in the white. Professional football is seen by youngsters as extremely lucrative and glamorous, and it would be an odd boy indeed, black or white, who would not, if he had the chance, rather be a pro football star than a bank teller or a plumber or a marginal life-insurance salesman. But what if the alternative were to be a millionaire businessman or lawyer (or doctor), a supreme court justice, governor, U.S. senator? (It must be admitted, in the last-named cases, that it may be possible for a professional athlete to "eat his cake and have it too" in terms of subsequently achieving high political office; cf. the case of New Jersey's Senator Bill Bradley.)

Here is where the very different socio-economic position of Average Black with Athletic Ability versus his white counterpart comes in. He knows what it takes to play football, and if his race will not bar him, he basically knows what it takes to be a professional football player. (*Now*, of course, he has prominent black footballers as examples, too.) The lofty reaches of the business and professional world are a mystery to him; it is unlikely that a parent, a relative, or a friend of his family can, by offering a believable personal example close at hand, make that sort of thing something at which he wants to aim instead of professional sports.

For males in poverty who possess athletic skill, utilizing that skill has long been an obvious avenue of escape from poverty, not only for the individual but for his enthusiastic family. Take boxing, for example. The higher up the socio-economic ladder, the more oriented the family will be toward directing the youngster toward preparation for a professional career; attitudes change as to the relative merits of football practice and academic study.

It may be that the average black youngster with pro football potential not only *perceives* the way he ought to aim differently than does his white counterpart, but also that his perception is *correct:* that is, if the controversial researchers Jensen and Shockley are correct, professions requiring mental acuity are relatively less promising avenues for blacks than for whites.

What conclusions, now, can we draw from the foregoing analysis, as to why there are so few whites playing professional football? First, we don't know exactly what the cause is, and it seems reasonable from our survey to suspect a combination of factors. The last dealt with, the socio-economic, seems to make a lot of sense, but from the evidence it would certainly seem that there may be something to the belief that, in terms of the high level of physical prowess required in pro football, the Negro race has received more than its share.

A second conclusion is that there is certainly no reason to assume that foul play is involved. While it is always possible that an individual coach has discriminated in some instance against a white player, no specific instance has come to light, and positing such discrimination as the reason for the striking overall "racial imbalance" in professional football is patently absurd.

A third conclusion is that there certainly seems no basis for any court orders requiring the hiring of certain numbers of white football players. Nor would it appear reasonable or just for football teams to begin a policy of giving whites a competitive advantage over blacks in try-outs for teams, whiteness, say, being worth five points. There is good reason to believe that such a policy, in addition to being unfair to the Negroes not selected, would result in poorer football.

Last, since it is possible that there are talented whites out there who would, if they understood the opportunity better, direct themselves toward pro football, football owners and managers, if they suspect they are missing the boat in failing to tap a great pool of talent from which superior players for their teams could be recruited, would be well advised to implement some kind of "affirmative action" program. If it turns up white players better qualified than the Negroes who would otherwise be signed up, then the whites will be signed up instead and the level of football will rise. It would not seem that owners and managers should be required by law to do this, however. No important public interest is involved.

Now let us try to apply the above analysis to the matter of Negroes and medical school admission. *Mutatis mutandis,* the alternative explanations are as follows:

1. Medical-school admissions officers are deliberately admitting less-qualified whites instead of better-qualified blacks for racial reasons.

2. Although no deliberate discrimination is involved, the criteria used in the admission of applicants are such as to lead to the selection of less-qualified whites instead of better-qualified blacks because the criteria fail to properly measure the true qualifications of applicants for the practice of medicine, and further fail in such a way as to penalize black applicants systematically.

3. A far smaller percentage of blacks than of whites possess the very high qualifications required to qualify for admission.

   a. Because, in terms of ability to practice medicine, the black race as a whole, or on the average, is inferior to the white.

   (1) Inherently: God gave the white race better medicine-practicing aptitude.

   (2) Not quite inherently, but almost, and for practical purposes the same thing.

   (3) Whether or not (1) or (2), in fact, in the case of this generation, at this point in time, whether due to poor diet, lack of mental exercise, or whatever.

   b. Whether or not a. is true, the different distribution of this ability in the two races is such that a disproportionately small number of Negroes possess the exceptional ability required.

4. Whether or not 3. is the case, of those who are available for, or apply for, medical school, a disproportionately small percentage of qualified persons are black.

   a. Because, due to the notorious anti-black policies of medical schools in the past, a high percentage of qualified blacks are discouraged from applying.

   b. For other reasons.

Again, we can separate out the obviously implausible rather easily. While undoubtedly 1. happens from time to time, even today, the academic world is about the last place one would expect to find racism so pervasive as to account for the great disparity in admissions that has been noticed.

Point 2. seems quite implausible. Medical schools in general want the best students they can get, for one thing because the glory of alumni reflects on the school, and the procedures they have chosen represent their best effort to select accordingly. (In those cases where favoritism may still be shown toward children of alumni, the admission of whites is likely to be furthered, but such favoritism neither seems a significant factor overall nor would help the white sons and daughters of non-alumni vis-à-vis similarly situated blacks.) No one has ever come up with alternative selection criteria together with a reasoned case that their use would ensure selection of the best applicants, nor shown why it should be that an apparent aptitude to practice medicine, as measured in admissions procedures, should correlate with an actual aptitude in the case of whites but not in that of blacks. For that matter, there are medical schools and there are medical schools. There must be some Negro doctors who were turned down at their first-choice school and went elsewhere and received their degrees and went into practice. A showing that in fact they are on average better doctors than those admitted to their first-choice schools instead of them would go far toward lending some plausibility to what otherwise can only be called a totally implausible allegation with no factual basis whatsoever. If it is unreasonable to expect some correlation between the measurable qualifications, including grades and test scores, of a twenty-two-year-old college graduate and that graduate's actual qualifications to practice medicine, a lot of time and money could be saved by simply admitting to medical school by lottery.

(Apropos of qualifications, the Davis people made a great point of stressing that, even under their quota system, "everyone who was admitted was qualified." This is, of course, an almost completely meaningless statement. It may mean that they have the intellectual capacity to pass their courses, receive their degrees, and be admitted to practice medicine. In that sense, there are many people who are qualified to practice medicine in this country: and if they'd "had the grades to get into medical school" they would be practicing medicine: it's the limited number of places in medical school, and admitting only the *best* qualified, that admissions procedures are all about.)

Point 3. would seem as reasonable to consider in this case as with the black athletes. Here again, where, as with pro football, very high qualifications are involved, the bell-shaped curve of standard distribution would magnify the effect of even a very small average difference between the races. Here, too, however, instead of 3.a.(3) being altogether implausible as in the football analysis, it offers a *very* plausible explanation, so that no inherent Negro inferiority in this area need be assumed: the nurture *is,* of Negro younsters in this country, on the average, inferior to white, in that quality of nurture is pretty directly correlated with socio-economic level and the average Negro's is lower than the average white's. Lack of encouragement at home, poor diet, crowding, etc., can give rise to poor habits of study and thought; thus, even in the case of a Negro college graduate planning to go to medical school, there still could be, on the average, inferior qualification.

Point 4. also looks promising. Not a.; it does not seem all that plausible. In the case of schools in areas of the country where racial segregation was practiced, everyone now knows that it is over; while a black student might still hesitate to apply to a deep South medical school, we are basically talking about UC-Davis and other non-Southern medical schools, and, though many formerly restricted the percentage of Jewish students they admitted, none, as far as I know, ever discriminated against Negro applicants. (Any Negro who, in this age of "affirmative action," doesn't apply to a northern medical school because he or she thinks they discriminated against his race in the past and probably are still up to that sort of thing would have to be so far out of touch with reality as not to be able to distinguish bubonic plague from measles!)

But b. seems to make a lot of sense, as did the corresponding explanation in the professional football analysis above. (Indeed, there may even be some blacks playing football professionally who, had they been directed toward a medical career, would have ended up easily being accepted at Davis under the regular admissions program!) Take two equally bright youngsters, one white, the other black. The black's father, in his day, aspired to be, not a doctor, but—something his father thought realistic for a Negro—a Pullman porter on the Twentieth Century Limited—the "Century." The white's father aspired to be, and became, a doctor. For the white youngster, the most natural thing in the world is to follow in his father's footsteps, and on top of that, he has the advantage of his father's help and advice in connection with his studies. The black youngster is in a more difficult situation. In the first place, the Twentieth Century Limited has been discontinued. In the second place, and less facetiously and more fundamentally, he is understandably not keenly interested in such service-type work, but he is not on easy and familiar terms, from contact with family and family friends, with the various professional alternatives. It is not that the doctor he goes to is not black (as he probably isn't), just as the one-time absence of black professional football players didn't stop blacks from pursuing their interest in football. In fact, our black youngster probably knows well that there *are* black doctors, and lawyers (there was even one decades ago in "Amos 'n' Andy," although it must be acknowledged that Algonquin J. Calhoun did not project a high level of professional competence), and congressmen, etc.: the problem is, that these possibilities are much less likely to come alive for him in his lower socio-economic milieu (a problem faced by the son of a white janitor or bus driver, too). It may even be—who knows?—that for cultural reasons a very high percentage of Negroes view the practice of medicine, with all its exposure to sick or injured people, with aversion.

At any rate, again as with football, some conclusions—not altogether dissimilar—can be drawn. Again, we don't know the real cause of so few blacks qualifying for medical schools, but a combination of factors is reasonable to suspect. Again, no foul play seems to be involved; whatever may be the case in this or that isolated instance, there is no evidence that anti-black discrimination in admissions offices is a factor. Again, there seems no basis for quotas or systems of preference; such policies would necessarily be unfair to non-minorities, too, and, if objective measurement of aptitude has any meaning, would reduce the level of medicine in this country. (As far as medical services in the Negro community are concerned, there is no more reason to expect that a first-rate Negro doctor will spend his life in Negro slum practice than that a first-rate white doctor will. While it can be argued that a marginally competent Negro admitted to practice will be more likely to practice in a ghetto, since that is more likely to be the best he can do, it hardly seems to make sense to promote that sort of medical care for poor blacks, when the price is one less more-competent white physician: after all, many of the country's best urban hospitals are near black ghettos, so that their residents have easy access to them.)

Last, on the assumption that an untapped pool of black medical talent may be waiting out there, there is a case to be made for taking steps to bring the opportunities in medicine to blacks' attention. But since there is as much reason to assume such an untapped pool among poor whites, this is not an effort that should be confined to blacks. Nor, obviously, is there a sound case to be made for selecting less-qualified applicants of whatever race.

Giving preference to the poor of whatever race seems to be quite widespread in a variety of areas. While individuals may quite properly indulge their charitable impulses in any legal way, we did not inaugurate a government to take it upon itself to improve on the distribution of the goods of this life which occurred naturally. Furthermore, the assumption that the words "deserving poor" always belong together seems based on a highly objectionable view of the fairness of our socio-economic system. There are undeserving poor and deserving rich.

But arguments about the propriety of government wealth redistribution aside, the point needs to be made, with regard to giving a certain degree of preference, whether in employment or admission to medical school, to a poor person, that this practice can *only* be justified, as far as getting the best-qualified people and maximizing the level of competence is concerned (and let it not be forgotten that the competitiveness of the American economy in the world is becoming increasingly questionable), on the assumption that poverty is responsible for that degree of inferiority in the candidate's objectively-measured qualifications *and* that his apparent inferiority is temporary. Joe Blow's score was low, and he comes from a poor family; but it may be that Joe's score would have been no better had his father been a millionaire. Or, poverty may indeed have been at the root of Joe's poor performance, but now that the twig has been bent and the foundation laid, Joe *may* never catch up.

Obviously, the earlier on in his life we are talking about giving Joe favored treatment, the more optimistic it is reasonable to be with regard to his prospects for fully overcoming his early handicap: Joe has been retarded by poverty; he has started picking up speed; the process of acceleration will accelerate. Unfortunately, this doesn't always happen; the unfortunate people who were once called "retarded" as a euphemism for "feeble-minded" (and who now seem to be referred to either even more euphemistically as "exceptional" or more honestly as "handicapped") generally never do pick up speed significantly. It is one thing to admit a poor performer from a poor family to a prep school on a scholarship; it is quite another when one is talking about medical school admission; we can only be amazed when a black law school graduate, age twenty-five, after twenty years of education, blames the cultural disadvantage of being born black for his inability to pass the bar examination.

In terms of the overall good of society, it is not such a good idea to be so obsessed with avoiding the waste of the talents and potential of the poor that a larger waste occurs, that of the talents and potential of the better-off. And let it not be forgotten that if someone requires special coaching and remedial classes to keep up, some other person has to use time and talent to provide those things and cannot use them to do other things.

Looking back at our comparative analyses of racial imbalance in football teams and medical schools, it becomes obvious how foolish and wrong-headed we are when we jump to conclusions about "discrimination" in such cases; and how counter-productive, in terms of the overall good of society, are quotas and other preferential-treatment systems, whether governmentally required or freely adopted by well-meaning people. Why should a group's representation in a particular occupation be proportional to its population? So many factors, from historical accident to cultural patterns and all the rest, have a bearing. Every now and then someone rediscovers that there are not many Jews in the executive ranks of large commercial banks and public utility companies, or that some suburb has hardly any Negroes living in it, and the conclusion jumped to is always that bankers are bigots and so are suburban real estate agents. But there is an "overrepresentation" of Jews in retailing and investment banking, and Fresno has more Armenians per capita than any other American city: is the answer a quota system for Gentiles in retailing and a ban on further sales of homes in Fresno to Armenians?

Just as quotas are not rational, neither, of course, is the elimination or weakening of reasonable standards. It can, in fact, be called mind-boggling that such weakening would be seriously suggested. Yet it has been and continues to be; the following tongue-in-cheek response, written in 1971 after I read this news item, is not irrelevant today.

In a speech . . . [Vice President Spiro] Agnew commented on developments in Pennsylvania, where some public officials and lawyers are calling for abolition of the bar examination. They have charged that the tests are "culturally biased" against Negroes and that a high percentage of them do not pass, and they have suggested that all persons who gain law degrees should be licensed to practice.

New York Times Service, February 1, 1971

A MODEST PROPOSAL

It is without a great deal of surprise that we read of this latest extension of the cultural bias principle. This is, after all, merely a logical step in the progression of its application, and this may well represent the next great area of progress in the field of Negro rights. There have been stirrings of this sort in a variety of places for some years: according to J. Edgar Hoover, he was pressed in the 1960s by then Attorney-General Robert Kennedy to lower the standards for FBI agents so that more Negroes would qualify; a recent *U.S. News & World Report* article surveys the nationwide effort to attract more Negroes to police forces, notes that difficulty in passing examinations has been a hindrance in this regard, and refers to suggestions that the examinations be made easier; in San Francisco, a spokesman for Negro postal employees charges that dismissals of employees for absenteeism are "racist," because most persons thus discharged are Negroes, whose lifestyles and difficulty in finding babysitters make their absenteeism inevitable.

Eight black college graduates from Chicago filed a lawsuit against the Civil Service Commission yesterday, contending the Federal service entrance examination is 'culturally and racially discriminatory.' . . . Supported by the Lawyers' Committee for Civil Rights Under Law, they complain that the . . . Commission has failed to comply adequately with federal executive orders requiring equal employment opportunity. Statistics cited in the legal brief indicate that while 49 per cent of all people who take the test pass, only 3 per cent of those who attended black colleges do so. As a result, they say, only 1.2 per cent of all federal employees in the high grades of GS 16 to 18 are black.
—Times-Post Service, February 5, 1971

Perhaps we shall soon see a spate of magazine articles about the "racial imbalance" of the bar, and of medicine, dentistry, and the accounting profession; and it can be safely anticipated that, once matters are expressed in these terms, the pressure for action to correct the problem will become well-nigh irresistible, sooner or later.

Racial imbalance, after all, has come to be recognized as one of the *summa mala* of modern American life, an evil so nasty as to call for correction by whatever means are needed. Under California law, for example, going beyond the federal mandate to eliminate only deliberately caused imbalance, school authorities have a positive duty to correct any racial imbalance by any means necessary. It is no excuse that a school is racially imbalanced because no white, or no black, lives within a mile of it; in that case, to the joy of transportation entrepreneurs, children must be driven back and forth in buses, and even financial difficulties in the school district will not deter the provision of funds for buses, whatever urgent needs must fall by the wayside as a result. Nor is the consumption of student time, disruption of parent-teacher communication, or anything else deemed any justification for standing in the way of the correction of racial imbalance.*

*Hitherto, attention has been paid only to race in the broad sense. But for someone convinced that a proper "mix" of children of different colors is crucially important, it is only a small further step to being concerned about the proportions of youngsters of various ethnic backgrounds within the colors: Irish, Italian, Polish, etc. We have so far been spared the suggestion that an infusion of Lithuanian children, so lacking in the racial balance of Brooklyn elementary schools, should be obtained from the Midwest by early-morning jet, to be sent home again in the afternoon.

This terrible ogre of "imbalance" needs to be banished not only from our schools but also from other key areas of American life, such as the professions. Just as the fact of children living two miles away is no excuse for their not attending a particular school so that it may stop being racially imbalanced, so the fact that some men and women cannot pass the bar examination is no excuse for their not being admitted to the bar so that it may stop being racially imbalanced. One can with confidence look ahead to the discovery of area after area, profession after profession, that suffers from racial imbalance, produced by culturally biased examinations; and then to demands, ultimata, demonstrations, seizures of buildings, bombings, riots, and exhortations from the pulpits, editorial columns, and television screen; in short, to a continual uproar for years to come: unless something is done.

It cannot be expected that the arguments that the elimination of examinations and standards will debase the professions by admitting to them unqualified individuals, or that the unqualified individuals will not be able to operate effectively, will carry much weight. The principle is already quite well established that lack of preparation for a certain level of instruction on the part of a Negro, and a decline in overall standards at that level that results from his or her admission, are not valid reasons for exclusion.

After all, some years ago, it was discovered that, due to cultural bias in IQ tests, Negro elementary school children did less well on them than did white; but it would not do to put them into the slow readers group as a result; that would be demoralizing for them; and furthermore their innate ability to learn was not, could not be, properly represented by their showing on those culturally biased tests; and if keeping them with the faster readers did slow up those children a bit, too bad, and anyway the Negro youngsters would get over their slowness pretty soon. It must be agreed that, while it was too bad to see the testing of students stop, in a way, keeping slower and faster learners together made a good deal of sense. It would not be the end of the world if the fast readers were held back a little, and even though it might be difficult for a "slow" child to cope with the fast track (after all, let's face it, standard textbooks *do* use normal English, not Harlem patois, so that a child who did poorly on an intelligence test, culturally biased though it might be, *did* have a handicap in facing learning materials and classroom work), he needed the encouragement and the exposure.

Of course, this approach of disregarding performance as measured hardly stopped with elementary school. Throughout junior high and high school, the accepted practice in public schools has become to move students one grade ahead each year, regardless of ability and achievement. The effect on the overall level of education in a particular grade, of course, was not considered particularly important; although an increasing tendency on the part of public school board members to send their own children to private schools has been noted.

Since 1970, and particularly heartwarming to the concerned, forward-looking segment of the population, we have seen important developments at City College of New York. This institution for many years prided itself on being a first-class college although charging virtually nothing to those partaking of its education; admission was confined to students meeting stringent academic qualifications; *i.e.*, it took more than a high school diploma of dubious worth to get in. It was found, of course, that this resulted in a racially unbalanced student body; admissions procedures were, it was clear, culturally biased; there were demands and demonstrations. The obvious solution, "open enrollment," which was implemented in 1970, was aimed at facilitating the admission of unqualified Negroes and Puerto Ricans. There was opposition, on the grounds that this policy would ruin the college, but the anti-imbalance element carried the day. The ability of the new students to do the work, and the effect of their presence on the general level of the institution, were not deemed worth worrying about.

Many of the best private universities, throughout the country, are now moving, in their separate ways, to eliminate racial imbalance from their student bodies, by straightforwardly admitting unqualified Negroes (and, depending on locality, Puerto Ricans or Chicanos), although not unqualified whites. This is, of course, a more direct means to eliminate racial imbalance than simply admitting a certain number of unqualified students regardless of race, creed, or color.

Recognizing, among other things, that the most prestigious universities in the country have thus wholeheartedly embraced the racial balance concept even for themselves, it is hard to see that it will be possible to stand against it in the long run anywhere. It therefore seems reasonable for the country to spare itself years of struggle, with serious effects on blood pressure, digestion, and window panes and stonework, by simply eliminating all professional standards forthwith, perhaps along the lines proposed by the enlightened Pennsylvania officials and lawyers for their state's legal profession.

Eliminating all standards may seem a drastic step, but upon reflection, we are assured, it will be seen that only thus can a really telling body blow be dealt that old demon, cultural bias. This old fellow is tricky, devious, and persistent; attempts to devise tests totally free of cultural bias (that is, tests on which Negroes will score on average as well as whites) have to date, at least to my knowledge, proved unavailing. In the Pennsylvania case, we have Negroes who have gone through grammar school, junior high school, high school, college, and law school; and still too high a percentage of them fail the bar examination, due, as the Pennsylvania authorities point out, to the cultural bias of the examination. The thing is unbeatable, head-on; you have to make an end run, by simply eliminating the examinations where cultural bias rears its ugly head.

Of course there will be people who argue that in any case a person who is unable to pass the bar examination in a given state is liable to have difficulty practicing law effectively in that state, since the examination is based on the law as it is. This is, of course, true, but, given the paramount importance of eliminating imbalance, irrelevant. People will also argue that the bar, or the dental profession, or the level of riverboat navigation, as the case may be, will be degraded by eliminating examinations. This is also true, but, again, irrelevant, since these downgradings are minor compared to the need to achieve racial balance and compensate for centuries of oppression.

In any case, it will immediately be pointed out by clergymen, commentators, liberal politicians, Negro leaders, and the like, that people who use such arguments are racists; if, for example, an opponent of open admission to the medical profession inveighs against the danger to human life posed by "unqualified surgeons," it will be charged that he really means "black surgeons," and that his words are "code words for racism," "designed to appeal to all the worst instincts of mankind." (This reasoning has ample precedent: *vide* the 1968 New York mayoral campaign, where certain candidates spoke against "crime in the streets," and were accused of racism, on the grounds that, since in fact most crime in the streets in New York is committed by Negroes and Puerto Ricans, opponents of crime in the streets were necessarily anti-Negro and Puerto Rican racists.)

The solution of automatically admitting all persons who complete curricula designed to prepare them for a profession to that profession, along the Pennsylvania lines, is as simple as it is effective. There may be a problem in erms of admission to some of the institutions offering these courses; out if some of them should balk, public pressure, the cutting off of government funds, and, if necessary, a court order, should suffice to get their doors open on an "open admissions" basis. If there should be a shortage of places in some field, the federal government can easily use federal funds to set up institutions offering easy, quick equivalent courses, not only in professional areas such as law and medicine, but also in any area where heretofore an examination had to be passed to qualify the would-be practitioner, such as airplane flying, pharmacy, plumbing, and truck driving. Certainly, lack of funds should no more keep a person from preparing for a chosen career than lack of aptitude in passing culturally biased examinations, and the taxpayers, seeing what is right, will surely not begrudge the funds required.

Once students enroll in these courses, it may confidently be predicted that, especially in this age of pass-fail grading, all who stay around will graduate, particularly since concerned, liberal faculty members will be exceedingly reluctant to fail a student and thereby discourage him, alienate him, and deprive him of an opportunity to practice his chosen profession. Needless to say, all diplomas must be regarded as equal for this purpose; the Pennsylvania anti-bar examination people assuredly would not propose to disqualify a Negro merely because his law degree was from an obscure correspondence course law school.

For that matter, perhaps even requiring courses before allowing practice will prove to be tinged with cultural bias, or "culturally and racially discriminatory." As the San Francisco post office man would point out, Negroes have a different lifestyle, on average, than whites; it may be culturally discriminatory to expect them to spend their time—they are understandably impatient now—in classes, paying attention to a teacher, especially if the teacher is white.

The new system of immediate open admission to all professional and semi-professional areas (and to any area where an examination is presently required, whether it involve the position of forest ranger, streetcar conductor, or building inspector) will have the tremendously salutary effect of sparing the nation the turmoil that would inevitably be produced by a laborious, step-by-step struggle to break down professional standards piecemeal; it will also eliminate the expense of administering examinations, and can thus be billed as a sweeping economy measure.

Prophets of gloom and doom, who can be counted on to attack any progressive measure, will probably try to scare the people with a scenario about a man who gets up in the morning, gets an electric shock from the light switch, scalds himself when he turns on the cold water faucet, thinks the ham, although passed by the Department of Agriculture inspector, tastes funny, strikes his head on an excessively low doorway on the way out, hails a cab whose driver has no idea how to get downtown, is hit by a truck-trailer driven by a helpless driver, gets to his office and finds that the mail has not been delivered, is chagrined to peruse a balance sheet with entries reading "currant assets . . . fixed assets . . . unfixed assets . . . deprecation," and finds that his lawyer has filed papers in the wrong state, and that the IRS man has lost all his tax material; the lights in the office do not work and the electrician, who proclaims that the light bulbs have all been made in Watts and points proudly to the name at the top of each bulb, does not inspire confidence . . .

Of course, there *will* inevitably be some difficulties caused by the new no-examination situation; but, as the saying goes, you can't make an omelette without breaking some eggs. There should be no great problem in the legal field. To be sure, it can be very annoying to retain a lawyer to recover the cost of a faulty television set and find that he used the wrong form and your marriage has been dissolved instead. But this sort of thing is not likely to happen often. And, while it is admittedly no fun to be represented by an incompetent, many legal matters involve adversary proceedings, and you may get lucky: it may be your opponent who is represented by an incompetent. It all ought to even out in the long run, as perhaps the Pennsylvania gentlemen have in mind. As for dentistry, there is liable to be somewhat more pain in the dentist's chair, but this will serve to give people a keener understanding of the suffering of Negroes during centuries of oppression.

Medicine presents, on the surface, more of a problem: a toothache is one thing, but it can have very serious effects on a person's health if his surgeon removes his heart or his liver instead of his appendix. But a mistake of this magnitude is unlikely to be made twice on the same person, and you can't live forever anyway. Similarly, improperly compounded prescriptions are just a problem people will have to live with. If they can; some, unfortunately, will inject themselves with rubbing alcohol instead of insulin.

People will just have to accustom themselves to slightly different levels of service in a variety of areas, but Americans are eager to do what is right, whatever sacrifices it may entail. The practice of giving examinations, all of which it can safely be assumed are culturally biased, has been a widespread one in our society: accountant, architect, building inspector, airplane pilot, civil servant, engineer, fireman, harbor pilot, policeman, river pilot, stockbroker, truck driver, veterinarian: all these, and many more, involve examinations.

A difficulty may unfortunately arise in the form of people not wanting to have anything to do with even very able new lawyers, electricians, doctors, etc., (particularly, given the reason the examinations were eliminated, those of minority races) in the belief that they would not have been able to pass the examination, had one been still required, and are probably incompetent. This attitude, or a precursor of it, has already been noticed in employer attitudes toward high school diplomas. It is to be hoped that the climate of enlightened public opinion will serve to counteract this tendency, by making people feel it to be their duty to employ newly-practicing professionals and semi-professionals, and implying that racism is probably at the heart of anyone's failure to do so at least part of the time. If it becomes necessary, however, it would be easy enough to set up a quota system of some sort and have everyone from lawyers to plumbers and accountants assigned to the would-be user from a central, racially-balanced pool. Some will complain that a man should be able to choose his local lawyer if he wants, but people said that a child should be able to attend the neighborhood school, too. First things first.

The above facetious "modest proposal" has not yet been extensively implemented; we are still in an era of attacks on standards and the devising of ways around them, such as quota systems. We need to keep in mind is that we have standards, and we seek the best-qualified people, for sound and proper reasons; that there is no reason to expect races to be represented in every occupation from sports to medicine in exact proportion to their share of the population; and that the lowering of reasonable standards, no matter how well-intentioned the reason, neither furthers justice nor benefits society.

10

Popular Attitudes

It is probably correct to say that most of the fundamental causes of the disruption of the *economic* environment—minimum wage laws, "fair labor practices" legislation, and federal involvement in the economy, for example—were, at least when the implementing legislation was passed, approved of by the majority of Americans. Whether this would have been the case if it had been understood how the resulting disruption would affect people's economic self-interest in the long and even in the short run is another matter. That is largely irrelevant, however. The man in the street is not and never will be an economic expert, and tampering with the economy, like building a canal, is generally done at the behest of a pressure group or particular interest that knows very well what it wants. This is, of course, all the more reason for a policy of "hands off the environment." To labor unions anxious to reduce the threat of competition from non-union labor, constant increases in the minimum wage make sense; to persons interested in developing their inland town into an ocean port, a trans-Florida canal makes sense. In the one case, widespread joblessness among the unskilled is the result, and in the other, the ruin of a river; for in both cases the environment has been tampered with.

While there is general concurrence in the tampering with the economic environment (with the probable exception of generous interpretations of welfare laws), there is no such thing in the case of the socio-political landscape, where recent changes have no obvious beneficiaries except various minorities and the majority is the fairly obvious and apparent loser. Not only do the vast majority of Americans still lead their lives by the old rules and precepts (which is crucial to the fact that our system still runs as well as it does), they abhor the new precepts.

Time and again sociologists have surveyed the attitudes of the bulk of the population and come away absolutely horrified at the level of enlightenment they found. In one famous study, it was found that the vast majority of Americans would not allow a Communist to teach in their school! Even with slanted questions and the extent to which the man in the street is increasingly getting the idea, via the media, of what he *ought* to be thinking, the attitudes of the population come through loud, clear, and—to a liberal—dismaying. By a better than two-to-one margin, in the mid-1970s, California voters voted to restore the death penalty; and then, in 1978, by a margin nearly twice as large, to extend its application.

The man in the street does not regard welfare recipients as unfortunate victims of an unjust system, or of racial discrimination; he regards them as, on the whole, a bunch of shiftless, characterless misfits. He is not struck with feelings of guilt at being shown that, although Negroes constitute 8 per cent of the population of Hick

Center, they fill only 1 per cent of the managerial positions in the Hick Center lead smelter, or any of the plethora of similar facts currently being discovered by well-meaning people and trumpeted as incontrovertible and damning proof of racial discrimination; he regards it, in many cases, as only natural that Negroes should be underrepresented in many positions, since, after all, they are, at least in terms of current preparation for such positions, inferior to whites on average, as he sees it. He probably has not read of Professor Jensen's researches, or of the baffling fifteen-point IQ differential, but forms his views from observation.

The man in the street has no patience with rioters; if he were running the TV networks, he would not devote great amounts of time to giving radicals a chance to mouth their sentiments to the nation. He applauded the police in the Chicago convention riots, even after he was presented with as one-sided a television presentation of the event as possible.* He would like to see hippies and vagrants rousted from the streets, rioters firmly dealt with, radical professors fired, unruly and disruptive students expelled, etc., etc.; in short, he would like to see things run rather differently than they are and *very* radically differently than the TV programs, and the magazine articles, and the preachers, and the "experts" who are quoted at such length in the news columns of the *New York Times* would like to see them. As to the media, the man in the street applauded Spiro Agnew's attacks; indeed, he had been muttering much the same thing for years himself.

How is it, then, that there is this gulf, this gap, between the country as a whole and the "opinion-making elite"? Here we have, in the social and political area, one set of basic values and views shared by the great bulk of the people; and another, violently at odds with the

---

*I happened to be in Chicago at the time of the riot and in fact was at the Conrad Hilton Hotel when the police cleared the intersection of Michigan and Balbo Avenues, having earlier been outside between the police and the demonstrators. It had occurred to me that there were safer places to be, since a major intersection like that presumably could not be allowed to be blocked indefinitely, and therefore I was inside when the famous charge occurred. My reaction was that the police used a good deal of vigor, but, after having seen "kids" in their versions of Viet Cong uniforms, with helmets, and what had been done to the Grant Park stonework, and being aware of what the police had had to put up with, I thought that not unreasonable. After having dinner and returning to my room, I turned on the television and learned, with some disappointment, that I had missed the real excitement; the newsmen, and everyone else interviewed, were obviously talking about some terrible outrage perpetrated by the police somewhere in the city. I kept watching, anxious to learn what had happened and where, when it finally dawned on me, to my amazement, that what everyone was talking about in tones of such outrage was what I had seen.

first, shared by the bulk of the articulate opinion makers and imping-ing to a substantial degree upon the socio-political environment, to the immense chagrin and frustration of the population at large. How has this come about?

11

The Role of the "Intellectuals":

Attempts at Definition

I f there is one thing that has been crucial in the trend of our times, it has been the attitude of the "intellectuals"—that articulate opinion-shaping force, sometimes known as the "vocal minority." This includes teachers, professors, journalists, writers, playwrights, clergy, commentators. Without really significant exception, this force, in the post-World War II years, has been what can be called "liberal."

Many have attempted to define "liberal." Some, looking at particu-lar controversies at particular points in time, have tried to define the word in terms of centralizers versus decentralizers, isolationists ver-sus interventionists or internationalists, free-speechers versus cen-sorship advocates, etc. This is a normal academic approach that often makes sense, but only if we can take at face value what those involved in those controversies are saying.

But we cannot do this if we want to deal with fact instead of fancy. Put, as above, in 1950-ish terms of "isolationism versus interna-tionalism," the "liberals" would presumably fall into the category of internationalists—as opposed to mean isolationists wanting to cut down foreign aid and jealously guard American sovereignty. But put the dichotomy as "isolationists versus interventionists" and you get, in the images fashioned by current liberal journalism, "liberals" the other way around—on the isolationist side, as opposed to those who supposedly wish to intervene all over the world, usually to prop up friendly regimes. But what then about Israel? Or Rhodesia/ Zimbabwe? Then the "liberal" is found to be an "interventionist," in the former case seeking to assist a foreign state and in the latter to topple and restructure a foreign government.

In the age of the aristocratic Federalist party, the "liberals" were those in favor of states' rights. Similarly on the matter of President Grover Cleveland sending federal troops to get the mails moving in the 1893 Pullman strike, over the opposition of Governor Altgeld of Illinois. But as soon as one uses "states' rights" in its modern context, it is the other way around; liberals want more federal power so as to overcome the backwardness, racism, and responsiveness to local moneyed interests of the statehouses. Local rule can be very bad. But it was a different matter, a few years ago, when upstate New York Republicans trampled on Mayor John V. Lindsay's progressivism in New York City.

Neither how one stands on foreign involvements on grounds of principle, nor how one stands on decentralization of governmental power, nor any such matters really get to the heart of what is a liberal or a conservative, in a meaningful sense, in the United States today. The stands people take on such issues really are a matter of "whose ox is gored": intervention against fascism—against the Rhodesian government or against Somoza in Nicaragua, say—is one thing; intervention against communism is another. Federal overriding of state authority in Little Rock or Mississippi is one thing; federal overriding of state authority like President Cleveland's is another.

"Whose ox is gored." Liberals have certain oxen with whom they identify and certain *bêtes noirs* toward whom their feelings are quite different, and therein is the real nature of our "liberals." Good people, or oxen that must not be gored, include Negroes, Mexicans, Indians, and similar unassimilated, or, rather more to the point, relatively unsuccessful racial groups; persons on a political spectrum ranging from liberal virtually all the way left; countries dominated by such ideology, or inhabited by such racial groups (although a left-wing country of white people, like Russia or Yugoslavia, takes precedence over a right-wing country of darker people, such as Brazil); and the *lumpenproletariat*. The "liberal's" heart is down there with the underdogs, the little fellows.

Bêtes noirs include rich people, unless they are liberal; white people (Chinese and Japanese too) of unenlightened (un-"liberal") views (the bulk of the American people fall into this category, under the patronizing title "Middle America"); any member of a generally depressed ethnic group, especially if he has worked his way upward, who fails to agree that his people have had a really raw deal and that all of their troubles are of other peoples' making; persons whose views are to the right of the "liberals' "; and countries dominated by conservative ideology.

A "liberal" may also tell you that what distinguishes him from a conservative is that he is for freedom. This is hogwash. The "liberals," indeed, are for some freedoms: the freedom of an employee to wear his hair long or otherwise violate his employers' rules without losing his job, the freedom of hippies to sunbathe in the nude, the freedom of pornographers to market their product, the freedom of people to demonstrate threateningly and even violently in the streets against "nukes" or for "affirmative action" and more welfare or whatever the current "cause" is; the freedom of the likely criminal from conditions that make his conviction, if guilty, more likely; the freedom of foreign countries to seize American corporations' properties.

Liberals are emphatically not for freedom of employers to select their employees, the freedom of society to repress disorder and crime, the freedom of the landlord to select tenants, the freedom of children to go to school in their own neighborhoods, the freedom of white racists in Mississippi to march in the streets, or the freedom of ITT to try to replace a Chilean government likely to confiscate its properties in that country.

It all boils down to the sacred oxen and the *bêtes noirs*. There are a few purists in the liberal throng who do try hard to promote at least the rights of public demonstration and free speech for extremists on the right, but this does not detract from the basic fact about liberals in general where "freedoms" are involved: that it is not freedoms as such but rather the apparent interests of the groups they favor that concern them.

Tortuous reasoning is often required to keep the innocence of these sacred oxen unsullied. An unenlightened observer, for example, might wonder whether oppressed Negro families might not, through systematic saving and frugality, better their lot, as so many varieties of despised immigrants successfully did in an age of child labor, sweatshops, and a total absence of Job Corps, free college education, compulsory high school, and Head Start and Tail Start programs, to name a few. It is difficult to get an explanation from a liberal on this matter other than a statement like "that was different," or "discrimination is worse for Negroes," or a suggestion that anyone who asks such a question must be a racist, or a refusal to accept that the questioner can be serious.

The conviction that the less-well-off in American society—and throughout the world—are in their condition through no fault of their own can fairly be called a basic article of faith of the liberal creed. That creed, as it emerges from a study of the sacred oxen, is underdogism, which may be called egalitarianism or the yearning to level; its *essential* article of faith is that the natural ordering of society in a free enterprise, captalist system is inherently unjust. Our system does not really generally give "to each according to his ability," and, to the extent that it does, it still fails, for "to each according to his need" is the appropriate principle. Either way the system is unjust. This important point must not be overlooked. It is central to the outrage and indignation that issue from the liberal community whenever the startling discovery is made that this or that group of people—the itinerant wild berry-pickers of Kentucky, this month's stars may be—is not very well off financially. The impoverished, particularly if Negro, Mexican, Indian, etc., are seen as almost entirely free from any blame in connection with any of their actions, no matter how outrageous. The concept of blame has been only selectively eradicated in the liberals' minds, for clearly such groups as policemen, landlords, white people in general, inadequately "militant" Negroes (whites are "extremist," Negroes are "militant"), white Rhodesians, Chilean or Brazilian leaders, and employees and stockholders of Dow Chemical Company are just a few of those exposed to withering contempt and obloquy for their sins. *"Toute comprendre, c'est tout pardonner"* applies only to the sacred oxen, not to the *bêtes noirs*.

It is also interesting and instructive to note the differences in the degree to which members of the two classifications are vulnerable to criticism or ridicule. The "Middle America" group is fair game for clever commentators and writers, who continually poke fun at Lithuanian and Polish steel workers, etc., their bowling and other recreational propensities, their potbellies, their taste in food and furniture; but just try to find an article in a major magazine ridiculing the speech, dress, and diet of Negroes, or satirizing their life-style! If you will recall a typical "Polish joke" and tell it, or imagine it told by a comedian, with "Pole" replaced by "black" you will see the point.

Given liberal underdogism, with its sacred oxen, basically those on the bottom, and the achievement of sanctity through wholeheartedly identifying with them, the position that they are there through no fault of their own is essential. Suffering per se may be sad, but it is not enough to guarantee sympathy even from the greatest "bleeding heart" liberal. That liberal is quite prepared to see Nazi extermination experts, Ku Klux Klan nightriders, child molesters, poisoners of pets

(provided their constitutional rights are not violated), and other per-
petrators of extremely unpleasant acts suffer as a result of their
misdeeds, without developing the sympathy that he feels toward the
ordinary imprisoned mugger; nor have liberals' hemophiliac hearts
bled very much for the skid-road derelict, whom even they find it
difficult to see as a victim of oppression. You cannot get that good
warm feeling inside from identifying with a sufferer who all *too*
obviously brought it all on himself.

It is ironically the very success which liberalism has had over the
years that makes the underdogism that current liberalism amounts to
such an irrational doctrine; if in fact today the Ku Klux Klan were
rampant in the South, child labor and sweatshops near-universal,
business totally indifferent to social causes, unions weak and near-
nonexistent, welfare confined to the "poor farm," and education
beyond grammar school the exception rather than the rule, the attitudes of today's liberals would make a great deal more sense. Para-
doxically, the success of the liberals in changing for the better the
world that was makes the current liberals' attitudes totally inappropriate to the world that is.

12

The Role of The "Intellectuals":

Attempts at Explanation

I f the "liberalism" of those who
dominate the group known as "intellectuals" is characterized by an
uncritical favoritism toward, and identification with, the "underdog,"
founded on a conviction that the American capitalist system is fundamentally unjust, where did this come from? These views, after all,
are not commonsense views, nor are they views grounded on a grasp
of elementary, or advanced, economics. Anyone with eyes can see
innumerable examples of persons from the most fashionable "disad-

vantaged" groups who, simply by hard work and application, have worked their way to prosperity. There are Negro millionaires in this country, and there were Negro millionaires in 1920. The way in which economic advancement can be achieved is not a secret known only to members of an occult lodge. The nature of the country as literally and actually a land of opportunity has been amply demonstrated by the progress made by illiterate, impoverished immigrants in times when few of today's benevolent programs for the betterment of the poor existed; and anyone who doubts that personal progress is possible today has not looked around and seen how many of today's leaders in business and the professions come from very modest backgrounds. Indeed, current waves of immigrants, many non-English-speaking, are already producing their own "success stories."

The conviction that this is an unjust society in which being poor is *per se* an entitlement to sympathy and to being identified with by "enlightened" people simply cannot come from honest observation. You need to wear ideological colored glasses to look around and reach that conviction. Even stupidity or naïvete will not normally do the job by itself. (In terms of personal characteristics needed by a liberal, a certain amount of will-power and determination, so that what is seen is only what one wants to see based on prior ideological commitment, are perhaps necessary.)

Not normally, but there may well be cases where naiveté, in the sense of economic ignorance, *is* fundamental to a liberal's under-dogism. Consider clergymen who seem anything but liberal theologically or temperamentally but who continually convey the idea that all individuals and nations that are well-off should be giving much of their wealth to "the poor." It is as if they have no understanding of how a modern free enterprise economy functions and assume that somehow worldly goods have been apportioned by sheer happenstance. Perhaps their concept of economic life comes from Biblical references to the static agricultural economy of ancient Palestine.

But devout, economically naive clergymen are not a major part of our American liberal community. What about the rest? We have to deal here to a considerable extent with psychology, but we can make some observations and suggest some hypotheses. One hypothesis is that liberals indulge in their views as a cure for guilt feelings. One manifestation of this concerns wealth: you feel guilty for having wealth without effort, and compensate by a devotion to the poor.

Another aspect is less straightforward. I have known people who were entirely obnoxious and unpleasant to nearly all they dealt with, yet espoused the most liberal views on groups they had no dealings with. (But also those they did in some cases, like one woman who supported the Negro rights movements but treated her Negro maid atrociously.) The theory here is that if you are a bastard and feel uneasy about it, you can feel good again and feel like a wonderful person by being an ardent liberal. This also entitles you to be mean to people who do not share your views as long as you regard them as bad as a result.

Though these "guilt" theories do, I think, account for many people's liberalism, they are necessarily very incomplete; I have known very agreeable, pleasant people who were liberals, and also plenty of people whose liberalism could scarcely be attributed to guilt over inherited wealth.

There is, of course, the obvious class-interest explanation for liberalism, so obvious it is redundant to mention it: one in poverty, or feeling strong ties by birth, childhood experiences, etc., to those who are, may absorb liberal views as part of his or her heritage or as a means of promoting personal interests; but this is certainly not the reason for the liberalism of the intelligentsia.

In the case of our young people, including today's generation of college students, it can be argued that in fact they do look at their country through specially colored glasses provided by their teachers. There is a good deal of truth to this that accounts for a lot of the simple-minded liberalism of the young as well as for the liberalism of those who never shed the political views their teachers gave them. Teachers are predominantly liberals.

The college generation of the 1950s, to which I belonged, was, I recall, definitely exposed to enlightenment from its teachers also. Not, of course, that we were constantly bombarded with left-wing propaganda in the classrooms. The typical teacher taught his subject and did not discuss politics except in the case of subjects whose content included the stuff of current political discussion, such as economics and political science. Nor were all our teachers who expressed political views to us liberals. At Stanford we had as visiting professor of political science the late eminent Willmoore Kendall, then of Yale, some of whose views would have had to be called reactionary rather than conservative. (They would become particularly virulent at gatherings such as Young Republican parties. I recall his announcing that he was in favor of slavery on the grounds that, as he put it, since some people were born slaves, the law ought to recognize that fact; on another occasion I argued with him about public schools: he was against them, not wanting his tax dollars to go to educate "some slum-dweller's brats.")

But, by and large, the political views our teachers expressed to us were liberal. For every Willmoore Kendall (who was not offered a professorship, by the way), there were at least two toward the opposite end of the political spectrum, such as, at Stanford, pacifist political scientist Mulford Q. Sibley or physics professor Albert V. Baez, whose daughter Joan was at the time refusing to participate in civil defense drills at Palo Alto High School. Professor Baez was a skilled debater on such issues of the day as nuclear testing. But our teachers' liberalism had comparatively little effect on us; our liberal teachers could do no more than repeatedly, and vainly, bewail our "apathy"—by which they meant our failure to agree that the causes they were enthusiastic about merited our support.

Perhaps the difference between that generation and those attending college in the 1960s and 1970s, in addition to the absence of the galvanizing effect of the Vietnam war, was partly that faculties had become more liberal and partly that our parents still were respected by us sufficiently that we had a tendency to continue with the attitudes and values they had raised us with, regardless of what our professors preached, whereas the latter group yearned to be told that what their parents believed in—if by then they had any strong beliefs at all, that is—was garbage. But that is the subject of another book. The question is, *how did their teachers, (and the other members of the predominantly liberal opinion-forming group), come by their convictions?*

Let us focus initially on teachers, since their role in spreading political views is so obvious. Now, the predominant liberalism of the academic world cannot be explained entirely as a reaction to the Great Depression, by any manner or means; particularly as a similar phenomenon occurs and recurs throughout history without the coincidence of comparable economic troubles.

But there was a significant leftward shift in the academic community in the 1930s and the role of the Great Depression in the formation of the predominant liberalism of today's opinion-molding class should not be ignored. That was a terribly traumatic experience for all who underwent it, and it was natural for a fair percentage of those who were in the habit of seeking the Why of things to reach the conclusion that the God of Capitalism had feet of clay and go over to the new Communist *Weltanschauung*. The adoption of this new faith was widespread in the academic community, as was disillusionment with the old god of *laissez-faire* capitalism and traditional values generally.

Given the leftward bias of the 1930s and the fact that progress and acceptance in the academic world are substantially dependent, as in most places, on sharing the values of one's colleagues and one's seniors, a continuing tendency in that direction would naturally result. The liberal orientation of the liberal arts faculties in particular at the average college is no secret, nor the intolerance of these enlightened people toward conservatives ("How could any intelligent person vote for Nixon?"), and a conservative young person attracted to academic life must have second thoughts and probably will decide against it, on that ground alone, unless the calling to the academic life is extremely strong. As a current example of the difficulties of academic life for the non-liberal, consider the 1980 outcry at Harvard against the proposed appointment as professor of economics and director of the Harvard Institute for International Development of an economist who had consulted with former students who held positions in the Chilean government. After it all, the economist chose not to accept the position. Can anyone recall a case of academic outrage at a major university on account of a professor's involvement with an undemocratic socialist or communist regime? A few days ago, my wife and I had dinner with an old Stanford acquaintance, now a professor in a midwestern university, and his wife. He was a Kennedy supporter and a believer in further extending the role of government; "You are the only intelligent, educated person I know who is planning to vote for Reagan," he declared. But he did express some very sensible views on foreign policy questions. "But," he hastened to add, "that's just between you and me. I mean that: in my position, you can't say things like that publicly."

But, while the Depression is a reasonably convincing explanation for the marked lurch leftward of the "intellectuals" in the 1930s, and consequently and subsequently for a certain tendency on their part to remain left, it alone cannot adequately explain all of their continuing (and pre-Depression) tendency in that direction.

Helping in this regard, certainly, are the "we-are-the-brightest-and-know-best-but-they-won't-listen-to-us-out-there and a-stockbroker-makes-more-money-than-a-professor" alienation effects. Feeling that they are not receiving from society the attention and respect to which their wisdom entitles them accentuates their tendency to dislike and distrust the world outside.

Also, liberalism tends to go in directions that are perceived as *new*, thus appealing to the kind of peculiar intellectual pride that is convinced it can improve on anything and has a basic unwillingness to accept and use what has already been developed, even where it can for all intents and purposes be considered perfected. This serves to incline the intellectual community toward liberalism. There is an interesting parallel in architecture; earlier this century and up through the 1920s, public buildings, as well as private office buildings, generally were built in the classic style, the forms and ornamentation going back to the Renaissance and ultimately to the Greeks and Romans; whereas, commencing with the 1930s, the decade that saw the strong leftward lurch of the intellectual community politically, practically no such structures have been built. It is as if, regardless of what most people find attractive, no self-respecting architect would design a county courthouse in the "style of the past." "It must represent and reflect our times." If "our times" include diminished attractiveness and an unwillingness to learn from and use the accomplishments of the past, then much modern architecture indeed well reflects "our times."

But is this all? The Depression; people's natural tendency to avoid occupations where their views would be a liability; academic resentment based on compensation and respect; intellectual pride; are they all that can be adduced to explain the predominance of liberalism in the academic community? Perhaps there are further reasons why, today, liberals are particularly likely to enter the teaching world and teachers to express liberal views. Let us explore these areas.

Ego needs, of course, are an important matter for all people. Good, old-fashioned snobbism is, indeed, very much alive today, however much people may be conditioned to deny to themselves, as well as to others, that they are guilty of it. Status seeking is alive and well today, everywhere from Greenwich to Dogpatch.

But how can it work for the ego needs of an educated person? He has read Vance Packard's *The Status Seekers* and smiled knowingly. He knows, in his heart, too, that the gaucheries of his economic and educational inferiors are not really their fault, and that it is not nice to snicker at the quaint ways of the poor.

The academic community, through which the college graduate moves for four years at least, is not a community given to socioeconomic snobbery. In the nature of things, being a college professor is not the way to make a fortune, and those primarily motivated by the more materialistic values of middle-class America, and by those of American business (which to a large extent are those of traditional America: "the business of America is business," said Calvin Coolidge, and Babbitt, caricature that he was, was not unrepresentative of a basic American attitude), are not likely to be professors. Nor are they likely to be members of other occupations whose "wave length" professors share and whose views also shape the climate of the intellectual world of which professors are a part. And therefore, while some conventional (socio-economic) snobbery may creep in, professors generally will not indulge their egos by looking down on their colleagues whose homes are less expensively furnished or who stay at the wrong hotel when at Biarritz.

So our educated citizen spends four years in college. This is not only a period during which he is part of an academic community (although he is not likely, unless he is planning an academic career, to think of himself as part of *the* academic community), it is also a period in which he has the time, and is likely to be given the encouragement, to read magazines and books and other products of the intellectual community, academic and non-academic. If passing through on the way to a business career, or a profession like law, the student may at least pick up the idea that there are many important things besides wealth or social position and perhaps be less inclined to think uncharitably of socio-economic inferiors, but the graduate's life will be achievement-oriented in largely a material sense, and major satisfaction will come from succeeding in business, or in a profession.

If, however, graduates have really immersed themselves in the quite different culture of Academe—as many, but by no means all, of the brightest students do—they will often come away, whether or not remaining in the academic world, marching to a very different drummer than this down-to-earth, business-oriented country as a whole. They will perhaps feel that business generally is a nasty thing, and that they must avoid it and instead do something "creative" or "meaningful"—like being a journalist, or a writer, or a "poverty lawyer," or a teacher, or a social worker, or a city planner.

Without disparaging the amount of creativity and meaningfulness in such occupations, or suggesting that they are not important or there is anything wrong with wanting to use one's analytical or literary talents, for example, full time, it must be said that the idea that such occupations have a monopoly on such characteristics is not only wrong but indicates a total missing of the point of the capitalist system. A government planner, working with the elements in his sphere, devotes himself to accomplishing as much as possible, at least partly motivated by desire for recognition and promotion, and this is considered fine and meaningful by many; a businessman, managing the resources at his disposal, seeks to use them in the most effective way, his objective being maximized profit, and this is seen as "just business."

The operation of the economy, the use of existing human and material resources to satisfy human wants as well as possible, is a matter of immense importance from every standpoint, including that of supporting an intellectual, opinion-influencing part of society; and this is done best by private enterprise. The manager of a business is in charge of utilizing resources in his sphere, which becomes a larger sphere the more successful the manager. Unfortunately, that one entrepreneur who ("creatively") founds a business that gives remunerative work to 1,000 people has done more to promote social uplift than ten welfare workers "working with" their "clients" is overlooked by many who seek "meaningful" occupations.

This sheds some light on the question of why more liberals than others tend to go into "meaningful" areas: for those who appreciate the value of business enterprise and understand the vital contribution bankers and business leaders make to the welfare and progress of the people of the country, and who are therefore at home with the existing economic system and oriented toward its values (we might call them "conservatives"), business is a leading contender as a career; while those who write business off and feel that things like teaching, writing, and government work are the *only* "meaningful" activities have all got to be channeled into the "intelligentsia" areas of professional intellectualism. For them, there is no alternative represented by the business world, which draws to it many people, apolitical or of conservative bent, who could be first-class journalists, teachers, etc., but choose a business career instead. It is not that only liberals make good teachers and newspaper reporters, but rather that conservatives have more alternatives to being teachers and newspaper reporters.

Is there more that can be said, given the foregoing discussion, as to why teachers have such a pronounced liberal tendency? Very possibly. Let us pursue the matter of ego needs and return to the educated person who has absorbed the values of Academe and has chosen *not* to enter the world in which achievement, wealth, etc. give the deep ego satisfaction of being able to look down on others.

As everyone knows, the typical university community is as full of petty snobbery as any other place; human nature is human nature. But the rules forbid looking down on a colleague because his house is poorly (cost-wise) furnished; a professor with substantial outside income would hardly look down on his less fortunate colleague. (For that matter, professors cannot look down on members of the outside world for these reasons either.) All that has been left behind, in eschewing the outside world. How then to get that deep good feeling that comes from being better than someone else?

It would be wrong to disregard the satisfaction that comes to a member of the academic world from accomplishment. To have a book published that is widely hailed is a great source of satisfaction. Even to have a book published that is not widely hailed but is favorably reviewed and reasonably widely read by those in a special field is satisfying. Promotions, first to assistant professor from lecturer, then to associate professor, then to full professor, are much sought after; there are particularly prestigious chairs to which professors can be appointed as a great honor. Promotions involve teaching ability, writing ability, politics, and the passage of time. They may also involve moving to another university. Let no one think that ambition and the yearning for fame and recognition are not present in universities and that the academic community consists entirely of quiet scholars and teachers unmoved by and unmotivated by promotions.

But: 1. It is true that the university is characterized by an atmosphere of less ambition and striving than the everyday business world; and 2. seniority plays an important part in promotions; and 3. accomplishment is departmental: that is, while it is true that you have just been appointed a full professor of French at thirty-four, this hardly entitles you to look down on your colleague who is only an associate professor of chemistry at thirty-nine. The business world is primarily interested in making money, and it is no source of satisfaction to a typical businessman to be running the most profitable railroad car manufacturer in the area (or even the country) if it is barely profitable; or to be making more money than anyone else in the city bus business, if that is very little. The point is that accomplishment and achievement do not function as givers of ego satisfaction in the academic world in quite the way they do in the business world, and that as a result the inhabitants of the academic world have a special need for something in the world of ideas that will provide for their status and ego needs. Whence is this to come?

The answer is fashion: and especially, for people whose profession is dealing with ideas, fashion in ideas: here, certainly, liberalism plays an important part. The liberal who possesses enlightened ideas and is "forward-looking" and "right-thinking" can automatically look down on anyone, regardless of origin, race, color, or creed, who does not possess such ideas. Here is the solution to the ego needs of the man or woman who has forsaken the more conventional American society. Here are fashions that really set the chic apart from the gauche in a realm that matters; here is something of the mind that works better for the intellectual than Louis XVI furniture, country houses, and Rolls-Royces work for the businessman. Indeed, these fashions may bring especially satisfying relief to an academic who has heard the old saw, "Those who can do; those who can't teach" and feels defensive.

There may be resentment, also, of the material wealth of those in business. Enlightened views enable the academic to feel *good* again.

This is not to say that professors are bereft of the ego benefits of fashion in other areas. In dress, in vacation habits and hobbies, in home furnishings, they have opportunities to demonstrate superiority; but note: see the professor: well-worn old tweeds, elbow patches, a pipe, interesting artifacts decorating the home, furniture not necessarily very expensive, but demonstrative of either excellent or exceptional taste, or making the statement that the professor cannot be bothered with such things. *Almost everything giving status in fashion or oneupmanship in dress, furniture, etc. in the academic world goes back to and is a statement about the ideas and values of the professors, not about their accomplishments and achievements.* Hence, the prevalence of "inverse snobbism" on college campuses: those academics are making the statement that their values are superior to those of the materialist, money-seeking world outside and that they have no use for elaborate and expensive living. The professor who could afford the best hotel but stays at the little *pensione* and drops that fact in conversation may, of course, be making a statement about his political philosophy too; but apart from that he is making a statement about his values and ideas, whereas the businessman who stays at the Grand Hotel and drops that fact is making a statement about his success as a businessman. (If he just stays there and does not make a point of letting others know that, he probably just believes in having as enjoyable a stay in a city as possible, which, after all, is the normal, sensible, natural, straightforward approach to staying at hotels.)

A professor can have the most advanced and satisfying views on the subject of organic chemistry, but this will do him no real good ego-wise, as it will only enable him to look down upon less-advanced organic chemistry scholars, a piddling thing. Political matters, however, affect all and interest nearly all, so that superiority in ideas *here* really does the job. Anyone who has seen one of the Pharisees of modern liberalism confront with scorn and contempt an unenlightened adversary knows how true it often is that liberalism is the snobbism of the intellectual. It is ideally suited for its role. It is not readily obtainable; as noted above, in fact, today's "underdogism" requires an act of will, veritably, shutting off the vulgar common sense, so that it possesses a certain inherent exclusivity.

The use of the word "Pharisees" above is more than a happenstance. While current liberalism—underdogism, that is—can in the case of some persons best be thought of as their snobbism, it can also become, in effect, a religion: indeed, it can take hold of people like a religion; or perhaps I should say "like a religion used to"! First, the initial exposure, then favorable reaction, commitment, and a growing and increasingly zealous devotion, combined with growing loathing for the unclean and evil men outside the fold.*

Of course, the mind of the real zealot is not open to the possibility that his religion is false, and a suggestion that it is is met with rage at the sacrilege of the blaspheming unbeliever. Witness the reaction of liberals to Nobel Prize winner Shockley's theory that Negro intelligence is inferior, on average, to white: the man is shouted down and shunned by the Academy as though a leper or possessed by an unclean spirit. Similar is the reaction to the works of Professors Larsen of the University of California and Herrnstein of Harvard on the relative importance of heredity and environment on intelligence. Professor Herrnstein was prevented from speaking at Oxford University by an angry mob of chanting zealots who were determined to prevent blasphemy from being uttered.

When underdogism has become a person's religion, it is a demanding one, a jealous mistress whose adherents must have no other god before it or with it. Take the case of activist liberals among the Catholic clergy. One by one, sooner or later, the god of liberalism seems to release them from their commitments to the lesser religion. The newspapers over the last couple of years have had one story after another about Catholic priests leaving the priesthood to marry or just going ahead and getting married; they are usually identified as prominent in some liberal cause. Father Philip Berrigan, prominent in the anti-Vietnam War movement, subsequently married the nun with whom apparently he had been living for some time; Reverend Austin Morris, S.J., of San Francisco, who became a member of the California bar specializing in defending the poor and downtrodden criminal, revealed a couple of years ago that he had married in Las Vegas a cocktail waitress from Clancy's Bar; she was pregnant at the time. Father James Groppi, who achieved fame as the leader of black demonstrations in Milwaukee in the 1960s, subsequently left the priesthood.** No man can serve two masters.

*Norman Podhoretz, editor of *Commentary* magazine, ably discusses the fanatical intolerance of the New York radical intellectual community in his book *Breaking Ranks* (New York: Harper & Row, 1979).

**My file of amusing typographical errors has one from the time local aldermen were Groppi's target: "Tension had built up as Father Groppi directed Negro pickets in demonstrations against older men who had voted against open housing. . . ." (August 1, 1967)

By its nature, academic liberalism typically builds on itself, and in one direction: given the largely inherent anti-business bias of an academic community of those who eschewed business and the more mundane and lucrative professional careers, professors are not likely to get their kicks from being more conservative than their fellows; rather, they will get them from being more *liberal*. Last year Professor Jones may have gotten his kicks from looking down on those who could not grasp the government's obligation to give Negroes preferential hiring; this year, those who do not heartily approve of the Black Panthers and condemn "white liberals" who fail to do so. A certain alacrity is needed to maintain the most advanced position, but the rewards are great. (What may be called a flexible reasoning process is a prerequisite too; can you imagine what the reaction of a university faculty would be to a program of "affirmative action" designed to increase the percentage of whites on the faculty while at the same time "not discriminating against qualified minority group members"? They would scream that this was an absurd fraud, and that any sophomore could see that a contradiction in terms was involved.)

A delicious side effect of advanced liberal views, from the standpoint of the fashionable liberal, is that one is not only entitled to look down on less enlightened people intellectually, but in other ways as well. If a liberal encounters someone to the left, he treats him with respect, because of his inherent bias and—perhaps—because he senses that he may be there next year. But anyone to the right is fair game. Somehow, to the complete liberal, "honest differences of opinion" occur only from himself leftward, and to hold views rightward marks the holder, automatically, as something of a *bad* person. Conservatives, as noted above, are *bêtes noirs*, and the worst is too good for them. If a Southern white espouses segregation, or states' rights, it is immediately proper, for example, to reproduce his dialect in print so as to ridicule his speech: "Ah don't dislike Nigras." But Negroes are sacred oxen, so you will not find the *New York Times* accurately quoting a "welfare mother" as saying, "Ah demands mo' money, ah does."

The limitless contempt for "Middle America" so noticeable among fashionable intellectuals is permissible under this general license. Here is a fine way—the only permissible way—to savor some of that satisfying old liquor, socio-economic snobbery, while at the same time floating on the heights of advanced liberalism. References by bright young Vassar and Smith graduates, campaign workers in John V. Lindsay's last mayoral campaign in New York City in 1969, simply reeked of disdain for the *icky* people who were supporting John Marchi and, especially, Mario Procaccino. These young liberals were quoted in the *New York Times* and no one as far as I know made an issue of it back in New York, although I was struck by it at the time. It was permitted, and not in violation of the Rules of Liberalism, for the icky people were backing a rather conservative candidate. (Just turn it around and picture the rich and reactionary scion of an old family running for office on a *very conservative* platform against a fat little Italian son of poor immigrants who calls indignantly for more understanding and gentleness in the treatment of the poor and those in trouble with the law; and then have Yale and Vassar supporters of the aristocrat snicker in print at the poor, fat, smelly supporters of the little Italian; and imagine what the reaction would be!)*

Middle-class Americans of unenlightened views can be ridiculed and looked down on for their very middle-class characteristics; in addition, of course, any person of unenlightened views can be hit with any name-calling desired. Harriet Van Horne, writing in August 1970 in her syndicated column, referred to the initial pleasure of being in California instead of in stifling, smelly New York; but, she went on, what was very disturbing was the large number of "political primitives" she met at social gatherings. Conservatives are not like people to the left, whom we must "listen to."

This, then, appears to be a fundamental part of the liberal academic genesis, and one that has a significant bearing on the consistently noticeable leftward bias of the academic community: the desire to be fashionable ideologically and entitled to bask in one's intellectual with-it-ness (or, in the language of a less with-it age, superiority) and look down on the common herd. The desire to be in fashion is pervasive and powerful: why do women (and some men) wear strange new styles upon ascertaining that they are the newest fashion?** Of course, in those cases where liberal "underdogism" reaches the status of religion to the afflicted person, filling spiritual needs and shaping his or her whole outlook, its power is obvious.

---

*Marchi, campaigning on a pledge to reduce crime and make the streets safer, was, it may be recalled, accused by John Lindsay of "appealing to the basest instincts of mankind," part of the reasoning being that, since minorities were responsible for most of New York's violent crime, Marchi was really attacking those racial groups.

**The fact that this phenomenon is so much more common among women than among men supports the theory that lack of achievement-related satisfaction in the intellectual community, especially the academic world, is an important cause of the snobbery of ideas, and the fashionableness of liberalism, among the academic community.

Of course, we are covering a complex and broad question and it would be obvious foolishness to lump all "liberal intellectuals" together. We have examined a variety of factors that have an apparent bearing on the intellectual community's political orientation, and they will be of widely varying significance with different individuals. We can only hope, by touching on various hypotheses and factors, to shed some light on a rather baffling phenomenon, the relative political silliness of professional thinkers. While we have focused primarily on the academic community, much that has been said applies, *mutatis mutandis*, to the rest of the intellectual world, and furthermore Academe is a major, and very influential, part of that world.

A little speculation as to why liberalism apparently has never significantly infected the non-intellectual part of the population may be in place here. For one thing, underdogism flies in the face of common sense and experience, and it takes abstraction from the nitty-gritty, everyday world, both physically and in terms of how one earns one's living, to allow the mind of override them. For another, the rest of the population is more achievement-oriented, measured to some extent in terms of power but principally in money and what it brings in terms of living standards, and it gets the satisfaction it needs through accomplishment in these areas, as noted above.

One final fact that also deserves mention is an external one. While it would be simple-minded to say that American liberals hold or espouse their political beliefs, or actively work to promote them with regard to this or that cause, because they are doing Moscow's bidding, or that, in general, they *would* deliberately do Moscow's bidding, it would also be simple-minded to say that there is *no* connection between Moscow's efforts and what liberals believe, espouse and work for; particularly where specific causes and their timing are concerned.

In case one is tempted to believe that covert action to bring about desired effects in foreign countries occurs only in fiction, let it be remembered that the CIA was roundly belabored for doing such things as using local operatives and adherents to stir up movements whose activity furthered American interests, and that in these covert-action areas it has been our adversaries, the Russians, who have historically been far more experienced, sophisticated, and effective. It strains credulity to suppose that Moscow does not use and has not used every means at its disposal to shape American public opinion and activity in ways favoring the interests of what is sometimes called "international Communism," basically meaning the Russian-directed communist movement. (Yes, Virginia, there *is* such a thing!)

It stands to reason, therefore, that not every liberal cause always gets off the ground and flies strictly on its own merits (as perceived by the domestic liberal community) and out of the underdogism of the intellectual community. The sincere, non-communist liberal very likely holds his basic beliefs without any help from deliberate communists; his belief on a particular *issue*, his application of his basic belief to a particular situation (his move, say, from being against right-wing dictators in general to being particularly worked up against General Somoza), just *may* owe something, however, to an article, for example, that did not appear solely as the chance writing of a conscientious journalist. It is even more possible that, when our liberal friend gets involved in a specific movement that has international implications, some of those who are affecting its direction are very definitely marching to a Russian drummer (e.g., the Fair Play for Cuba Committee).

Only a very naive person would believe that all the stop-the-war-in-Vietnam hullabaloo, which was so crucial in bringing about the communist victory there, "just happened" without anyone who was actually seeking that communist victory being significantly involved. There are also remarkable coincidences, in which one reads a great deal in the American press about the evils of this or that foreign regime at just about the time that a revolutionary movement (which often turns out, at least subsequently, to have been communist in origin) is getting under way in earnest in that country: so that, when the chips are finally down, there has developed a large number of indignant Americans who would oppose any American effort to rescue that regime.*

A prominent Washington columnist had a series of columns exposing the evils of the Somoza government in Nicaragua a few months before the final anti-Somoza offensive began. Presumably he merely thought it was a good time to rake that particularly greedy dictator over the coals in the press; but could those interested in the overthrow of Somoza not in the interests of good government and fair play but in order to create a communist government in Managua have somehow played a part in getting that columnist interested in the subject at that time? One can only wonder, but one certainly cannot rule out the possibility.

There has been considerable publicity in the press, in early 1980, about the "social injustice" in El Salvador, which is very near Nicaragua, and we have for some time been hearing much about the

*One hopes that the widely publicized showing in May 1980 of the film *Death of a Princess*, which shows Saudi Arabia in an unfavorable light, will not turn out to be a case in point.

repressive governments of South Korea and the Philippines, the former of which borders an aggressive and heavily-armed communist country and the latter of which has a significant problem with domestic insurrectionists. Yet we read nearly nothing about the bad qualities of communist and socialist governments—no continued exposés of the arbitrariness of government, corruption, etc.

And of course our efforts in Vietnam were carried on in the face of a constant diet of press exposés of the evils of our allies. I will return to this point later in discussing the significance of the outcome of that war and refer to it here only in connection with the remarkable coincidences between the flowering of causes among the American liberal community and what can be assumed to be the specific current objectives of the Soviet Union. Our typical liberal friend's ideas and beliefs are basically his own, and his current causes, major and minor in terms of feeling and commitment, are not selected to benefit international Communism; but some who have that objective *may* have played a part in getting those causes going.

In early 1980, a veteran of the anti-Vietnam War movement looked out over a vast anti-nuclear power rally in Washington and commented to the effect that this was the first time his kind of people had gotten really stirred up since the Vietnam War ended. How peculiar, I could not help thinking. Surely an effective shutdown of nuclear power production in the United States would remove a tremendous hope of getting out from under being disproportionately dependent on Near Eastern oil and on whomever controls it.

Is it conceivable that the present governments in the area could be seeking to foment anti-nuclear sentiment in the United States? That is rather implausible, but there is a major power in the world, one which is certainly happy to see us dependent on Near Eastern oil, one which in fact is rapidly gaining power in that area of the world itself and obviously is very interested in so doing; the same power, in fact, which had so much to gain from the success of the *last* movement which, according to the old activist, had really stirred up these people and this very liberal segment of American society. It is interesting that a group of visitors to Teheran in early 1980, whose leader declared, "We congratulate the students (those holding the American Embassy personnel hostage) for their bold and courageous effort," included representatives of the militantly anti-nuclear Clamshell Alliance.

It is, indeed, not far-fetched to recognize that the springing up of this cause, like the springing up of the anti-Vietnam War cause, may not be 100 per cent domestic or innocent in origin. Too much should not be made of this factor; American liberals are quite capable of believing, and getting very stirred up about, remarkable things without the intervention of "sinister forces" at all, and without con-sciously seeking to assist foreign countries or "un-American" ideologies; but neither should this factor be regarded as non-existent.*

In summary, there appear a variety of reasons why individual Americans hold the rather nonsensical ideas about "underdogs" and the concomitant unfairness of our economic system that are such an essential part of current "liberalism"; a major reason is the orientation of the opinion-molding intellectual community in general and the teaching community in particular. This group's view of matters, in turn, appears to stem from an assortment of factors, some historical and some inherent in the nature of contemporary intellectual orienta-tion, and including significant elements of specialized status-seeking and substitute religion.

13

Digression on Liberalism in Business

In the light of our analysis of why the intellectual community tends to hold liberal views in the first part of the preceding chapter, it is interesting and alarming to observe the

*Along this line, what is one to make of the late Supreme Court Justice William O. Douglas's will, which was made public in 1980? He left land in Nova Scotia for the use of scholars from all over the world, *with preference to those from Iran, Vietnam, China, Russia, and Mongolia.* Now, the justice was always a strong civil liberties man, and among those whose civil liberties his opinions and rulings enhanced were American communists: was he, in his will, revealing where his heart had been, all along? One is loath to believe such a thing of a former Supreme Court justice. But why would a sincere and consistent civil libertarian single out those totalitarian countries for special treatment? Perhaps he felt that freedom-loving scholars living under such oppressive regimes were particularly deserving of a place of refuge. But was he then unaware that anti-totalitarian scholars in communist countries are not able to travel freely around the world? Perhaps, in his latter years, he was not himself, politically and/or intellectually; in that case, one has to wonder how long he was on the bench, helping to shape our institutions, in that condition.

rise in recent decades in liberal thinking among top business leaders, a striking departure from the past which does not appear reflected among small businessmen. It seems to have become the vogue among leaders of giant corporations—although apparently less now than a couple of years ago—to mouth the latest liberal cliches and deliver forward-looking pronouncements as to the social responsibilities of business (whereas Samuel Gompers once said that the worst crime a company could commit against workingmen was to fail to operate at a profit). Presumably, at the corporate heights, abstraction from the nitty-gritty everyday world occurs; but still, why the need to massage the ego with the latest liberal fashions of the realm of ideas? These big business statesmen did not think these things up—they are not original with them. They have picked them up from the liberal intelligentsia. But why? Are they no longer given the ego satisfaction they need from achievement? Have their businesses perhaps reached the point of "maturity" where further progress, if it occurs at all, is too insignificant to provide the satisfaction they need? There are certainly signs, such as the decline of the dollar, that drive and progress in American industry are faltering badly. Men who preside over stagnation need something other than their business careers to make them happy.

There are, of course, many influences at work on business leaders who make liberal statements. Some may have a yearning to be well thought of by the intellectual and academic communities; a very unhealthy thing considering the political folly of those communities: grown men should know better. Some, being ignorant and naive politically, may simply be bamboozled by the stuff they hear from the "articulate opinion-leaders," or perhaps from their own children, who are heavily exposed to it at leading universities. People, business leaders included, can obviously be liberals for all kinds of reasons, as we have seen. *But*—to wrap this digression up—it will be remembered that we were dealing with why the intelligentsia was predominantly liberal, and one explanation adduced was that by virtue of their being separate from the achievement-oriented bulk of the country, they had a particular need to have their ego needs—their need to feel better than other people—fulfilled through wearing that latest fashions in political ideas; *and* to the extent that this may come into play in business leaders' liberal statements, it would be an alarming commentary about American big business.

After all, it is generally accepted that when a company's leadership starts getting absorbed in fancy offices, private planes, etc., etc., it is a bad sign for the company's future, for it shows that the leaders are no longer getting the satisfaction they need from building the business, which indicates either that the leaders can see that prospects are no longer exciting or that the business will soon suffer in any case from neglect by its top management. The same is true of liberal political games.

Political activity on the conservative side by company leaders is a natural thing, as profits can be destroyed by bad laws as quickly as by bad products. The economic ecology is a legitimate concern of business leaders. Too much time spent by its heads in politicking for conservative causes can also harm a business, obviously, but it is a commonsense and reasonable thing for a business leader to do, as opposed to playing with liberal fads.

In the 1920s, as a glance at newspapers of the era will show, business leaders were highly respected in the United States in their own right. Their pronouncements on matters of political and economic importance made front-page news, rather than being relegated to the business pages. Businessmen in that climate had no need to parrot liberal clichés in order to feel the satisfaction or approbation from the world of "opinion-makers," being themselves basically part of that world—that is to say, the more articulate and effective parts of that world, those who devoted themselves to the spoken and printed word on a full-time basis, were in tune with, rather than hostile to, the businessman's values.

Of course, taken as a whole, business leaders of no country at any time have been known for exceptional political savvy; they tend to be short- to reasonably long-run profit maximizers, period: short indeed in the case of Lenin's famous capitalists, who, he said, would compete to sell the rope with which they were to be hanged, much longer in many other cases. (Of course, while the rope merchant would be acting irrationally and suicidally if he were the only source of supply for the rope, he is actually acting reasonably when many other rope merchants, foreign and domestic, are available, eager to make the sale. This situation is rather analogous to the recent competition among countries to sell sophisticated machinery, electronic equipment, etc., to the Soviet Union, and to make the loans to finance the purchases; the Kama River plant, which manufactured trucks used by the Russian Army in its invasion of Afghanistan in 1980, utilized sophisticated U.S. equipment paid for by a $154 million Export-Import Bank loan. After the Afghanistan invasion, a major stumbling block in the way of all attempts to "punish" Russia economically continues to be the ready availability of products from alternative sources in other countries. Argentina, for example, greatly increased its grain exports to the Soviet Union subsequent to the U.S. embargo. Considering that even outcast Rhodesia was able to sell and buy what it needed abroad, "if we don't sell it, someone else will" is obviously apt.)

Perhaps part of the problem today is that too many of "the best and the brightest," in the liberal arts sense, who perhaps could and would think beyond trends in earnings per share, price/earnings ratios, and stock prices, etc., have been discouraged during their education from considering a business career; perhaps part of the problem is that, in a world of large corporations with management answerable to large or small armies of stockholders, it is not seen as the place of a manager to go beyond profit-maximizing responsibilities. At any rate, former President Richard Nixon was probably right on target in his 1979 analysis of the shortcomings of what he referred to as the 200,000-person "opinion elite" of the United States, in dismissing the effectiveness of America's corporate leadership, vis-à-vis the Soviet Union, in terms of Kosygin's being able to have them all for breakfast.

14

The Role of the Intelligentsia: The Significance of New York

No discussion which seeks better to understand not only how the liberal minority has succeeded in imposing its views on the country but why it is that the liberal minority has those views in the first place would be complete without at least some glance at New York City; for it is New York City that, while not our political capital, is nevertheless to a great degree the center that affects and influences the whole country, and feeds especially the country's vocal liberal minority. Here is the nerve center of American television, newspapers, magazines, book publishing, advertising, fashion, and business and finance.

New York, to be sure, is not one city. In terms of absolute numbers of people, in fact, it is not that extremely liberal a city; for example, in the mayoral election of 1968, which presented a particularly clear conservative-liberal choice, Mayor Lindsay's two relatively conservative opponents, one a rather colorless Republican and the other a colorful Democrat of apparently somewhat limited skill and stature, received, between them, about 60 per cent of the vote to 40 per cent for the dynamic, youthful, impeccably liberal incumbent, John Lindsay. (Of course, Mr. Lindsay had been making quite a mess of running New York City, and that didn't help him; but the ideological issues appeared dominant.) Again, in 1966, a system involving a civilian police review board, installed by the city, was submitted to a referendum by petition of the required number of citizens; despite wholehearted support from the Mayor, all leading politicians, including New York's two U.S. senators, and the *New York Times*, the thing lost 2-1.

Out in the middle-class areas like Staten Island and Queens are large numbers of reasonably normal people with reasonably normal political ideas. But this is not the New York that dominates the news and dominates political discussion where decisions are made in New York; and plays such a crucial role in affecting the life of the nation (probably more, in terms of fundamental causes, than Washington). The influential New York is the New York of Manhattan; of the people who make up the nerve center of so much of America's endeavors. This New York is liberal in the extreme. In the 1972 Nixon landslide, in which he carried every state but Massachusetts, Nixon was narrowly outpolled by George McGovern in New York City as a whole, but he lost Manhattan by a two-to-one margin.

This is the New York City for which the *New York Times* speaks, the *New York Times* which in the mid-1960's called socialist Norman Thomas "the conscience of America" in an editorial, and which can be depended on to defend and promote every liberal cause, whether abolishing capital punishment, overthrowing Batista, overthrowing Somoza, or concentrating on opposing "police brutality" in the midst of a crime wave. Liberal New York's heart goes out to welfare recipients, accused violent criminals of minority races, convicted murderers, and the "downtrodden" in general; it has little use for the relatively well-off: after all, if there are people one thinks of as "downtrodden," there have to be those, by definition it would seem, who have trodden them down, and they are entitled to little sympathy. Judges give light sentences, and huge riots can occur with no one being charged in court at all.

Under the dominant influence of liberalism, things are done in

152   TAMPERING WITH THE MACHINERY

New York that boggle the mind. In 1964 and 1965, when I lived in New York, much of the East experienced drought conditions. A serious water shortage developed in New York City; people were being urged to conserve water in every possible way—save bath water and use it to flush the toilet, etc. One day there were articles in the newspapers dealing with a proposal to install water meters: I discovered that no one had to pay for water in New York! Then-Mayor Robert Wagner declared, rejecting such a regressive sort of thing as water meters, "Free water is part of the social philosophy of the people of New York."

There have been many striking manifestations of that extremely liberal social philosophy. In 1966, a brand-new, "showcase" school opened in East Harlem; local extremists objected violently to the fact that the principal, a respected educator with experience in the Harlem schools, was white; a clamor for "community control," meaning a takeover of the schools by local rabble-rousers, grew. The school board's response was basically to give up control of schools in black areas and acquiesce in the wholesale ouster of white administrators and teachers.

In 1969, when demonstrations favoring everything from "open admissions" to a separate institution which would provide easy degrees to minority students effectively disrupted New York City's huge City College for extended periods, the authorities avoided summoning police and sought to avoid the scheduling of examinations that those demonstrating and boycotting would miss. When thousands of New Yorkers took advantage of the 1977 power blackout to go on a looting spree, the police were directed to use extreme restraint, with the result that 1,400 stores were looted and 418 police injured, eighteen seriously; enlightened New Yorkers, including the editors of the *New York Times*, took a very sympathetic view of the looters, and soon a major thrust of the discussion had become charges that those held in jail in connection with rioting and looting had insufficiently agreeable accommodations.

Throughout the entire post-World War II period, New York City, alone among American municipalities, retained rent control, and a stringent form of it at that. While this system has obviously turned once liveable housing into slums by making proper maintenance, let alone improvements, uneconomic, and actually led to the abandonment of block after block of buildings, totalling many square miles, destroying housing and undermining the city's tax base, the political climate of New York City is such that there is no discernible prospect for an end to this ruinous idiocy.

Why is New York liberal in the extreme? A full analysis of that question would justify a separate book. All we can do here is mention a few key points.

1. New York is heavily Jewish. One-third of New York City's Democratic voters (and 25 per cent of New York State's) are Jewish, as are over one million out of the population of eight million. This is in fact close to 20 percent of the entire Jewish population of the United States. The news columns of the *New York Times* contain many stories dealing with Jewish religious developments, matters affecting Israel, etc., etc. An uninformed visitor might think that this was simply because the paper's internationally-minded readers happen to take an interest in these things, as they might in tribal conditions in the Upper Volta. This is hardly the case; it reflects the ethnic composition of the city.

It is an undisputed fact that the Jewish community in the United States is far, far more liberal than any other group (outside of groups whose devotion to welfare, for example, reflects simply their own direct and immediate interests as they see it, such as poor Negroes), racial or religious. This reflects in part history; the anti-Semitic movements in the Western world have tended to be on the right, from the Spanish Inquisition to the forces which framed Captain Dreyfus to the Russian Czars to the Pétainists to Hitler. (The economic policies of the leader of "National Socialism" would hardly have pleased a Calvin Coolidge, but he is certainly generally regarded as a man of the right.) It is a natural reaction for Jews to give their support to the left almost as a reflex action.

Furthermore, Jews are everywhere, except in Israel, a minority, and a noticeable and identifiable one, and it is natural to be devoted to civil liberties and minority rights as a sensible and rational matter of self-interest. (It may be noted, now that devotion to the Negro has carried so far that this now in some respects specially-privileged species is starting to trample on the rights of ordinary Northern city-dwellers and on those of intellectually capable Jews, that a change is occurring in Jewish attitudes toward "minority rights," particularly among those directly affected by proposals to help blacks at what amounts to Jewish expense. A proposal that low-cost housing be plunked down in the midst of a middle-class Jewish area in Queens arouses furious opposition from those in the area, while liberals, Jewish and Gentile, in Manhattan deplore the "racism" of the Jews who see their neighborhood threatened. Similarly, Jews have begun realizing that quota systems designed to admit less-qualified Negroes to institutions of higher learning mean that someone else, very often qualified Jewish students, cannot get in, and opposition to these quotas is now appearing loud and clear in the Jewish community, as it is to quota systems in hiring.)

Furthermore, it is probably a safe generalization that, at least in the case of the large percentage of Jews whose religion has come to be more and more a kind of humanism than the stern Judaism of Orthodoxy, the idea that people should be reasonably patient about difficult conditions on earth in the anticipation of a happy eternity is not present; therefore, the achievement of justice here and now becomes a matter of particular urgency.

This liberalism of the Jews is of far more significance than if we were talking, say, about the Irish, or the Poles, because, for whatever reason, Jews are far more heavily represented in intellectual occupations than other nationalities. The Irish and Italians in New York are quite conservative, but that has little bearing on New York's journalism, book writing and publishing, etc., while the fact that the Jews of New York are strongly liberal has every bearing.

2. New York has a strong tradition of immigration. From time almost immemorial, New York has been the mecca for emigrants from areas where they were not happy: Irish, Italians, Eastern European Jews, Negroes, Puerto Ricans. Plenty of immigrants, both recently and long ago, of course have reached other areas of the country, and other big cities, too, like Chicago. But New York has always been the pre-eminent Mecca for them, meaning both that there has tended to be a higher percentage of these new arrivals and that New York has received them in their most impoverished, unassimilated state. From a political standpoint, this has had a bearing: in the old days, unassimilated poor immigrants represented a source of votes to the ward-heeler with food, etc. to offer, and nowadays, when the public treasury is much more open to the needs of the poor, the poor represent votes to politicians who can offer them things at the expense of the taxpayers. It would seem reasonable to regard New York's "melting pot" history as a contributing cause of the city's liberalism. To some extent we are dealing with a "chicken and egg" situation here, inasmuch as the city's liberalism with welfare benefits, etc. has acted as a magnet to current poor immigrants such as Puerto Ricans and southern Negroes. But its original history would seem to have helped bring this present liberalism about.

3. New York City has lots of poor people and lots of minority races.

4. New York is very crowded. People are living in close proximity not only to others like them, but to all races and classes. Harlem is

within relatively easy walking distance of the best part of Fifth Avenue. Black slums are close to middle-class areas. Upper-income commuters from the suburbs and beyond, in almost all cases, pass through slums on their way to and from work each day. As a result, educated and/or prosperous New Yorkers are constantly confronted with a hopeless-looking kind of poverty and with lots of dark faces, and it seems likely that in their minds poor people and poverty and minority races loom larger than they would without 3. and 4. The elite in general either live in a small area of Manhattan or commute; and in either case, oddly enough, those of other socio-economic levels most visible to them are not the middle class but the black and Puerto Rican poor: as neighbors in the case of the Manhattanites and as dwellers along the railway tracks on the way into the city in the case of commuters. This may have something to do with the tendency of these people to act as if the middle class does not really exist.

5. New York is a crummy place to live if you do not have a lot of money. Not only is it crowded, as noted above, and containing a high percentage of poor people, but, in addition, it has lousy weather—tropical summers and Arctic winters—and is dirty and smelly. Everything is terribly expensive. Also, the pace of life is terribly rushed and everything is hard to do. It is hard to get to work; it involves long commutes and/or miserable riding in horribly crowded subways where in summer the temperature may be 105 degrees. You are surrounded by grim, possessed people moving at high speeds. And there is such population density in the whole area—not only New York City but the whole metropolitan area—that it is difficult and time-consuming to get to a place of peace and quiet.

Many of those who live in New York and are well-off will tell you that they hate the city and think it a terrible place to live and raise a family, but they are there anyway because they think they will make more money there. A substantial percentage of people with that order of priorities in the population mix with which one comes into contact does not improve the quality of life even for the rich. (It may be that this set of values has something to do with what appears to be the high incidence among children of prosperous New Yorkers of alienation, sometimes to the extent of turning against the whole socio-economic and political system of the United States, as in the case of the girl who was blown up working with explosives in her parents' upper east side townhouse.)

This kind of environment magnifies human frailties. It may be that the harassed middle-class New Yorker, who because of the melting-pot history is far more likely than elsewhere in the country to have been born in a slum himself and struggled out of it, is less relaxed toward threats to his hard-won way of life than a small-town middle-class "wasp" would be, and, as a result, strikes the prosperous liberal who reads of his battle against a public-housing project as a less sympathetic figure because he is angry and desperate, which in turn helps feed that liberal gentleman's distaste for "Middle America." But also, certainly, the horror of poverty must be magnified to someone who finds that $50,000 a year is the minimum level required to support civilized life where he is living. The middle-class man is indeed making far less, but still he is receiving far more than the black slum-dwellers the affluent commuter sees lying half-naked on the fire-escapes of their railroad flats trying to find relief from the stifling heat as he whizzes past in his air-conditioned commuter car, and this may have something to do with the rich liberal's strong sympathy with these, to him, more obvious victims of an unpleasant urban environment.

With all these factors present, the process seems to feed on itself in terms of liberalism in the intellectual elite in New York. It is a mutually reinforcing thing, pulling the magazine, television, newspaper, drama, etc., people together in New York City. They talk to each other. They read the *New York Times*. They read the utterances of local politicians, welfare advocates, and each other. In a way, it is like a liberal college faculty.

But whereas a liberal college faculty directly pollutes only its college and perhaps its college town as well, New York City pollutes the entire country. Not only the major magazines, but the news gathering services, the television networks—everything from lecture bureaus to sports league headquarters—are in New York. Even new fads generally get started in New York, or, if they do not get started there, they get the imprimatur of chic, in the *New York Times, W,* or *Women's Wear Daily,* or *New York* and *The New Yorker* that really starts the ball rolling in terms of national acceptance.

The liberal bias of the national news media has been amply studied and described and need not be gone into here. Apart from the uniformly liberal editorial pages, this bias of course includes comments and asides, and tones of voice, of television commentators and "anchor men," burying versus playing up news items, and the marvelous technique of entirely turning the import of a story around. At one point some years ago, President Nixon made a speech in which he attacked some person or group. The *New York Times* gave this story a fairly prominent place. But the headline was not "Nixon Attacks

_____." Rather it was, "Clergymen Decry Nixon Slur on _____."
The whole thing was stood on its head and the issue was made the
alleged impropriety of Nixon's remarks rather than the alleged
wrongdoing of his original target. (New York has no monopoly on
this technique; I remember a *San Francisco Chronicle* story on a riot in
Isla Vista at the time of the University of California–Santa Barbara
troubles. There had been a riot and the police had apparently dealt
firmly with it. Was the heading "Students Riot"? No. "Police Get
Tough With Students"? No. It was something like "Widespread Outcry Against Police Tactics.")

15

How Was It Able to Happen?

T he damaging of the political-
social and economic ecologies of the country has been brought about
by a combination of factors that have worked very differently, and
played roles of vastly differing importance, in the two areas.

ECONOMIC ENVIRONMENT

In the economic area, as gone into above, some of the anti-
ecological influences cited—labor legislation and the minimum-wage
laws—arose fairly directly through the political processes of passage
and signing of legislation in response to the demands of voters and of
voters' political groups—primarily labor unions, commencing in an
unusual period, the Depression. Promoting the growth of labor
unions at that time was intellectually fashionable, and once that had
been done, the labor unions themselves grew strong and, through
their political arms like COPE, became factors for more such legislation. Nor was welfare created by court decision, although its availability has been extended by court decisions with respect to such things
as residency requirements. Again, it is the people's elected representatives in Washington who have embarked the federal govern-

ment on involvement in practically every area of human life. So, in this economic area, while the press and the "intelligentsia" played an important supporting role, more or less conscious acts of the people, acting through their elected representatives, have been involved. They did not know that clear-cutting would cause erosion, and even now as they complain about the erosion, most do not understand the connection between clear-cutting and the subsequent erosion, but they did want the clear-cutting.

The situation is similar to anti-pollution and better-mileage legislation, which has imposed crippling burdens on industry generally and put the automobile industry, in particular, at a competitive disadvantage vis-à-vis foreign manufacturers, who are not subject to the same government requirements as to the average fuel economy of the cars they sell in the American market. (Some of the interferences with the economy have of course been done almost entirely at the behest of special interests, without any general popular consensus at all; such is the case with the 1978 trigger price system for steel, which has helped steel industry profitability in the short run at the expense of raising the costs of all steel users—machinery and automobile makers are examples—and reducing their ability to cope with foreign competition.)

It would be a mistake, however, particularly in the matter of bringing the federal government into every area of human activity, to underestimate the importance of the liberal press and so forth. Members of Congress live in the East most of the year, read the liberal *New York Times* and *Washington Post,* and are exposed to the whole of the New York-Washington liberal atmosphere (ironically, in what may be a vicious circle, the more they involve the federal government in local affairs, the harder they have to work, the more matters that come under their purview, the less time they have to take recesses and get back to healthier areas of the country, and the more their thinking is shaped by the liberal New York-Washington climate!), and the New York and Washington media are expert in creating the impression, in anyone constantly exposed to them, of an overwhelming national groundswell in favor of their pet project or bill of the season. It is very doubtful that a majority of Americans, or anywhere near a majority, were in favor of the sweeping civil rights acts of the Johnson administration, but the barrage from the heavy artillery of the liberal media and the "Establishment" was so deafening, so overwhelming, coupled with well-organized and operated mass marches and the like, that members of Congress, far from their constituencies and the grassroots, were swept along. This concerns directly the political-social rather than the economic environment, but the case in point is very instructive, in that it shows how the legions of enlightenment converge on Congress to get crucial legislation passed. (And woe to the opposition if they are using a filibuster in the Senate! That becomes an arrogant, blatant attempt to use the quirks of antiquated parliamentary law to defeat the will of the people; whereas if liberals are filibustering against a defense bill, that is a matter of dedicated men utilizing their time-honored rights, the sacred rights of the minority, to educate and arouse the people in opposition to the Pentagon lobby, etc.)

New York Mayor Edward Koch, formerly a very, very liberal congressman, acknowledged how the process had worked in remarks early in 1980. Referring to his own role in supporting liberal legislation, he confessed, "I was dumb. We all were. Who knew? We got carried away with what the sociologists were telling us . . . we have permitted a small number of people, generally gifted, elitist, to dominate the society. This was their view. It was never the majority view."

Of course, we are getting to the point now, with regard to the growing plague of government interference with the economy, where things are happening that are going far beyond what the people have wanted. Things are developing their own momentum, involving (1) an intervention-oriented bureaucracy (which is hardly surprising; it would be most remarkable if an unusually high percentage of those in governmental regulatory employment did *not* believe their work to be wonderful and crucially important; (2) the natural tendency of public employees to enlarge their function, their staffs, and their responsibilities and remuneration; (3) the pressures of the interested parties and groups that have benefited from federal programs and want more; and (4) the involvement of many members of Congress in the whole process in terms of the segments of the political base on which they depend for reelection, if not as regards nationwide regulatory programs and the like, then at least in terms of "bringing home the bacon" for their own districts—in which endeavor others' votes are important: and those votes are hard to come by if you steadfastly oppose the federal programs that are near and dear to your colleague's heart because in *his* district the public employee unions and the education lobby are crucially important.

SOCIO-POLITICAL ENVIRONMENT

The socio-political environment, unlike the economic, has been drastically altered without the electorate or their elected representatives, in general, being involved at all. This has come about largely through (1) court decisions, as we have noted earlier; (2) creation of a social climate through the press, etc., apart from political processes, and (3) administrative fiat. Examples of (1) are the many court decisions expanding criminals' rights and eliminating obscenity and vagrancy statutes, discussed at some length earlier; of (2), the barrage of books and television programs attacking traditional American values; of (3), the "affirmative action" programs which the Department of Justice has been twisting the arms of business and educational institutions to implement. Much has been written about the total perversion of the clear intent of Congress that such quota systems represent, yet the process goes merrily on.

But regardless of the operative method, the legions of enlightenment have played a very important role in preventing effective reaction by the majority. Certainly there was a majority in the country averse to, for example, the *Miranda* ruling of the Supreme Court, which, of course, a constitutional amendment could have reversed, far greater than majorities in favor of recent constitutional amendments dealing with the presidential succession and the two-term limit (or in favor of the Equal Rights Amendment, which certainly has come extremely close to ratification). Similarly in the case of the ruling prohibiting non-denominational prayer in the public schools; similarly in the case of busing to produce "racial balance." Similarly with the ruling striking down the existing capital punishment laws. In fact, judging from the overwhelming passage in California of an initiative repealing a state "fair-housing" law, the same can even be said about the great Lyndon Johnson "civil rights" bill.

But efforts to implement the public will in these cases never get to first base, or at least not to second base. The basic reason would seem quite clearly to be that the great opinion-molding apparatus of American liberalism was not available to promote that implementation; rather, it was brought into operation, to the extent needed, on the other side.

Not much needed to be done, considering that without the apparatus to keep the causes alive and fan them, they largely flickered and went out of their own accord. The attention span of the average person is not that great. People are absorbed in their own personal concerns—work, family, baseball, what have you. Without being constantly given new stimuli either in print or on television, they lose interest in even something about which, initially, they feel furiously indignant. (Hostages in Iran are an example.)

But certain legislators, in both the school busing and school prayer matters, did persist, and the media did a fairly good job of portraying the latter as misguided religious zealots or rather silly fundamentalist types (leading liberal clergymen made well-publicized appearances before committees of Congress to testify against allowing any prayers in public schools) and the former as bigots. A congressman who votes in response to a liberal pressure group's demands is being responsive to his constituency; when he votes in response to the evident deep feelings of a majority of his constituents, he is sinking to demagoguery or catering to the baser instincts of the people.

What the media were able to do in the case of President Nixon was an impressive demonstration of their power, as well as of their selectivity in its exercise. In the case of Lyndon Johnson and Bobby Baker, in striking contrast with the Nixon case, no such constant refanning of the fires, day after day, week after week, month after month, was seen; nor was it seen in any other cause that went against the views and wishes of enlightened liberaldom. (It can be imagined whether the matter would have been let drop for years had Senator Richard Nixon been at the wheel at Chappaquiddick!) We can see therefore just how potent a force the "pro-ecology" forces are up against, and how it is that it has been possible to do so much, so fast, so much against the grain and against the wishes of the American majority. The power of the opinion-molding apparatus of liberalism is tremendous, and it basically favors the destruction of the traditional American socio-political environment.

This is, of course, not the whole story; the fact must be faced that many advocates of what we are here calling economic "ecology" are such not out of a "sincere, honest desire for the common good," but for their own financial good, and are not prepared to give time or effort or money beyond their own area of concern. The shipping people do not like the idea of subsidies for farmers, but they think subsidies for the shipping companies are wonderful. The construction industry wants as many tax (or borrowed) billions of dollars spent to promote public works and housing as possible. Each area of the country, each city, each congressional district, has a pet project that it wants, and it appears ready to sit down at the tables and play and hope that it will be able to be a net gainer versus the rest of the country, against all the odds. Indeed, considering first the amount siphoned off by the bureaucracy, second, the amount of inevitable bureaucratic waste, and third, the vigorous efforts of all other parts of the country who are also playing the game to win, a locality has far, far better a chance of coming out ahead by playing roulette in Reno than through the government-spending route.

Even in the area of socio-political ecology, where the "ecologists" are admittedly in a better position since they are more or less on an even footing with their opponents in emotional commitment, there is the problem that there are very few defenders of the traditional environment who clearly have nothing better to do with their time than work, work, work against the polluters. Yet the woods are full of rather non-gainfully employed (often very articulate, too, being the products of lots of education and good schools) folk who can spend pretty much all of their time circulating petitions and working on behalf of, say, a new welfare program or against a nuclear energy project; whereas the socio-political ecologist is likely working hard to support a family, and is very likely operating in a culture where status and ego-fulfillment depend to a considerable extent on financial position and material standard of living.

16

Encouraging Signs

There are now, in 1980, encouraging signs that the tide of pollution of the economic and socio-political environments in the United States is starting to ebb. It is too early to say that what we are seeing is the beginning of a real long-run trend, but present indications are encouraging. In the economic area, we seem to be seeing a growing degree of sophistication as to the end results of policies, a turning away from the simple-minded seizing on assorted nostrums without grasping or considering their ultimate consequences, coupled with a decline in the economic and political power of organized labor—a force consisting of many and varied parts, some of which have an actual vested interest in economic policies that are harmful to the economy as a whole. The latter phenomenon is perhaps related to the former, as the greater economic sophistication in the country generally is found also in the work force itself. In the socio-political area we are witnessing, at long last, a rising up on the part of the "man in the street" against the long-dominant liberal ideology, most noticeably perhaps in the form of the passage of Proposition 13 in California in 1978 and signs of a realistic attitude toward the usurpations of the judiciary. Diminished radicalism on university campuses may be another reflection of this resurgence of common sense thinking.

The signs of growing economic sophistication are many. There seems to be more and more talk about the ill effects of constantly rising minimum wages, coming now from representatives of the black community, so adversely affected by minimum wage levels, as well as from those who have been saying the same thing for so long. An example is Walter Williams, the black Temple University economist I quoted on page 18; he has been ably making the point that the rising minimum wage guarantees maximum unemployment for the young and unskilled, particularly blacks.

In a striking change from its former orientation of looking to government rather than to private industry for help in achieving the objectives stated in its name, the National Association for the Advancement of Colored People recently took a position in favor of the de-regulation of energy prices: sensibly, the NAACP appears to be recognizing that, with artificial, government-imposed barriers to Negro advancement gone, a healthy, expanding private economy to provide real jobs is of great importance to Negroes.

Understanding what makes the economy tick and being willing to do what clearly should be done to foster economic health, even in the face of the cheap shots of demagoguery, seems frequently present in Congress, too, these days: and it probably reflects on the economic sophistication not only of members of Congress, but also, given that politicians do not in general have a political death wish, of the American people.

It is obvious that capital gains taxes foster misallocation of capital resources initially and other resources ultimately. For example, the other day a knowledgeable lawyer friend of mine mentioned that he was holding a certain oil stock. I commented that I had heard that that particular company had been doing quite poorly lately in terms of market share. Yes, he said, the stock was going nowhere, but he had got it years ago at such a low price that he did not want to sell and incur the attendant capital gains tax. The result, of course, in situations like this, is that on the one hand the "locking in" of stockholders keeps the stock of the stagnant company at a higher level than would otherwise prevail, facilitating its raising of capital; and on the other, the locked-in capital is not available for the financing of promising new ventures which should provide new jobs in expanding areas. The capital gains tax is a governmentally-provided impediment to the fulfilling by the market mechanism of its capital-allocating function, and the higher the tax, the worse the impediment. No other industrialized capitalist country imposes a capital gains tax.

Yet, because by definition a capital gains tax is a tax on the "haves," it has been a darling of the liberal wealth-redistributors and a virtual sacred cow of the practical politician. But in 1978, even in the face of President Carter's demagoguery about "huge savings for millionaires and a pittance for the average man," Congress did provide substantial relief from the tax without suffering for it politically. This says something very encouraging.

Another encouraging sign, the following year, was the move in Congress to curb the excesses of the Federal Trade Commission. On the other hand, the continuing of so much energy-price regulation, the passage of the "windfall profits" tax, and the willingness to keep the failing Chrysler Corporation afloat (as, perhaps, an American version of the Leyland Motors disaster in Great Britain), are disappointing reminders that we have a long way to go.

The United States is tremendously fortunate in having been spared domination by the ruinous class-struggle, "them" and "us" orientation so typified by modern Great Britain. In America, it has been said, if a workingman sees someone driving a Cadillac, he says to himself, "Someday I will have a Cadillac," whereas if an English worker sees someone driving a Rolls Royce, he says to himself, "Someday that Rolls Royce will be taken away from him." The United States has basically been spared domination by the politics of envy. George McGovern was shocked that his proposals for confiscatory taxation were spurned by the American people in 1972. These fools, he seemed to be sputtering in disbelief, must think that someday *they're* going to be making that kind of money.

Most Americans do expect to become better off, and not without reason, and therefore without being foolish so to think. Politicians are finding that people with little immediate personal benefit from lower capital gains taxes nevertheless like the idea, with the thought in mind that someday they will be situated to benefit and that, if they are not, their children will be. They simply do not regard themselves as being permanently frozen in their current position, so that their chief goal becomes to seize the property of those who are better off.

A recent article in *National Review* mentioned its author's having been present at a gathering of bright and prominent British Labor Party thinkers. The discussion touched on a new industry that was developing. Left in private hands, development would be rapid, but (note that in the United States the word would be, in responsible circles, "and," if the matter came up at all) there would be "new millionaires" as a result: and the consensus was that, of course, development would just have to be less rapid, so that the predominant evil, the creation of new millionaires, could be avoided.

The atmosphere of hope, of belief in the possibility of personal progress, belief in the "American dream," is of course crucial if increased economic sophistication is to be a constructive force. Indeed, it may well be argued that in an environment of stagnation or depression, a nearly superhuman degree of economic sophistication would be required to bring about support for what would normally be called sound, long-run policies in keeping with principles of free market economics. (If we go further and envision a completely different ball game, in which the principles of free market economics no longer apply, then of course "economic sophistication" would be whatever was in line with the new reality.)

Perhaps this is why the Great Depression coincides with the birth of a wave of British-type "haves and have-nots" politics on a massive scale in the United States. Not only did individuals' hopes for their own progress dissolve in the general situation of depression, but it even seemed to many that the basic economic laws that had determined what *was* sound policy for the long run had been repealed or had been found to have been based on fallacy. As the Depression recedes further and further into the past and those nurtured in and on it become fewer and fewer, the politics it spawned may tend to fade away, too.

An interesting current phenomenon that may well be related is the decline of the labor union movement as a political force in the United States. Since 1977 it has lost several very important battles in Congress, including those involving common situs picketing, cargo preference, and the "labor law reform" measure designed to facilitate organizing, as business interests waged a determined and effective struggle to prevent a predominantly Democratic Congress from delivering these long-fought-for goodies to organized labor. Numerically, union membership has declined to 19.4 per cent of the nonagricultural labor force, from 23 per cent ten years ago; in 1978, unions won only 45.9 per cent of National Labor Relations Board verification elections versus 57.1 per cent in 1968.

Economic sophistication on the part of today's workers, coupled with the availability of lessons from the last few decades and a shift of the U.S. economy toward service as opposed to manufacturing jobs, seems a significant cause of union decline. With the Depression and its legacy of class-struggle thinking fading into the past, many workers, thinking in rational economic terms, simply see no reason to join a union and pay their dues to what many now see as an organization largely devoted to furthering the economic interests of those who run it. There has been a great deal of publicity of late about the huge salaries drawn by union leaders, and about union corruption generally, that cannot have gone unnoticed by actual and potential union members.

But the lessons of the last few decades also must play an important part in shaping workers' attitudes toward union membership. To paraphrase Lincoln Steffens, "We have seen the labor union future, and it doesn't work." All too often, labor unions have functioned like too much mistletoe on an oak tree: bleeding the tree until tree and mistletoe die together. (Of course, some of these trees, with their mistletoe burdens, are kept more or less alive by federal sap infusions: Conrail, the residue of the U.S. merchant marine, and Amtrak, for example: but help from the federal sap is a sporadic business.)

A high percentage of Southern workers, in particular, feel that their prosperity and their hope for future prosperity are closely tied to the absence of unionism. After all, in the last ten years, states without right-to-work laws have lost 1,237,500 manufacturing jobs, while those with them have gained 938,200; and the flight of industry from union-ridden areas is an obvious phenomenon, a phenomenon which only became so noticeable, by the way, after large areas became union-ridden, usually subsequent to the New Deal labor legislation. This process seems to be continuing; in April 1980, taking note of the findings of a new union-commissioned report, United Auto Workers president Douglas Fraser said that companies "are abandoning the traditional unionized areas of the country." The New Deal was, in this way, a great boon to the South, whither so many companies in the Northeast fled. (It would be an oversimplification to attribute this phenomenon entirely to the lesser power of unions and ignore the importance of other aspects of "good business climate" in what are now being called the "Sunbelt" states: lower taxes, financing often made available by municipalities, etc.; even though all these factors stem from the same sort of economically sensible orientation.) It is an interesting fact that Atlanta-based Delta Airlines, the only major non-union carrier, earned over 25 per cent of the entire airline industry profit in 1979.

This shift of economic prosperity and growth away from areas of strong unions operates not only inter-regionally but also within a state and within an industry in one city. One suspects that one reason the San Francisco area, which sixty years ago was the pre-eminent center of California, has been so strikingly eclipsed since then by the Los Angeles area, is that unions have never attained the hold on Los Angeles that they have long had on San Francisco. (Ironically, the old-line unions now play only a modest role in San Francisco politics, since, with manufacturing largely driven out of that city to less union-ridden areas in other parts of the Bay Area or elsewhere, these unions have few members still residing in San Francisco.) Two years ago, with many non-union restaurants and chains thriving, Foster's, a chain of coffee shops in San Francisco, went bankrupt: the attorney for the defunct company stated proudly that the company had been a completely union operation.

A recent (October 23, 1978) article in the *Wall Street Journal* cited the case of a mine operator driven out of business in West Virginia by the frequent wildcat strikes, chronic absenteeism and other labor problems that organization by the United Mine Workers union of his small mine brought. Operating a non-union mine in the same area, he was achieving production per worker of nearly four times as many tons of coal as in the average UMW-organized underground mine; the miners, averaging earnings of $25,000 a year, were happy with their jobs. The operator planned to open additional mines. It is no wonder that, according to the article, non-UMW mines had by 1978 come to account for about 50 per cent of American soft coal production versus 30 per cent five years previously. Similar trends exist in other areas: non-union tire production reached 13.8 per cent in 1979 versus 7.1 per cent in 1975.

At any rate, given the tendency of labor unions to favor legislation that is harmful to the health of the economy in general, the decline in their power is an encouraging development in terms of the health of the economic environment.

Increased economic sophistication is not something that has come about all by itself. It is simply part of the general increase in sophistication that the last few decades have wrought, what with more years of education, the decline of illiteracy, and the omnipresence of television. While college board scores have been declining, and this has received much deserved attention, it is unquestionably true that the average working person today has far more years of schooling and is far more likely to be literate and to be knowledgeable in a variety of areas than was the case a generation ago. Furthermore, in the case of the population in general, it seems safe to say that the "loss of innocence" noted in contemporary America does include a certain degree of loss of economic naïveté: so that there would seem some silver lining along with so much—loss of faith in public institutions, cynicism, etc.—that is unfortunate.

In the economic area, of course, the various governmental impingements on the environment that have had such harmful consequences basically were done with the consent of the majority of the people; while they did not will the consequences, they did will the particular instances of tampering with the economic environment, so that greater economic sophistication, as well as the decline of influence of elements with a vested interest in counter-productive or counter-ecological measures, is crucial, in terms of hope for improvement in the future. In the socio-political area, the ravaging of the environment was basically done against the will of the majority of the people, so that it is signs of more determination and effectiveness in Americans making their wishes felt, rather than greater sophistication in their views, that are the encouraging signs.

To some extent, the passage of Proposition 13 in California in June 1978, and that of similar measures in other states in November of that year, was indeed a sign of greater economic sophistication: the people refused to be bamboozled by the barrage of self-serving prophecies of economic gloom and doom laid down by politicians, underwriters of municipal bonds, leaders of public employee unions, and others with a vested interest in keeping the public trough well-filled. The voters recognized the motivation behind those predictions and also were simply not buying the idea that prosperity requires taking the taxpayers' money and spending it on government jobs and government programs. And they also showed their sophistication by seeing through the specious argument that they should vote against Proposition 13 to avoid being deprived of desired services. The goods and services that most people want and are willing to pay for do not generally (with obvious exceptions such as fire and police protection) come from government at all; indeed, if one wants something, cheerfully acquiescing in higher taxes and then trying to get what is wanted from government is an awfully roundabout way of going about it.

Speaking of economic sophistication, there was quite a bit of it among Proposition 13's opponents too: not just among the knowledgeable, such as the Bank of America with its interest in municipal bond financing, where one would of course expect to find it, but also among the impecunious elements directly benefiting, in their small individual ways, from generous government spending: thus in an area such as San Francisco, with an unusually high percentage of persons feeding at the government trough relative to those required to keep it filled by their tax dollars, the proposition got a minority of the votes.

The overwhelming passage of Proposition 13, however, is most important as a demonstration, not of increased economic sophistication, but of political determination of the "I'm fed up and I'm not going to take it any more" sort. Certainly, people were interested in keeping their money rather than having the government spend it for them. But they seemed more interested in stopping the spending on, as they saw it, unwanted programs, unproductive bureaucrats, and unworthy recipients, than in personally saving money. An opponent of 13 would cry that its passage would mean the laying off of thousands of public employees, and people would say, "Yeah! Yeah!" with relish; and they would respond similarly when someone said, "Passage of 13 will mean eliminating all kinds of programs for the poor." The enthusiasm—the zest—shown for effects such as these seemed, to this observer at least, far greater than that for the financial savings promised.

The progress of Proposition 13 was watched with rising hope by overburdened taxpayers all over the country. I remember being back at the Harvard Business School for a reunion at the beginning of June 1978, just before the California election, and finding that the main topic of conversation one morning was the likely imminent passage of Proposition 13; classmates from several states indicated that they hoped something of the sort could be done in their states if the initiative passed in California.

There were indeed many signs in November 1978 that the "taxpayers' revolt" was a reality nationwide and that the people were determined to find ways to assert, finally, their right in a democratic country to control its course. Liberal Senator Charles Percy of Illinois, fighting for political survival against an opponent who seemed more in tune with the voters' new anti-spending mood, announced in desperation that he had gotten the message, seeking to assure the voters that he would have a different approach to government programs in the future. In California, it was only by a narrow margin that the ultra-liberal Rose Bird, a stranger to the bench before her appointment as chief justice, retained her job; a year later, a proposition limiting state spending, a successor to Proposition 13, won overwhelmingly.

By mid-1980, the California example had been taken up all over. "California's Proposition 13 tax revolt has unleashed a storm of similar activity in state capitals and the U.S. Congress," began an article in the May 1980 *Dun's Review*. It noted that in the two years preceding twenty-four states had reduced taxes, at least seven had imposed spending limits on their governments, and about fifty proposals to limit federal spending had been introduced in Congress. Specifically, property taxes had been rolled back or frozen in Florida, Kentucky, Nevada, New Mexico and Virginia, among others, and income taxes lowered in at least twelve states including Arkansas, Indiana, Kansas, Maryland, Mississippi and Vermont; a mixture of tax-cutting actions had been adopted by states including Alabama, Massachusetts, Missouri, North Dakota, and Wisconsin, with ceilings on spending imposed in Arizona, Hawaii, Michigan, Texas, and Utah, as well as California.

The path ahead is not an easy one. The judiciary will to a large degree continue to frustrate the will of the people by tortured interpretations and reinterpretations of the Constitution, state constitutions, and laws, and by utilizing various mechanisms to create delay. The predominantly liberal press will do its predominantly liberal work; for example, not a single major California paper either endorsed Proposition 13 or opposed the confirmation of Chief Justice Bird. The pulpit, now that such a large percentage of the clergy see themselves as social workers and wealth-redistribution activists rather than as moral shepherds and preachers of the Gospel, will do its bit: with utter predictability, the new dean of San Francisco's very liberal Episcopal Grace Cathedral, arriving from the eastern seaboard some months after the passage of Proposition 13 to take up his new post, began by chiding the people of California for having been so selfish and un-Christian as to have passed the proposition. And, of course, those many groups with a vested interest in continuing and accelerating the unfortunate trends of the last few decades will fight tooth and nail against their reversal. Still, the now-aroused majority will be a force to be reckoned with, to judge from recent developments.

This is particularly true to the extent that the initiative process is involved, and, now that Howard Jarvis's Proposition 13 has shown the way, more use of the process, taking advantage of its potential, can be anticipated in states which permit it. The great advantage of the initiative, from the standpoint of those in tune with the desires of the majority of the people, is that *all* the people are involved directly, through the ballot box, rather than only groups, such as legislators and judges, that are more inclined to liberal views, more susceptible of being influenced by the "enlightened elite," or with a vested interest in a status quo, including lots of money to pass around.

No sooner had Proposition 13 passed than it was discovered that the California state government in fact had a huge surplus, the product largely of progressive income tax rates in an inflationary era, and nothing was more natural than for state legislators to come to the rescue of their friends in local government by parceling out that surplus to replace the Proposition 13-slashed property tax revenues and permit a kind of "business as usual," substantially thwarting, for the time being, the will of the voters who passed Proposition 13 so overwhelmingly. Nevertheless, another Jarvis initiative, this one designed to cut state income tax rates in half, was soundly defeated in June 1980. Opponents, spearheaded by public employee interests, this time were able successfully to play on voters' concerns about the beginning recession and their natural reluctance to move too far too fast; also, curiously, something like the "cry wolf" principle in reverse may have come into play: having been lied to twice by politicians with an axe to grind, to the effect that a measure would be disastrous, many voters seemed to feel that the politicians must be telling the truth the third time. Nor did Howard Jarvis's excessive public abusiveness and cantankerousness reassure Californians about his proposal. No fundamental shift in the voters' mood, however, seems to be signaled; it continues to be the case that when the entire electorate is the arena, the liberals are much less able to cope.

In states whose constitutions do not provide for the initiative procedure, that avenue of course is not now open; but the successes of the "taxpayers' revolt" in states which do will undoubtedly serve both to encourage the taxpayers of other states to expect and demand similar relief and to warn their legislators to be responsive, as all state constitutions do provide procedures for their amendment.

A specific development of considerable interest concerning the activist California Supreme Court is its reversing its *Tanner* decision subsequent to public outrage (as noted on page 87, one justice changed his position); another, the way in which the public airing of more or less dirty linen (justices' petty bickering, etc.) before a commission that was set up to investigate the delay in the release of the original decision until after an election has, in the eyes of many, pulled that highly political court down from its former pedestal.

The standing of the California courts, at least, can also hardly be helped by the September 1979 arrest of State Court of Appeals Justice Paul Halvonik, a former A.C.L.U. regional counsel, and his lawyer wife on charges involving possession of cocaine and having over two hundred marijuana plants growing in pots at the Halvonik residence; this case ended with the jurist pleading no contest and resigning from the bench, his wife pleading guilty. In the June 3, 1980, California election, a judge in Contra Costa County who was considered excessively lenient was overwhelmingly defeated for reelection. Considering that the winner of the election was the thirty-nine-year-old chief assistant district attorney, the judge's post-election comment that "some young punk" had taken his job perhaps unwittingly confirmed voters' feelings that he was biased against the prosecution.

Lastly, reference should be made to the fact that a great deal of encouragement as to the future, at least for the relatively near term, can be drawn from the relative quiet of college campuses and the related fact that surveys indicate a substantial shift away from radicalism in student attitudes. With the nuclear power issue showing a fair amount of life on campuses and the possibility of draft registration being reinstituted, however, we had best keep our fingers crossed, remembering the turmoil of a decade ago, when the following parody seemed very much to the point:

Unrest in the academic world had become very commonplace by 1971, but, although the wave of violence which swept across the nation's junior high schools in the late 1960s, in protest against President Richard Nixon's decision to send additional military assistance to Thailand, shook the complacency of many, few expected the elementary schools to explode. To many in those days, the grammar school seemed immune to the kind of revolutionary activism that by the end of 1970 had led to the resignations of so many junior and senior high school principals and the nervous breakdowns of so many more.

That elementary school principals and teachers were sitting atop a live volcano was grasped only by a few forward-looking educators. "The elementary school is feudalist and colonialist," Eppa Sappinger, an intense young third-grade teacher, had declared in a seminar in November 1970. "These youngsters are denied all voice in their curriculum, in grading methods, and in the selection of faculty, and subject to arbitrary punishment without pretense of due process. Any attempt to redress grievances or negotiate is met with heavy-handed repression. The kids are not going to take being treated like second-class citizens much longer, and when the elementary schools go, look out."

Miss Sappinger's words fell on deaf ears. Among the entrenched, old-line school principals, few would even admit the possibility that the entire elementary school system might be in need of radical reconstitution. Student idealism and activism, such as that of the Pasadena second-graders in Longfellow Grammar School who announced that they would not come in from recess until President Nixon ended the Vietnam war, were typically met with ridicule and harsh disciplinary measures. The Pasadena youngsters were dragged bodily into the classroom and made to stay after school.

But this incident, in the spring of 1971, proved to be the spark that lit the entire elementary school system of the United States. That night, Vice President Spiro Agnew, in a typically divisive statement, had called a mob of Grand Rapids seventh-graders, who had thrown their principal into a fishpond to protest the use of ink remover made by Dow Chemical Company in the school print shop, "kindergarten babies." Now, in the wake of the brutal treatment of the Pasadena students (later to be known as the "Pasadena Sixteen"), this insulting reference threw fuel on the flames of discontent that were already engulfing Longfellow Grammar School.

By then virtually the entire student body had gone on strike. A committee headed by nine-year-old Grover Jones, defense minister of the school's Black Caucus, had drawn up a list of six non-negotiable demands on the administration headed by elderly Miss Margaret Whump.

"1. Longer receses.

2. No mor speling tests.

3. Black corses like Drums insted of reding.

4. Student selekshun of techers.

5. No disciplin or punishmens. Speshly stay after skul.

6. End war in VetNem."

Principal Whump's first reaction was to refuse to negotiate. She attempted to address the students, who were in the process of burning the American and California flags, but a shower of rocks forced her back inside. Throughout the next hour, as Principal Whump and her teachers conferred frantically ("We were desperately seeking a course that would not polarize the school, or alienate these young people further," explained Miss Sadie Klutz, the school counselor), a steady rain of rocks and bottles was aimed at school windows by the enraged students. Fires were set in garbage cans.

At 2:00 P.M., when it became clear that some of the fires were on the verge of spreading to the school annex, Principal Whump "reluctantly, and with a heavy heart," as she told newsmen later, called the police. "We had desperately hoped to avoid a confrontation," she explained.

In the melee that followed the arrival of the police several policemen received bites and bruised shins, several children were bruised, and the school was shut down.

TWELVE HURT AS POLICE CLUB CHILDREN, read one newspaper headline. It, and the evening TV news, also featured extensive interviews with Grover Jones, the strike leader. He was quoted, "if the ----- principal don't let us have what we want, now, we gonna burn the ----- school down and her and all the ----- with it." Other persons interviewed affirmed sagely that the tinder had been there all the time, legitimate grievances had too long been ignored, and the wonder of it was that the grammer schools hadn't exploded before.

The rest followed swiftly. In the wake of the widely publicized police brutality and the general heaping of blame on Vice President Agnew's inflammatory remark about "kindergarten babies," outraged grammar school students all over Pasadena, and then in schools across the nation, struck. A "Manifesto of Elementary Educators" rapidly gained thousands of signatures of grammar school principals demanding an end to the Vietnam war, "if we are ever to regain the confidence of our elementary school children." It condemned police brutality and Agnew's "inflammatory rhetoric." Fifty-two elementary school principals journeyed to Washington and met with President Nixon, telling him that peace could not be restored to the grammar schools "until America heeds its idealistic young people and stops insulting them by defying them."

Some protested that many of the idealistic young people could not even read yet, but a highly respected grammar school principal, Miss Sheila McCarthy of the Hans Christian Anderson school in Green River, Connecticut, declared, "Those who say we should ignore the moral outrage of our young because they are young ignore the fact that, in their very youth, they are free from the corruption and hypocrisy that exposure to the world and the 'facts' brings. This is why enlightened America has looked to college students, and then to teen-agers, for moral leadership. Elementary school students have even less corruption of their natural idealism than high school students, and we should therefore heed them more, not less."

By now, demands for "No Homework, No Grades," closing the schools until the following fall, and an end to aid to Thailand had been added to the original demands as part of a nationwide elementary school manifesto. Grover Jones had catapulted to national prominence, having appeared on many television programs, on one of which he shocked conservative viewers by telling the president of Yale, "---- you, -------." Liberals pointed out that such language was merely "an eloquent expression," as the *New York Times* put it, of "the desperate disillusion and frustration of idealistic youth with the tired posturing of a hypocritical Establishment." While it was true, liberals admitted, that they had in 1964 belabored Senator Barry Goldwater mercilessly for "simple solutions to complex problems," and at first blush, the same criticism might appear levelable against youth's solutions, "this is different, because the instincts of youth are sound."

The crisis ended, of course, with President Nixon's conciliatory speech in which, urging nationwide closing of the schools, he expressed sorrow at "intemperate rhetoric in this Administration," and assured kindergarten children of his highest respect for their intelligence and moral instincts. He also announced an end to U.S. aid to Thailand and the establishment of a Commission on Young America. Among its appointed members were John Lindsay, Ted Kennedy, and several grammar school students, including Grover Jones.

While current draft registration and nuclear power rumblings remind us that there is still plenty of potential for mischief in our educational institutions, the fact that news stories resembling the foregoing parody are no longer part of our almost daily diet, as they were not so long ago, is certainly an encouraging sign. Another is the fact, noted in the June 1980 issue of *Dun's Review*, that many of today's brightest students are interested in business careers.

17

Some Alarming Signs

The encouraging signs mentioned in the preceding chapter are, of course, encouraging signs in the domestic context, and we have implicitly been making the assumption that the kind of society we have in the United States in the next few years and forward into the indefinite future will be determined, as in the past, by the interplay of domestic forces. Our cheer at seeing positive signs must be tempered, unfortunately, by the realization that current developments involving the United States in relation to the rest of the world make complacency inappropriate.

Putting it bluntly, the continuing deterioration of our military strength vis-à-vis that of the Soviet Union, combined with the apparent erosion of our will to use American power to make the world safe for this country, its interests, its values, its friends, and its own survival over the long run, raises the possibility, not to be dismissed out of hand, that much of our discussion of domestic matters may not be relevant for the long run. Political machinations in the latter years of the Athenian republic, or in the Roman Empire *circa* 400 A.D., or in the high councils of the Austro-Hungarian government in 1910, were destined to have relatively little bearing on the kind of societies that prevailed in those lands for the next generation of their inhabitants.

Militarily, we have gone in the last thirty years from a position of total and overwhelming superiority to one of modest superiority to one of rough equivalence to one of decided inferiority, and there is no sign of a change in this trend. An article in the November 20, 1978, *Fortune*, "What It Means to Be Number Two,"* cited chapter and verse very well. Not only is the Soviet Union outspending us dramatically (considering that, inadequate as the pay of our military personnel is, on the whole, it comprises a much larger percentage of total military spending than is the case in Russia) in armaments, but it has gone in also for a no-nonsense program of extensive civil defense preparation, so that impact on the civilian population and on industry in the event of a nuclear exchange with the United States would be of a much lower order of magnitude than in the United States. Current testimony by high-ranking U.S. Air Force officers indicates that our ability to retaliate against Soviet targets in the event we were hit by a Soviet "first-strike" has declined dramatically—been more than halved—in the last three years, thanks in large part to such unilateral disarmament moves by the Carter Administration as canceling the B-1 bomber and preventing aircraft carrier construction; it will, they feel, be 1985 at the earliest before we regain the 1977 levels of retaliatory potential.

This is a particularly ominous situation when one considers the different mentalities of communist and American liberal leadership. On the one hand, people agonize about the snail darter, the constitutional rights of obviously guilty sadistic mass murderers, and the welfare in wartime of North Vietnamese rice farmers; on the other, orders for the ruthless crushing of Czechs and Hungarians (and Afghans) are given without batting an eyelash, it would seem, and dissidents are promptly consigned to the horrors of the Gulag Archi-

*By Fred Charles Iklé, former director of the U. S. Arms Control and Disarmament Agency.

pelago. Take the more ruthless leader, with the more cavalier attitude toward human life, and give him military advantage and a relatively secure civil-defense situation; and put him eye-ball-to-eyeball with the gentle liberal leader, and who do you think is going to blink? Given a game of "Chicken," with one car full of tough punks with no great regard for human life and the other driven by a gentle clergyman, with children from his orphanage in the back seat, you know who's going to win, particularly if the punks' car is of much more solid construction than the clergyman's and the punks, and the clergyman, know it.

Although military inferiority does not normally conduce to a robust national will, history is full of case after case of the militarily inferior side in a conflict fighting through to victory; but the deterioration of the American will is a factor quite independent of the shifting military balance of power: indeed, declining military power is largely a consequence of our loss of will, rather than the other way around. We fought and won World War II; we took effective action against communist expansion in the postwar years in a variety of ways. We sent warships to remind the Communist Chinese of our commitment to the freedom of Taiwan; we fought the communists in Korea, but only to a stalemate (we thought *that* was bad back then!); we prevailed at least partially in the Cuban missile crisis. (But only partially: instead of overthrowing a communist government in the Western Hemisphere, as with Guatemala in the 1950s, we acquiesced in Cuba's communism in the 1960s.)

And then we let ourselves be ignominiously beaten in Indo-China in the 1970s and gave the Panama Canal away: Assistant Secretary of State William D. Rogers spoke of the need to avoid a confrontation with Panama (Confrontation with *Panama*? Yes, that's what the man said). And of course we have been watching ineffectually while Soviet and Cuban forces have intervened in Angola, and the Horn of Africa, etc. And now we have abrogated our defense treaty with Taiwan; and we have watched helplessly as Iran has gone to pieces, and actually helped in the apparently communist-led revolution in Nicaragua; and, after initially declaring that the presence of a Russian combat brigade in Cuba was unacceptable, endeavored to minimize that presence in Cuba and rationalize acquiescence in it. ("Maybe instead of removing their troups, it would be all right if they agreed not to use them aggressively?" was actually suggested by a State Department source: this when the very presence of the combat troops there in the first place violated an agreement!)

The losing of Indo-China, of course, is intimately linked with

Watergate and with the phenomena of domestic politics discussed earlier in this book. The lamentable history of those years has been excellently analyzed by Colin Gray in his article in *National Review*, "Looking Back on a Lost Opportunity," May 12, 1978. The failure to seek decisive or speedy victory; the pursuit of ineffectual half-measures based on a total failure to grasp the determination of our adversaries; the readiness to give the enemy time to recover when in trouble; the demanding of infinite patience on the part of the American people in the face of a hostile press and an absence of discernible progress: these all played a part in bringing about disaster. In a sense, Watergate was an American Dreyfus Case. In both cases, the good, solid people on the conservative side of the political spectrum were on the side that turned out to be wrong, and ended up discredited as a result of the muckraking of leftist journalists; in both cases, a sudden and dramatic loss of political power by the discredited side resulted. In the American case, the result occurred primarily in the field of foreign affairs rather than in domestic policy: we abandoned Indo-China to communist rule.

The resulting trauma of ignominious defeat in Vietnam has cast its shadow subsequently. The wrong conclusions entirely were drawn, of course: by people who wanted to draw them, and also by well-intentioned people who simply didn't know any better, or who believed the wrong analysis. The right conclusion, of course, would have been that little wars, if the decision is made to fight them, must be fought in such a way as to achieve victory as quickly as possible, with the least discomfort to allies and self as possible; other obvious conclusions would have been that a highly-motivated adversary will not quit by being made uncomfortable: you must eliminate his ability to carry on the struggle; and, that if you are afraid to do the job effectively with an adversary lest his big brother enter the fight, you don't belong in the fight in the first place, for what will happen in the end is that many people will conclude, not that you were afraid of big brother (which would be bad enough), but that you were such a joke that little brother was able to beat you: even worse.

No doubt, in fact, there were people who felt that if we couldn't handle the North Vietnamese, we'd better watch out for the Panamanians; and, boy, we'd better not try to do anything in Africa. (The question of how it is that Russians and Cubans are able to operate effectively in Africa while we cannot hope to do so is interesting.)

At any rate, we have gotten to the point where people have been starting to talk about the "Finlandization" of this country, and it is this situation that starts one thinking about what the future holds for us. On December 15, 1978, the *Wall Street Journal* ran an excellent editorial on this theme, pointing to President Carter's acquiescence in the presence of Russian aircraft with a nuclear-delivery capability in Cuba (on the lame excuse that we don't know that they and their personnel are actually able to accomplish what their hardware is suited to do), Secretary of State Vance's efforts to stop the British from making an arms sale to China that Russia opposed ("screaming outrage . . . doing the Russians' dirty work for them by pressuring our own ally."), our helplessness for months on end in the Iranian turmoil, and so forth. Finland exists as an internally non-communist state by Soviet sufferance, and knows how to behave and that it is not to act contrary to Soviet wishes in world affairs; if present trends of military strength and will continue, how long will it be before we reach the same sort of position? And after a period of that, isolated in a basically communist world, would we be in a position to insist on the integrity of our non-communist domestic institutions? Allan Drury, in his novel *Come Nineveh, Come Tyre,* paints a chilling scenario of this sort.

In terms of becoming surrounded by an unfriendly world (which in the real world is what tends to happen when you lose the ability or will effectively either to operate covertly or, failing that, to respond to force with force), matters have been moving with alarming speed in 1979 and 1980. Looking close to home, the new post-Somoza Nicaraguan government, in April 1980, sent a delegation to the Soviet Union which joined its host government in a joint statement condemning the United States ("imperialist and reactionary forces") for objecting to the Russian occupation of Afghanistan: a rather clear indication of the new government's orientation. Next door, El Salvador is, as this is written, sinking further and further into disorder. Looking at the rest of Central America, there is enough externally-encouraged disorder in one country after another that it does not require a very vivid imagination to see how easily a red wave could roll up to Mexico's southern border.

Across the world, whence comes so much of our oil, in 1980 we see Soviet power thrusting unafraid into Afghanistan, up to the Pakistanian and Iranian borders, with Iran itself no longer controlled by the Shah's government but rather, to the extent it can be said to be controlled at all, by violently anti-American fanatics, with communist elements active. Saudi Arabia and the other oil states of the Persian Gulf are not much farther; again, not much imagination is needed to devise a scenario involving at least other Irans if not Afghanistans in those states. Can those in the area, after the events of 1979 and 1980, feel any confidence that we would be able to cope any better there?

According to Senator Henry Jackson, Kuwait is now, as I write in June 1980, negotiating a long-term oil supply agreement with Russia, and a Saudi faction is holding secret talks with the Soviets.* If our access to the oil of this area were cut off, we would obviously be in a pretty sorry state indeed.

There is no question but that we have fallen far and fast. We are going to need to shore up our position significantly in order to be entitled to be confident that the long-run future of our domestic environment will remain ours to control.

18

Vietnam and After: The Red Light at the End of The Tunnel

If we were to look solely at the end of the United States' efforts in Vietnam and seek to draw conclusions about the future from it, we would end up with a gloomy prognosis. To inject a note of hope, an observer at the time of Munich and the subsequent German dismemberment of the remains of Czechoslovakia in the late 1930s would probably have reached similarly gloomy conclusions as to the will and prospects of Great Britain and France, particularly in the light of the whole history of the 1930s and such things as the famous Oxford Union "King and Country" resolution ("Resolved, that this house would not fight for King and Country": it passed overwhelmingly). Those conclusions would have been right in the case of France, but emphatically not in the case of Great Britain, whose heart, it turned out, was still sound.

But in terms of what the Vietnamese finale *implied*, there can be little argument. In the face of the commitment of the United States through several Administrations; after the expenditure of 50,000

*According to William Quandt, formerly the Middle East expert on the National Security Staff, "The risk is that the countries in the region will decide the Soviet Union is the ascendant power and conclude they must deal with it.

American lives and several times that number of allied losses under our leadership (to say nothing of the cost in wounded, maimed-for-life, and money); regardless of the implications in the Far East and elsewhere of such a resounding and catastrophic American defeat; the United States first pulled the rug from under the South Vietnamese and then ignominiously ran away. Who can forget those photographs of the helicopter evacuation from our Saigon embassy? We also remember that American warships were sent to remove refugees, a few days after the fall of Saigon; that the victorious communists sent word to us to steer clear of their shore (until recently the shore of our ally the Republic of South Vietnam under a peace settlement for which Secretary of State Kissinger had received a Nobel Peace Prize); and that on orders from Washington the humanitarian effort was stopped.

British Brigadier General Thompson, an expert on Southeast Asia, called what we were witnessing in the American disengagement from Vietnam "The greatest retreat since Napoleon retreated from Moscow."

There were those who pointed out that the South Vietnamese did not fight very well. Yet, after all, if war-weariness understandably struck the United States after a relatively brief time with relatively modest sacrifices in relation to the size and strength of the country as a whole, what criticism can fairly be directed at the hapless South Vietnamese? After all, it was on their soil, not that of the Communist North Vietnamese, that the war had been going on for ten years and more. It was their villages that had been ruined, their lives that had been disrupted, year after year; it was their wives and children that had been killed. And for what, under the no-win policy of their American leaders? For the right to continue to fight and have their land torn up into the indefinite future?

The North Vietnamese, on the other hand, fought on other people's soil and for an objective in which their principal supporter fully concurred, namely, victory; after which all the strife would be over and the work of building and consolidating their Brave New World could go on in peace, with the rice crops of the Mekong Delta in the bargain. Fighting for ultimate victory, under a disciplined dictatorship, with a big brother who backs you to the hilt in that goal, on someone else's soil, is something people can do rather well: Just a little more sacrifice, perhaps, now, and then at last victory will have been achieved and it all will have been worthwile. But take that away and what do you have?

Some years ago, it was argued that we ought not to get involved in Laos because the Laotians were not sufficiently motivated in terms of fighting on their own behalf, and at that time the Laotians were contrasted with the South Vietnamese. If only the Laotians were motivated to fight for themselves like the South Vietnamese, went the refrain then, why of course we would favor helping them. But. . . .

Thus it seemed to me particularly absurd of Congressman Pete McCloskey, in a late 1973 talk to a Harvard alumni group, to cite the superior motivation and fighting abilities of the North Vietnamese, in suggesting that, for Southeast Asia at that point in time, Communism appeared to be the "superior system." Even granting the superior fighting qualities and dedication of the communist North Vietnamese, since when did such grounds determine whose side we ought to favor? The Germans showed more dedication and fighting ability than the French in both world wars, and it would be hard to find fault with the determination of the Japanese Empire. Would Athens have deserved our support against Sparta, or the Roman Empire against the barbarians? If ability to win without our help is the necessary qualification for our help, we hardly need trouble ourselves with any matters beyond our borders: if they need our help, they don't deserve it; and we can just leave success on the battlefield to determine which way of life is superior.

We can amuse ourselves to some extent by making up newspaper headlines for the World War II years (1939–1945) applying the critical standards that later were used by opponents of our involvement in Vietnam. For example:

POLITICAL PRISONERS MISTREATED IN BRITAIN,
CONGRESSMEN CHARGE
MEMBER OF SIR OSWALD MOSELY GROUP POINTS OUT "TIGER CAGES"

USE OF AMERICAN WARSHIPS TO PROTECT BRITISH SHIPPING IN
NORTH ATLANTIC CALLED "RECKLESS BRINKMANSHIP"

ROOSEVELT ORDERS HALT IN BOMBING OF GERMANY, SAYS WILL
MEET HITLER "ANY TIME, ANY PLACE" TO TALK PEACE
GERMANS SPURN PLEA, DEMAND TOTAL U.S. WITHDRAWAL FROM BRITAIN

NORTH AFRICA INVASION CONDEMNED AS "ESCALATION,"
WIDENING OF WAR"; UPROAR GROWS IN COLLEGES
MANY STUDENTS CARRY NAZI FLAGS
Ending of War Only Way to Campus Peace, Say Educators

SENATORS ATTACK U.S. SUPPORT OF "UNDEMOCRATIC,
COLONIALIST" BRITISH REGIME
CLASS SYSTEM, OPPRESSION IN INDIA HIT

FRENCH COLLAPSE PROVES ALLIES HAVE NO WILL TO FIGHT,
EXPERTS CHARGE
INVOLVEMENT IN GROUND WAR IN EUROPE ATTACKED

NORTH AFRICAN VILLAGERS SUFFER HEAVILY IN
ALLIED OFFENSIVES
ALLIES ACCUSED OF BRUTALITY, ATROCITIES
Thousands Homeless
Clamor Against War Grows

"BRITISHIZATION" KEY ROOSEVELT POLICY
PRESIDENT REITERATES WE SEEK NO VICTORY
Senators Attack Policy, Demand Total Disengagement

It would seem quite a safe bet indeed that if this sort of attitude toward the war and our allies had prevailed in World War II, the outcome would have been very different indeed.

One pretty much had to profess indifference to whether Southeast Asia came under Communist domination to justify walking away from Vietnam; and many were equal to that task. Not long after the Saigon debacle, Senator Mike Mansfield suggested that it was time for the removal of American troops from Taiwan and for talks between the Communist and Nationalist governments looking toward the reunification of the island with mainland China; a steady diet of news about the corruption and undemocratic nature of the Philippine government and society appeared to be aimed at conditioning the American public to possible new developments there. Now, of course, the Carter renunciation of the defense treaty with the Republic of China takes American disengagement from opposition to communism in that part of the world one step further.

But just a minute. Why did we fight World War II against the Japanese? It is probably not speculation but fact to say that if the United States had acquiesced in the extension of the Greater East Asia Co-Prosperity Sphere south into Indo-China, instead of adamantly letting the Japanese know that we would not countenance it, there would have been no Pearl Harbor, no war with Japan, and none of the tremendous losses of life and treasure of the Pacific campaigns. Indeed, if we had simply made it clear to the Japanese that we had no objection to their expansion into Southeast Asia (to which, indeed, on the superior fighting ability and motivation test, they were patently entitled), all the unpleasant tension and confrontation with that rising and effective power could have been avoided.

And if it does not matter to us whether Southeast Asia is communist, it should *a fortiori* not have mattered whether it was under Japanese hegemony. While Imperial Japan represented, as does

Chinese or Russian communism, totalitarian dictatorship, it did include the system of private property, under which very rapid economic progress was occurring; so that from the standpoint of trade and business, the Greater East Asia Co-Prosperity Sphere might well have been preferable to a communist Southeast Asia.

Furthermore, Imperial Japan did not carry with it an ideology that infected the inhabitants of occupied countries to any great degree. The Japanese were not very nice to them, in the first place, and in any case their system was one of overlordship by Japanese. Unlike the aggressively Communist North Vietnamese of today, the North Vietnamese under Japanese occupation during World War II did not become ardent disciples of the imperialism of the occupying Japanese, ready to fight to spread it to neighboring countries. Thus, inherently, Japanese imperialism was not the kind of self-generating force for ongoing encroachment that communism has been.

In fact, in terms of humanitarian considerations, looking back on Mao Tse-Tung's domestic purges, North Vietnamese atrocities, and in particular observing the incredible barbarism of Communist China's Cambodian representative Pol Pot, one would have to say that the atrocities of the Imperial Japanese Army were rather tame by comparison.

It is, in sum, more than marginally depressing, and ominous that this country's collapse of will in Indo-China had the effect of rendering useless not only the post-World War II sacrifices there of ourselves and our allies, but also, to a very large extent, those of the Pacific war of 1941–1945.

19

Looking Ahead:

A Strange Contrast Again

There are signs that the United States is beginning to make some progress in coming out of its spell of Vietnam-induced collapse of will and morale, and that some normal red blood is beginning to circulate again. It may be that with countries in situations like ours after Vietnam the process of recovery bears some similarity to the oft-cited example of some alcoholics: that in some sense they have to hit bottom, where they finally see what has become of them, before they can finally pull themselves together and start the road back. The drunk awakens in a drunk tank, surrounded by skid-road types; or perhaps open his eyes in the gutter, where he finds that some small urchins are throwing rocks at him; and he finally gets a grip on himself.

I had begun to hope, prematurely as it turned out, that perhaps the events of early 1979: the murder of the American ambassador to Afghanistan, together with the first storming of our Tehran Embassy after the collapse of the Shah's government, and the perceived threat to the Saudi Arabian oil jugular, had finally had that galvanizing effect on the United States. Certainly there were more and more audible voices in Congress, as there had increasingly been in the country, calling for rearmament and self-assertion; even the Carter Administration, in 1979, moved briefly away from its passivity and paralysis to the extent of helping North Yemen against Communist South Yemen (formerly Aden), although, of course, there was no sign of any but a purely defensive aim—no sign of an objective of actually *winning* the confrontation through creating a non-communist South Yemen. (Subsequently, North Yemen itself has swung leftward; it abstained on the Moslem nations' U.N. resolution on Russia's invasion of Afghanistan and is apparently leaving the U.S. arms sent last year unused while signing a new weapons supply arrangement with Moscow.)

Before too long, however, the accustomed drift of American foreign policy began to reassert itself, at least as far as the Carter administration was concerned: supine in the face of the outrageous second seizure of the Tehran embassy in November 1979 (a clear act of war), mindlessly ruling out the use of force from the start, endlessly expressing impotence and childish optimism as to the hostages' release and talking about "economic sanctions" that everyone but the utterly naive knows have never worked. At this point, it must be quite clear to the world that any insults and indignities can be visited on the United States with impunity. The idea that hostility and aggression might cause painful consequences is simply not credible. Our last successful use of military power abroad was the 1958 landing in Lebanon; with our subsequent record, with which the Iranian desert rescue fiasco in April 1980 fitted right in,* and with the destruction of the CIA as an effective force, there is little reason for anyone to be afraid of us, no matter what they do to us. How can a country that agonizes and agonizes and agonizes about seemingly everything, and keeps giving money to those who rob it and spit in its face, have any credibility as a potential threat, or as a power to be feared? Willingness to give money away, to "throw money at problems" abroad as at home, is no substitute for the willingness to act forcibly when necessary.

It is small wonder that anti-American mobs burn embassies, generally psychotic elements release their frustrations on American persons and property, and pro-American elements decide to lie low, not stick their necks out, and avoid giving offense to those in tune with the times and apparently the wave of the future. The continuing humiliation endured by the United States with infinite patience could only be considered, in many quarters, proof that this country had reached a stage so lacking in spine and pride, and even elementary self-respect, that any identification with it would be folly of a suicidal sort.

Judging on the basis of American government action, or its absence, referring back to the analogy about the drunk at the beginning of this chapter, while this drunk seems now in an even more humiliating position than in 1979, with the abuse directed at him as he lies in the gutter redoubled after his feeble attempt to pull himself together (consider the limbs of dead American servicemen waved around by Iranian officials in Teheran), he still seems to be mumbling to himself that his restraint in lying there is the proper, mature course for a grown man who was guilty of arrogance toward little urchins in the past.

It is interesting to speculate on what the Soviet Union would have done had *its* embassy been seized and its personnel imprisoned. This is of course an academic question, since the very knowledge that no doubt something very unpleasant would result from such an act of war against Russia effectively deters those to whom such a thing might be tempting. But it would seem a reasonable speculation that, had the Soviet Union had an oil shortage and been thus outrageously provoked by an oil-producing nation, the occupation of Iran's oil fields and refining, storage, and shipment facilities would have seemed an appropriate punitive response, and one that, incidentally, would have gone far toward solving the oil shortage problem. (To the ˜

---

*While the failure of the mission seems due primarily to the Carter Administration's aversion to straightforward use of military force—Carter took pains to call it a "humanitarian mission"—resulting in the use of forces inadequate in the event of bad luck, the overall impression generally received was of military ineffectiveness.

extent that the Russians have talked, off the record and apparently frankly, about the question, they have not expressed such calculating expansionism. Former U.S. Senator John Tunney, now practicing law, reported that Russian bureaucrats he dealt with in Russia on clients' business told him they would have "gone in immediately and kicked the ---- out of the Iranians"; an unnamed Russian official was quoted in the press as saying, "There would have been very little left of Iran within twenty-four hours.")

Speaking of the Russians, despite their aggressiveness in so many areas, from Angola and Somalia to Yemen, and despite the destructive role played by the Soviet Union in fomenting anti-American sentiment so crucial to the Iranian crisis, and their chronic duplicity in arms control matters relating to SALT I, Jimmy Carter did not deviate from his support of the SALT I treaty until long after it had become clear that it was doomed in Congress. Here, truly, was a desperate optimist, resolutely refusing to believe that he was facing implacable enemies.

The Carter selection of economic sanctions and the like can be anticipated to have even less effect on Soviet aggressiveness than the earlier gentle pressures on Hanoi had on North Vietnamese expansionism, particularly as the whole approach is so half-hearted. "Despite the continuing presence of Soviet troops in Afghanistan," began an April 29, 1980, article in the *Wall Street Journal*, "the White House probably will announce this week that Moscow will be allowed to buy more U.S. grain. . . . Officials expect the President to agree to sell . . . another eight million metric tons, to avoid worsening relations with Moscow. . . ."*

As for the "we will use whatever means, including military force" declaration as to aggression toward the Persian Gulf, Moscow no doubt found it less than impressive, given President Carter's statement, in a news conference the following week, that in fact he could not say that we had, or would in the future have, the military ability to do the required job "unilaterally," the much-publicized testimony by top military men at the time that we might well lose a Near Eastern conflict with Russia, and the State Department's speedy disavowing Clark Clifford's statement that it "meant war" if the Soviet Union invaded more countries in the area. (Mr. Clifford apparently had not been adequately briefed and thought Jimmy Carter had meant what he said.)

*"President Kennedy told Congress today that if the United States did not sell wheat to the Soviet Union, cold war activity might be renewed."—*New York Times*, Oct. 11, 1963. *Plus ça change . . .*

Nor does the offering of sizable military aid to Pakistan, a country whose government and army were unable or unwilling to protect the U.S. Embassy against the November 1979 mob attack that left the embassy a ruin and two Americans dead, hold much promise.

The hope we are justified in entertaining that the United States may be approaching the end of its post-Vietnam paralysis has clearly to be derived from sources other than the Carter administration's posture. It was interesting to note that the predominant response of persons asked "What to do about Iran" in a "man in the street" newspaper survey in December 1979 was "use force." The "man in the street," unlike the foreign relations professionals, cannot understand why the United States needs to adopt a posture of whimpering impotence. Public opinion polls, as this is written in June 1980, indicate predominant support for more defense spending and for a stronger foreign policy, and one does not need psychic gifts to see a very good possibility that the Carter Administration will give way in 1981 to one more in tune with the mood of an America that once again has confidence and belief in itself and is tired of having sand, and worse, kicked in its face.

Former President Richard Nixon made some perceptive observations to reporters early in 1979. In essence, he said that the United States faced serious difficulties in the world; the heart of the country was still basically sound, but the condition of the opinion-molding and leadership elite was otherwise. Russian leaders would, he said, make mincemeat out of America's business leaders in a negotiation, while top labor leaders such as the late George Meany were seen as far more hard-headed; as to the rest of the country's leadership and opinion-forming elite, he had grave reservations.

A feeling of *déja vu* is engendered by these remarks. We have had occasion, on previous pages of this book, to remark on the striking contrast between what has become of the United States domestically and the views of the "man in the street" as to how the country should be run, particularly with respect to the far-reaching changes that have been wrought in the last couple of decades in what we have called its socio-political environment. We have also noted that this generally undesired transformation has been brought about through the efforts, and because of the views, of the "opinion-making elite," or "the intellectuals." And we have discussed the key methods and mechanics of that foisting of their views on the country.

And now we are encountering the same phenomenon in the area of this country's interactions with the rest of the world: the circle may be said to be closing. Now that we are seeing encouraging signs of a determination to restore the soundness of the domestic environment, we look up and see a growing threat to our entire environment coming from abroad, no longer even invisible beyond the horizon; and, *mirabile dictu*, it appears, not without foundation as will be observed, that it is our old friends, the liberal opinion-makers, who are largely responsible for this threat also, again marching to a very different drummer indeed than the people in general.

It is not that there is one set of liberal opinion-makers for the domestic sphere and another for the foreign; no, it is basically the same group of people. In attempting to analyze what the "liberalism" of this group really amounted to, earlier on in this book, examples of the underlying, pervading, simple-minded "underdogism," both domestic and foreign, were discussed. Just as, to this kind of liberal mind, the rebellious local Negro slum-dweller can as a practical matter do no wrong, so abroad can the Marxist African dictator or the socialist Indian demagogue do no wrong. The liberal's long love affair with the "militant" Negro, denouncing the white man for the ills of the country, had its counterpart in the liberal's long love affair with India and its often stridently anti-American Jawaharlal Nehru. "Tell us again how evil the United States is!"

It would follow, of course, if you believed that the United States was a selfish, unfair, racist, money-grubbing society, characterized by rampant social injustice and inequity, that you would be not only very receptive toward being told that by foreigners and inclined to respond favorably toward those showing that perceptiveness (and running their own countries apparently more in line with your sensitive understanding of social justice), but also very negative toward foreign countries wherein were rampant the same evils you so abhorred at home (that is, all relatively conservative, capitalist countries). If you really detested your country or what it stood for, you might even be inclined to overlook some of the faults of its adversaries, subconsciously or otherwise, on the principle that no country which is the sworn enemy of your evil country can be all that bad. (This would present an explanation for the insistence by some on the fringe that the Soviet Union really does not mistreat political dissidents, or that the most aggressive and far-reaching Soviet armament measures are only an understandable reaction to our own excesses and apparent hostility.)

In short, the predominant political orientation of America's opinion-making elite, particularly of those segments of it which have an effect on the conduct of our foreign affairs, may have quite a bit to do with the fact that, while we were able to resoundingly defeat

Imperial Japan and Nazi Germany ("unconditional surrender" was the only acceptable termination to *those* wars), we have never been able to win a war since, even against small and weak opponents; with the shrinking of the percentage of the globe whose countries' societies are characterized by capitalism and individual freedom (as opposed to state domination); and with the United States' general decline in relative power and influence in the world.

20

A Lamb Among the Wolves

The history of American involvement in the high-stakes poker game of world politics is an unusual one. It is also, depending on how one looks at it, a comic or a tragic one. It certainly has elements of both comedy and tragedy, and it is to some extent up to the spectator whether to laugh or to cry. A very apt cartoon representing the United States' entry into the game, around the time of World War I, might have shown the smoky back room of a frontier saloon, with a card table surrounded by a group of pre-eminently wily, clever, and crooked-looking card sharps. Up steps a newly-arrived tenderfoot from the East with lots of money in his pocket and a smile of trusting naïveté on his face asking whether he can join the game. Well, of course, we know the poor chap will get fleeced; and we can either laugh at the cartoon or shake our heads sadly when we think about the sad disillusionment with human nature, to say nothing of the loss of his money, that the young man faces. There has been so much at stake, and the United States has lost so much, in the world political game, that it is less easy to laugh, but the potential for comedy remains.

Like Little Lord Fauntleroy, the United States had a very sheltered early life, free from the necessity to cope at close quarters with formidable adversaries. The War of Independence, of course, was not a bed of roses, and the War of 1812 had its difficult moments, but basically America went through the first 125 or so years of its existence with nothing more serious to worry about than Mexicans and Indians in terms of foreign adversaries. Around the turn of the century there were the hapless Spaniards and then the Philippine insurgents: very analogous to the Mexicans and Indians, in fact. Vast oceans and days, if not weeks, of travel separated and protected us from the nations and the quarrels of the Eastern Hemisphere; as to our own, the comical Latin Americans were hardly a problem: the United States, a high official said around the turn of the century, is "practically sovereign in this hemisphere," and our concern was to prevent European powers from meddling in our sphere of influence, which of course was the point of the "Monroe Doctrine." Washington's valedictory advice on avoiding foreign alliances and entanglements had been well received and taken to heart, and our concerns were basically confined to our own sphere of influence, where there was no one our own size to pick on.

Though we were the biggest boy in that remote block and it was not wise to affront us, we were nevertheless very gentlemanly about not throwing our weight around past a well-defined point. We certainly expected the rights of our citizens, including their property rights, to be respected by our neighbors, but we were not about to extend our *de jure* sovereignty by annexation, as we could easily have done in the case of Mexico.

The handling of our relations with the major powers in the great world beyond the oceans was not a matter of crucial importance to the United States; it was not seen as a matter of crucial importance; and the country as a whole took little interest in the whole matter. We were busy conquering a continent and building (and fighting over whether there would be a division of) a nation. It is easy to think of the names of many who had key roles in the business of the day, from Morgan to Carnegie to Harriman to Stanford; and it is almost impossible to think of the name of a single United States secretary of state of the nineteenth century, after Monroe of Doctrine fame and Seward of Alaskan. Those of robust strength, those who thought big and typified the energy, self-confidence and drive of nineteenth-century America, did not tend toward State Department careers. But if those who did were more gentle and less driving and effectual men than would have been more typical of their country and its spirit, it was of no great concern to the country and, in the context of the times, of no great moment as far as the country's interests were concerned, given that we had plenty of work to do at home and no appetite for annexing our neighbors.

Woodrow Wilson, "this blind and deaf Don Quixote" to John Maynard Keynes and in some respects, in terms of liberal idealism in foreign policy, an early-day Jimmy Carter, took the country into World War I on the side of the Allies (as a result of a variety of factors ranging from Germany's ill-advised unlimited submarine warfare campaign to the Zimmerman telegram to long-standing ethnic and financial ties), pulled their chestnuts out of the fire for them, was played for a sucker by them at the peace conference, and left behind the seeds of World War II. "The new order had fouled the old," Harold Nicolson, a British diplomat at Versailles, wrote in his book *Peacemaking*, using, one assumes, a nautical metaphor.

The reaction of the United States, during the "Return to Normalcy" in the 1920s, was not to put together a team that could hold its own and perhaps win at high-stakes poker, but to eschew the game, shaking its head in disgust at those card-sharps on the other side of the waters. We felt comfortable in our isolation in a hemisphere where we did not have to worry about people our size. "Gentlemen do not read each other's mail," said an American secretary of state apropos of breaking a foreign diplomatic code. The fact that other players in the world game were not, in that sense, gentlemen and were in fact reading our mail was not a problem because we did not see ourselves as playing in their game or, if we did, as threatened by them. We could afford to be big, and sportsmanlike, about things like that. And while people joked about "striped-pants diplomats" and their effete ways, it was not generally felt that they jeopardized vital American interests. American minds were on making a financial killing in the 1920s and keeping the wolf from the door in the 1930s. Americans, never having been accustomed to see foreign relations as a matter of vital concern or having achieved a comfortable degree of understanding of it, continued to be content to "leave it to the experts," even if they were unenthusiastic about those "experts," from the impression they had of them.

The long, long period when it really *didn't* matter much how our foreign affairs with major powers were conducted; the resulting lack of interest in, and familiarity with, foreign affairs, on the part of the people generally, with the concomitant feeling that this was a strange area that had to be left to the experts, a situation that continues, to a significant extent, to this day: these factors go a long way toward explaining why the agencies of the United States government charged with the conduct of our relations with other countries, and the United States as a whole, have in the post-World War II years achieved, on the whole, such a dismal record in terms of affecting the development of world events along lines desired by the American people. "We lose at the conference table what we win on the battle-field," is an old complaint.

"Politics stops at the water's edge." What does this often-heard statement mean? Only that politics-for politics'-sake attempts to gain political advantage by "cheap shots" and making political hay by charges and statements that a politician well knows are not justified have no place where the vital interests of this country vis-à-vis the rest of the world are concerned? Of course, in that sense, that is a sound exhortation. But when people say "politics," they don't just mean that sort of politics. The statement also reflects the idea that foreign affairs is a kind of *terra incognita* to American political leaders, where they are not equipped to make judgments, so that its conduct should be left to the Executive Branch and to the specialists, the experts, in the Department of State and other foreign relations agencies, with Americans supporting whatever course the Executive Branch, through its agencies, decides to follow.

In that sense, the statement well expresses the attitude that, as noted above, Americans have long had toward foreign affairs. To a country whose interests—indeed, whose very survival—depended to a large extent on the effectiveness of its foreign ministry in advancing its interests in the continuing high-stakes poker game of *Realpolitik,* that fact being, from long experience and history, well understood by government and people alike, such an attitude would seem absurd and indeed suicidal. The idea of the foreign service of a European power in the 1890s consistently promoting developments that were anathema to its own country because it was marching to a different drummer and disdained the values and objectives of its country would have been unthinkable.

The leftward bias of American foreign policy since World War II partly reflects the general leftward position of the opinion-molding, "intellectual" community generally. For example, just as the press would portray an opponent of "civil rights" legislation as a racist villain or an opponent of a "social-welfare" law as a heartless "let-them-eat-cake" type, with a Martin Luther King or a Cesar Chavez as virtually a reincarnation of Jesus Christ, so it would paint a Fidel Castro as a George Washington (former U.S. Ambassador to the United Nations Andrew Young predicted that Americans would come to think of the Ayatollah Khomeini as a "saint") and a Batista as a tyrant without redeeming features; and the same clergymen whose hearts bleed all over their pulpits for the South African blacks will never criticize a Marxist dictator like Julius Nyerere (who, wearing his black Mao Tse-Tung outfit, was showered with adulation at a State Department-arranged reception at San Francisco's City Hall).

The American liberal community is not, of course, significantly different from its counterparts abroad in this hypocritical double standard. When Joshua Nkomo's guerillas successfully used a rocket to down a Rhodesian airliner with the death of over sixty noncombatant men, women, and children, the British Foreign Office had nothing critical to say; but when, months later, in April 1979, Rhodesian commandos destroyed Nkomo's house in Zambia (described as "a sprawling mansion in the tree-lined suburb of Woodlands near a local golf course" in the April 13, 1979, San Francisco *Examiner*), its spokesman fairly shook with indignation: "the decision . . . to attack Mr. Nkomo personally is a major and deplorable step in the escalation of the war and can only impede the chances of a negotiated settlement." He went on to predict "a deep sense of outrage throughout the Commonwealth."

But there is also another factor. Just as, in domestic matters, there are the courts to rule, if liberal legislation cannot possibly be enacted because of the overwhelming opposition of the people, that what such legislation would have brought about was in fact mandated by the Constitution all along, so, in foreign matters, we have the various foreign-relations instrumentalities of the federal government operating perhaps even further removed from popular control than the judiciary or the domestic bureaucracy.

And—and this is the significant point—this foreign-relations bureaucracy has views that are on the whole very different from the average citizen's. Just as with various other occupations, as noted previously, so, with this, a high percentage of those who go into it march to a different drummer than the American people as a whole in terms of their political orientation and values.

Many of those who make their careers in the State Department, Agency for International Development (AID), or other foreign-relations arms of the government are not only dedicated and patriotic Americans, but dedicated and patriotic Americans who share the values and goals of their countrymen generally. There are those, however, with whom it is otherwise. Some enter foreign service because all their young lives they have longed to shake the dust of this (as they see it) crude, unsophisticated, money-grubbing country from their feet and become, in a real sense, expatriates, free to live in a culturally superior world abroad. Some, ridden with guilt at our prosperity and power, have a burning desire to share, as best they can, American wealth, primarily of course not their own but that of their materialistic fellow-citizens, with the more deserving people abroad. Some see an opportunity to spread their values— egalitarianism, land reform, socialism, democracy—overseas. Some see an opportunity to immerse themselves in the purer, more spiritual and less materialistic air of the East. Some end up in the diplomatic area of the federal bureaucracy more or less by chance, the significant decision on their part having been to work at something meaningful and devoted to human betterment, which precluded anything as mundane as a business career.

Just as, as we noted in analyzing the predominant liberalism of the academic community and the domestic "intelligentsia" generally, certain occupations are predominantly peopled by "liberals" because other occupations in the mainstream of American life are unacceptable to them because of their views, so does this phenomenon operate with respect to the foreign-relations apparatus. A certain favoritism toward, or yearning for, things foreign also, as noted, plays a part in this area; so that there is a tendency for this country's interests to be entrusted, on the front lines so to speak, to people who sometimes are not only liberals but also, in a real sense, anti-American liberals.

No great insight is required to see that people thus motivated will be less than zealous in seeing to the careful use of the taxpayers' aid funds, or in fighting threats to the property interests of American businesses overseas; they will not be heartbroken to see a socialist man of the people overthrow a pro-American, conservative government, even if the man of the people expresses anti-American sentiments; and so forth. To the extent that the conduct of our foreign policy is in the hands of people who think foreign countries are superior, or that left-wing countries abroad are more enlightened than the United States, or that it is a wonderful thing when right-wing dictatorships are replaced by left-wing dictatorships, or that multinational corporations and capitalism generally are exploiters of the backward countries, or that government-to-government aid is a wonderful thing when it spares a foreign nation the need to suffer the indignity of maintaining conditions of property rights which are needed to attract private investment, or that America bears a terrible burden of guilt for its wealth and militaristic leanings, the defense of the interests of the United States, as most of its people would see them, is under a severe handicap. Just as in the case of the San Francisco welfare official who impressed a reporter as inclined gladly to give the welfare recipient the shirt off the taxpayer's back, so there are those who would gladly give foreign countries, especially poor, socialist, "developing" ones, the shirt off the American taxpayers back.

(This shirt, by the way, is given indirectly as well as directly; the World Bank, for example, which has already made loans to Communist Vietnam, is primarily American-funded: in this manner, assistance to hostile foreign governments which Congress would be unlikely to countenance on an open, direct basis is provided nevertheless.)

Take the current situation in Central America. In Nicaragua, the right-wing tyrant Somoza is gone, replaced by a government now openly communist in orientation (the only junta member without strong ties to the leftist Sandinista front resigned in April 1980, shortly after the return from Moscow of a delegation which joined in communiques following the Soviet line on almost all international issues); the State Department, and the Administration, continued to urge Congress to approve a $75 million loan to Nicaragua, while economic and military aid to right-wing Guatemala has been cut off.

Nearby, in El Salvador, the thrust of our foreign-policy establishment is even more strikingly divergent from that of American values generally. According to the March 31, 1980, issue of *Forbes* magazine, referring to a report of its Washington Bureau Chief Jerry Flint: "What is amazing, says Flint, is that the U.S. government insists on 'reforms' in [Central America] that would be impossible here at home and aren't likely to work. In El Salvador, for example, as payment for its support, the U.S. demands nationalization of the banks and expropriation, without real compensation, of large estates. 'These actions are likely to drive out the middle class, the entrepreneurs needed to create jobs, and they don't placate the Marxists,' says Flint. 'Worse, taking highly productive plantation land growing export crops such as cotton or sugar and turning it into tiny corn-and-bean plots isn't going to work. But that is what we insist upon.' " The U.S. Chamber of Commerce publication *Washington Report* states that businessmen in the area are convinced that the takeover by the present Salvadorean junta was engineered by the Carter Administration in the first place.

U.S. Ambassador Robert White, a career diplomat who had previously attracted attention in Paraguay for public criticism of the government and an unfriendly attitude toward the American business community, saw fit, in March 1980, in a speech to the American Chamber of Commerce in El Salvador, to accuse both the American and the Salvadorean business communities of responsibility for financing right-wing terrorist groups.

There is no sign that the policy orientation indicated by this sort of thing is something that has suddenly been foisted on the State Department against its collective will by the Carter Administration. There has always been a part of our foreign-policy apparatus with very little use for our undemocratic right-wing allies, from Franco to Chiang Kai-Shek to Pinochet, and this hard-on-capitalism, soft-on-socialism element at long last has an administration that is in tune with it.

To be sure, there *was* an Alger Hiss in the State Department, and it would be improbable that there was today not a *single* American diplomat marching secretly to a foreign beat. But the real problem does not seem to lie there; rather, it lies in the fact that, while many of our foreign-affairs people certainly do share our country's values wholeheartedly, those who do not impair our effectiveness in achieving American goals abroad.

21

Decades of Negative Accomplishment

Throughout the post-World War II years, there runs the same melancholy thread of opportunities missed, advantages squandered, and the long-run interests of the American people not furthered. What were the long-run interests of the American people after World War II? They were not so many-faceted that relatively brief summary is not feasible. One, certainly, was to have the likelihood of being forced to bear arms to defend American interests minimized. Another was to have, so far as possible, a "friendly world": one in which Americans might travel, and American individuals and business enterprises conduct their business, without molestation. It is safe to say that Americans also, with their strong sense of fair play, actively desired as just a world beyond their borders as possible; a world where people were not exploited or plundered; and also that the rest of the world be blessed with prosperity and happiness. Another vital interest of the United States was being in a safe position in terms of obtaining from foreign countries those products and materials important to the smooth running of the American economy and to the economic well-being of the American people.

Minimizing the extent of communism's domination of real estate manifestly made sense in terms of all these objectives. Involving as it did a major military power and militant ideology aimed at world domination (the doctrine of Marx being that the ultimate stage of communism could only occur when there were no more capitalist states to cope with, for which the "dictatorship of the proletariat" was required, precluding the "withering away of the state"), its strength represented the chief threat that Americans *would* be forced to fight another war; communist states were not available for Americans to travel and carry on business enterprises in, they deprived their citizens of basic rights and were bad for their prosperity as well, and they certainly could not be counted on to make raw materials and products available for America's economy.

While socialist, or non-capitalist, societies did not represent the same threat of potential war, they were certainly unsatisfactory on just about all the other grounds. To an American who was convinced that there was no better engine for economic progress than the capitalist system, nor any fairer distribution of material goods, opposition to the spread of socialism was a natural thing entirely apart from the obvious disadvantages from a business standpoint. Further, to the extent that socialism involved an attitude of anti-Americanism and/or receptivity toward communism, there were obvious implications in terms of the freedom of Americans to travel and the possible eventual consequences in terms of another war. Given American attitudes, which did not include the goal of territorial expansion, the best guarantee that another war would not be necessary was the absence of sufficient strength on the part of actual or potential adversaries.

In terms of the preceding brief summary of American interests as they might have been summarized thirty or so years ago, very little has gone right. From a situation of overwhelming and near-total American military superiority, including being the only possessor of the atomic bomb, with communism still confined to Eastern Europe and Asian Russia, we have gone to one of military inferiority in which two communist powers have nuclear weapons and the area of the world under outright communist domination has vastly expanded. Nor have we anywhere near as friendly a world from an American standpoint. Granted, travel to communist areas is now possible where it was impossible thirty years ago. Elsewhere, however, areas in which Americans and other Westerners could travel in safety then are not safe now. More significantly, in terms of where American business can operate, the spread of socialism and communism has foreclosed numerous opportunities; vast areas of the world, with immensely valuable and often vitally necessary raw materials, have fallen from friendly Western control to hostile and often anti-American nationalist domination, often socialist but even where not representing a reduction in the availability of their raw materials.

In terms of justice in the world beyond our borders, in immense areas, including much of Asia and by far the greater part of Africa, there has been a transition from relatively benevolent and efficient undemocratic rule by relatively civilized Europeans to relatively malevolent and inefficient undemocratic rule by relatively uncivilized natives, with deleterious effect on the inhabitants' liberties and economic prospects.* Of immense significance, in the aftermath of the successful wholesale repudiation of contractual obligations to the business entities, often American, that had discovered the oil and brought it to the surface, on the part of the backward countries where the oil was found, the Western world, the United States included, finds itself forced to pay ever-increasing tribute to a handful of backward foreign states in order to obtain the fuel it needs, with far-reaching dislocations of its economic life and reductions in standards of living. (While it has been suggested that the answer is to wait until the Arabs et al. have recycled their oil wealth into ownership of a large part of the Western world and then, turnabout being fair play, expropriate *them*, the present situation is certainly not one that Americans could have desired.)

And it was hardly necessary, even under "international law," to have acquiesced in the seizure of our oil assets. Not that "international law" is all that meaningful a concept, just as domestic law would be relatively meaningless were there no civil authorities to enforce it: in the international sphere, there being no enforcement authority, "international law" basically amounts to what the custom in the international community is, and there is plenty of precedent, much of it provided since World War II by our communist friends, for decisive intervention where vital interests were felt to be at stake, and even simply to further expansionist goals: foreign governments can be overthrown by revolutionary movements fomented, controlled, and supplied from abroad; armies, such as the North Vietnamese, can cross borders and operate under the guise of local revolutionists; there can be out-and-out invasion, as in Czechoslovakia or Hungary, whether or not under the guise of purported invitation by a purported government.

*Shiva Naipaul's book *North of South: An African Journey* (New York: Simon and Schuster, 1979) contains an interesting discussion of the retrogression that has occurred.

"It is the business of a diplomat," wrote French foreign minister Walewski to Bismarck in 1857, "to cloak the interests of his country in the language of universal justice," and much the same applies to the use of international law. I took the International Law course at Stanford University, which was taught by a fine, liberal professor to whom international law meant that big powers could properly do very little to "throw their weight around" with their smaller brethren. This was the accepted orientation of international law as he understood it and taught it. Being differently oriented, however, I took great pleasure in working from the basic, given tenets of international law to reach, usually, precisely the opposite conclusions, in analyzing and deciding the hypothetical cases presented in assignments and examinations. We could intervene militarily to protect our citizens' property rights, for example. The professor conceded that my conclusions were just as valid as his, gave me the highest grade in the class, and urged me to consider a career in international law.

This view of the total flexibility of international law did not strike me as recommending its practice as a worthwhile endeavor, but rather left me with the realization that "international law" is a relatively meaningless and unimpressive thing. It would have been entirely in accord with international law, coldly viewed as the summary of actual international usage, for the United States to have threatened an oil-producing country with occupation if it expropriated our oil companies and, if necessary, to have overtly carried out the threat; or to have engineered a coup or carried out an occupation under the thin guise of a local revolution. Things like this are done all the time for far less justifiable reasons than to preserve a country's economic lifeline.

But even in terms of a stricter definition of "international law," more in line with what my professor taught, taking of drastic action could have been justified. From time immemorial it has been an accepted tenet of international law that a power is entitled to intervene in defense of its nationals' interests, where a foreign country harms them in violation of international law. The acknowledged right of a sovereign state to expropriate the property of the nationals of other states has always been subject to the requirement that fair compensation be paid. Absent such, international law has been violated and intervention is proper. Britain and France, in the 1956 Suez invasion, were exercising that long-recognized right, a right the U.S. State Department, in a surge of holier-than-thou or more-gentle-to-little-countries-than-thou indignation, refused to acknowledge existed.

Considering the immense value of the oil rights of varying sorts—

long-term leases, etc.—possessed by American nationals (our oil companies), which immense value is indicated by the vast amounts being spent to obtain oil today, it would of course have been virtually impossible for the backward oil states to have paid the fair compensation required under international law.

Our nice, liberal government, however, of course had no intention of enforcing our nationals', our companies', rights to be either fairly compensated or not expropriated and thus acquiesced in what in large degree was the wholesale seizure of oil rights possessed by American, and European, interests, with the ghastly consequences for Free World economic health and political freedom of action (vis-à-vis Arab pressure in particular) that have occurred.

The need to pay vast sums to the oil-producing states not only has resulted in economic dislocations and a reduced standard of living, it also holds out the prospect, over the years, of a greater and greater portion of the Free World, from London real estate to American companies, becoming owned by those who took over the oil, as the money that buys the oil is "recycled."

The lord of a great estate pays ever-increasing amounts to the gypsy fuel dealer for the fuel to heat and light the great house wherein there is so much merrymaking, and sells off the lands piece by piece to pay the fuel dealer; at some point, if the process continues, the lord's heirs find that they have become tenants in their ancestral home, with the fuel dealer's heirs their landlords. The old lord had originally developed the fuel source, on the gypsy's worthless bog-land, on the understanding that they would share in the profits for many years to come; he allowed the gypsy to break the agreement and seize the source because he did not think he should assert himself against one so much weaker and smaller than himself; his heirs wish he had been more assertive.

Just as the environment in which Americans live has not gotten fouled up by chance, so the environment in which the American environment, in turn, operates, has not either. In fact, the same elements which have played such a prominent role in damaging the domestic environment have played a key role in damaging America's world environment (with, of course, much help from their counterparts in other Western countries).

This country's liberal-oriented foreign-policy establishment has furthered the deterioration of our world environment by such attitudes as a simple-minded anti-colonial mania, a relative indifference to the property rights of American nationals abroad, a general bias toward left-wing and against right-wing governments and countries abroad, and an orientation toward government-run as opposed to private enterprise economics.

The American man-in-the-street was never much of an anti-colonialist. Certainly, to judge from the popularity of films and books romanticizing the "white man's burden," the average American did not think it was a terrible thing that "the natives" should be governed by Europeans. The natives, after all, couldn't read or write; how could they be expected to govern themselves intelligently? If the British (or the French, or the Dutch) left, they would just set to killing each other again (as in fact had happened, with over a million dead, in the first great postwar withdrawal from empire, the British departure from India).

But the enlightened Americans saw things differently, just as they saw the situation of the black slum-dweller very differently than did the average American. If the natives of Uganda or the Congo seemed unready for self-government, that was just because of the bad effects of colonial rule; self-government would be good for them and any-way, they had a right to it. Whether it was the Dutch in the East Indies, or the French in Algeria, or the British in Uganda, or the Portuguese in Angola and Mozambique, the hand of the enlightened, forward-looking people who handled American foreign policy was against them.

For all the twaddle about the inevitability of independence, one of the smallest and weakest of the European nations, Portugal, held a vast African empire for better than a decade against a determined effort by terrorists trained and supported by the communist powers and operating from privileged sanctuaries in neighboring states; it was finally war-weariness with a "no-win" war in the homeland, which facilitated the success of a carefully planned communist coup, that turned the large areas of Angola and Mozambique over to com-munist governments, not defeat on the battlefield: and it would seem quite clear that had the United States used its influence with those neighboring states to cut off the flow of men and matériel to the rebels, the situation would early on have been as well controlled as was that in Rhodesia until the Portuguese collapse gave Rhodesia, in turn, terrorist-fostering and supplying states for neighbors. (What a handful of Cuban troops have been able to do by way of being what former U.N. ambassador Andrew Young called a "stabilizing influ-ence" in Angola also says a lot about how un-inevitable speedy African independence really was.)

Independence has been far from helpful to the hapless African man-in-the-street (or man-on-the-trail). Kwame Nkrumah, leader of what had been the British Colony of the Gold Coast, made the cover of *Time* about the time the country achieved independence as Ghana, to the accompaniment of high hopes for the future of this early recipient of independence. Twenty-three years later, a *Chicago Tribune* article on the Pope's 1980 African trip referred to "Ghana, a country that has been on a downhill course since attaining independence from Britain in 1957. Ghana has experienced four military coups, inept government and staggering corruption."

The March 26, 1980, issue of the *New York Times* contained articles about two African countries on successive pages. One began, "For two decades, since Chad achieved independence from France in 1960, a civil war between Moslems in the north and black animists and Christians in the south has scoured that impoverished African nation. . . . the latest fighting . . . has killed hundreds and forced the evacuation from the capital of nearly half of some 900 Westerners, including the American envoy. . . ."

The article on the previous page was about Uganda, liberated from eight years of Idi Amin's savagery by Julius Nyerere's troops a year ago and since occupied by them. "Today was National Unity Day. . . . No one is working, but few people worked yesterday. In the processing plants for coffee and sugar cane, two of the country's major crops, production on working days has been five percent of capacity. . . . Gunfire is heard every night—sometimes, like last night, all night. There are bodies in the streets in the mornings. . . . Crime is everywhere, and no sane businessman wears a watch to work. . . . A member of the Kampala City council . . . said yesterday that the pervasive view in the country was that a 'force with a different pigment than us should come here. We have had the experience of the Tanzanians, and now we need a force from a civilized country, a country like Canada or New Zealand.' "

The barbarism and economic chaos that "independence" has brought to Africa do not seem to bother American foreign-policy liberals at all, nor does the loss of or at least the diminished accessibility of African natural resources or the foreclosing, in many cases, of opportunities for American business activity. These things may and do bother American citizens quite a bit; but, as has been noted earlier, our foreign-affairs specialists tend to march to a different tune.

(As far as the quality of life in foreign countries is concerned, the typical American liberal is far more exercised about one questionable death in a South African prison than about 200,000 murdered Ugandans or 10,000 victims of religious warfare in Chad. Again here, their approach differs significantly from that of the average American.)

Since it manifestly is not the case, as the Portuguese case shows, that extremist, Marxist black rule is inevitable in Africa absent overwhelming external influence, the longtime State Department-Andrew Young-Jimmy Carter insistence that Rhodesia be turned over to Marxist terrorists who openly declared that they would have no free elections (partly on the grounds that the elections held by the Muzorewa government did not involve sufficiently pure democracy!) certainly could not really be justified on the grounds that since Marxist rule was inevitable we might as well be on the side of the victors (a splendid illustration of the Carter commitment to morality in foreign affairs, no?). Nor, of course, was that apparently cynical curry-favor-with-the-likely-victor approach the real motivation for the policy. Rather, the real motivation was a virulent form of the old get-the-white-man-out-of-the-backward countries enthusiasm that has influenced American foreign policy since World War II, with such adverse consequences in terms of American interests.

This burning desire to get the white man out of Africa, in particular, simply will not be stilled or gainsaid, in the liberal heart. The successful Rhodesian elections of early 1979 (such observers as American civil rights leader Bayard Rustin pronounced them fair) were obviously a great disappointment to these people, who had their hearts set on the total destruction of the former Rhodesia and its replacement with a black Marxist dictatorship, rather than any transition to a biracial government which failed to stomp and dispossess the formerly governing whites.

One reason, perhaps the main reason, they were so terribly disappointed was that they feared that successful elections would build up pressure in Congress for a change in Andrew Young's only-terrorists-and-Marxists-deserve-a-hearing policy. And, indeed, as they had feared, the Senate voted, by a lopsided margin, to urge the Administration to lift sanctions against Rhodesia, by then known as Rhodesia/Zimbabwe. (The sanctions proponents were never bothered by the buying of chrome from Russia to avoid buying it from Rhodesia, just as their enthusiasm for trade with Communist China was on a par with their aversion to trade with Rhodesia: the enemies, you see, are *not* to the left.) The Tory victory in England in May 1979 was also a blow to their hopes.

They still hoped to salvage something, though: an article in *Time*, in May 1979, suggested that if Zimbabwe-Rhodesia's new premier, Bishop Muzorewa, wanted to maximize his chances for recognition and the lifting of sanctions, he would do well to (in violation of commitments and the Rhodesian constitution, of course, but such things apparently count for nothing when white people are involved) get rid of the name of Rhodesia and wipe out the constitutional safeguards for the white minority that were in effect. If one Bokassa declares himself "Emperor Bokassa I" of the "Central African Empire," that presents no problems in terms of sanctions or recognition (if only democratic African countries were recognized by the United States, all but one or two embassies would be closed, of course), but if the white population of Rhodesia has some constitutional safeguards against being dispossessed, that is a screaming outrage.

With the decision of British Prime Minister Margaret Thatcher *not* to recognize the Muzurewa government, of course, the liberals' long struggle finally neared victory; under British pressure, and the assurance of some constitutional safeguards, the Muzorewa government caved in and agreed to new elections and Zimbabwe/Rhodesia became plain Zimbabwe under former terrorist Robert Mugabe's leadership, with the improbably named Reverend Canaan Banana as president.* Granted that is is always possible that the country could become another Kenya rather than another Tanzania or Uganda or Mozambique, the odds are not too good, particularly considering the May 1980 assertion by Justice Minister Simbi Mubako that the remaining constitutional safeguards for the white population should be removed on the grounds that they had been "accepted only at British insistence in talks to end the former Colony's status as Rhodesia."

Another thread that runs through our foreign policy of the post-World War II period is aversion to the free enterprise system and a corresponding infatuation with government, that is, socialized, action. It is no secret that foreign companies are eager to conduct business activities in backward countries ("less-developed," "under-developed," or currently, "developing") where they are allowed to operate without being robbed blind, and that such activities produce economic advancement in a quite efficient way: the progress of Hong Kong, Singapore, South Korea, and Taiwan are cases in point. They cannot, however, function in socialist quagmires. There are some fundamental conditions, including respect for basic property rights, that must be provided to induce foreign capital to invest in a backward country, or in any country, for that matter. One would see no problem here: if a country wished to benefit from our capital and

---

*The Rev. Mr. Banana, who has a master's degree from Wesley Theological Institute in Washington, D.C., is no run-of-the-mill clergyman; according to an April 12, 1980, United Press dispatch, "He is best known for his theology of revolution. He rewrote the Lord's Prayer and the adaptation says, 'Teach us to demand our share of the gold. Forgive us our docility.' "

know-how, it could provide conditions that made investment attractive; this would create profit opportunities for Americans and help the country onto the road to economic progress in the healthy, efficient, conducive-to-individual-rights, free-enterprise way that Americans believe in and that has worked so well here. If it chose to hamstring its development with statist, socialist nonsense, it would be the loser, and it might get the idea from its neighbors who were progressing under free enterprise that it should mend its ways.

As Ray Moseley of the *Chicago Tribune* wrote at the time of the Pope's 1980 African visit: "Kenya, the third stop for the pope, is one of the showcases of black Africa. It is a land where black, white and Asian live together in a modicum of racial harmony and where a conservative economic and political system based on private enterprise has yielded relative prosperity. . . . The pope ends his tour in the Ivory Coast, another of the few African success stories. The Ivory Coast, through intensive development of agriculture and through the use of thousands of French experts in its government and business administration, has achieved one of the highest per-capita incomes in Africa."

Many American foreign-policy people, however, have seen their mission in terms of taking the American taxpayer's money and distributing it to socialist governments abroad so that those governments would not be forced to sell their souls and open their countries to American and other capitalist exploiters. This is much of what "foreign aid" has been all about. India, in particular, which insisted on stifling its economy with a lethal combination of socialist ideology and rampant bureaucracy, was provided with billions of American dollars; and this pattern of Americans using American dollars to make the world safe for socialism was found in country after country. It continues today. A March 1979 *Wall Street Journal* article by a knowledgeable African scholar and former admirer of Tanzania's dictator Nyerere describes how the doctrinaire socialism of this ideologue in a Mao-Tse-Tung outfit had ruined the Tanzanian economy, while neighboring Kenya prospered with free-enterprise conditions. What kept botched-up Tanzania from starvation? Why, foreign (that is, basically, American) aid, and lots of it, in massive doses.

The position of this country in the cold, hard real world outside has of course not been helped over the years by the foreign aid program that lavished hundreds of billions of dollars on foreign countries. The same enlightened liberal people who were telling Americans that they should not have to work too hard, and that poor people were poor through no fault of their own, were also telling Americans that they had an obligation to help the poor abroad to almost the limit of their resources.

They were, of course, selective as to who the proper beneficiaries of this largesse were. Poor countries with left-wing governments were the outstanding candidates, while in the case of poor countries with right-wing governments it was of course understood that the people's miseries were the fault of their oppressive regimes, and while the people might not be to blame for their regimes, nevertheless assistance to such countries implied approval of their dictatorial regimes and was thus out. India, and Indonesia under Sukarno, deserved and got aid on a vast scale; similarly Bolivia once it showed its deserving qualities by plundering privately-owned property; but equally poor Paraguay, under military rule, never had much of a chance.

It was of course said that foreign aid was really in America's best interests. Certainly a very strong case can be made for the Marshall Plan, aimed at restoring viability to war-shattered economies of what had always been pretty advanced countries, well capable of handling economic matters with effectiveness.

In the case of backward countries, matters were otherwise. The danger was not that under the stresses of unaccustomed economic misery (as in war-torn Europe) otherwise politically literate and civilized people would turn to strange new isms; economic misery in these countries was not unusual, and the problem of communism generally appeared precisely where the people had moved from agricultural areas to higher wages offered through industrialization. But, it was said, more or less as an article of faith, that the way to fight communism *everywhere* is to advance industrialization and prosperity. This theory works so well that the first Latin American country to go communist by democratic vote was Chile, with the highest standard of living, the best-educated people, and the largest and most racially homogeneous middle class of any Latin American country.

But, of course, that is beside the point in a way because foreign aid as an engine of real economic growth is rather questionable. The ability of do-gooders and bureaucrats from the United States, working as a team with local members of these species, as well as rakeoff artists, to accomplish anything constructive is less than evident. For one thing, Americans of this ilk tend to operate on the theory that we must consider "real human needs," and that the profit motive is a rather nasty sort of thing, with the result that they ignore the only real engine for efficient economic progress in existence. Then too, it often occurs to a foreign country's rulers that they need not worry about providing conditions that will attract foreign private capital and know-how if these will be provided, and provided free, anyway; and the more they rob those who invested in their country and foul up their economy to the cheers of the street mob, the more piteous will their plight become and the more deserving they will become of free, no-strings-attached foreign aid.

This is not to say that good may not be done through providing a road, or draining a swamp, etc., any more than it is to deny that a particular government waterway project in the United States may be a fine thing. But in general, worthwhile projects can be financed privately, provided the country has not committed itself to theft as a way of life. (Even then, American corporations may hasten to invest, convinced that *they* can do business with this country, and ending up expropriated, poorer, sadder, and perhaps still no wiser.) Furthermore, to have sappy money instead of smart money, and be freed from the need to attract smart money, is poor fiscal and economic and political discipline.

Before falling back on saying that foreign aid should be engaged in to "help people" (which, of course, it tended not to do), liberals would say that we had to give foreign aid as part of a battle for the "minds and hearts of the underdeveloped world." If we didn't give them money, in other words, they wouldn't be our friends. Some claptrap was usually used to conjure up the picture of wise foreigners carefully weighing the merits of different systems on the basis of how much each gave them; but it really boiled down to buying friends.

The dissipation of assets through foreign aid has not merely encouraged statism and socialism abroad, hampering the economic development and misdirecting the political evolution of foreign countries; it has also meant that, instead of American dollars going abroad under private direction in ways that would subsequently bring returns back to the United States (which would help our balance of payments), the American resources that that money or goods represented have simply been lost. One of the reasons we have the balance-of-payments problems we do, with the dollar having sunk as far as it has in relation to the world's strong currencies, is that we gave away abroad, rather than intelligently invested, so much of our wealth.

The truth is starting to be nearly universally perceived in the United States these days that the efficient way to accomplish something is emphatically *not* to have it done by a government agency with no incentive for efficiency or economy; neither the Postal Service in particular, nor the federal government in general, is widely perceived as efficient in comparison with private industry. When we further reflect that the difference between the government bureaucracy in the United States and that in a backward country is the difference between night and day, we shake our heads over a majority of Congress letting itself be persuaded for so long that economic (as opposed to military, of course) "foreign aid" to socialist foreign governments is a wise use of the taxpayers' money.

There is an interesting parallel between the fanatical orientation of liberals toward blacks in matters African and their blacks-can-do-no-wrong attitude toward Negroes at home and their burning desire to lavish the taxpayer's money on the surly welfare class at home and on unfriendly socialist regimes abroad. And another parallel comes to mind as we analyze the striking failure of American foreign policy since the war to protect the country's interests effectively: that between impotence in the face of left-wing violence at home and the inability to achieve victory in Korea or Indo-China. The United States can cope quite effectively, on a no-nonsense, no-quarter basis, with domestic violence from the right (the Ku Klux Klan, for example) and with right-wing enemies abroad; it is not very effective against domestic violence from the left or communist enemies abroad. The bias of American "intellectuals" is fundamental to this phenomenon. Basically, the same group, with the same biases, has fouled up both our domestic environment and our country's world environment.

Our failures to achieve victory in Korea and Indo-China are not only results of the same inability to be ruthless toward foreign enemies on the left, but the two wars were directly related: it was after our accepting a stalemate in Korea that the main communist thrust in Indo-China, which culminated in the disastrous French defeat at Dien Bien Phu, was begun.

Our ability to cope with situations requiring military force, as well as our credibility as an effective power (which would normally preclude adventures on the part of adversaries which confront this country with the need to use military force to protect its vital interests: *si vis pacem, para bellum*), has been very significantly diminished by what has amounted to a policy of relative unilateral disarmament. Some systems have actually been scrapped; but for relative, rather than absolute, unilateral disarmament to occur, all that is necessary is to avoid forging ahead when one's adversary does so forge. Incredibly, much of what has been done by us along this line has been done with the objective of convincing our we-will-bury-you opponent of our good faith and lack of aggressive intent! It was not enough, in the eyes of people who thought like this, that we had obviously reconciled ourselves to seeking only to halt communism's spread, and had abandoned any efforts to roll back the Iron or Bamboo Curtains; it was not enough that we had, when we and we alone possessed the atomic bomb and could have delivered an ultimatum to the rest of the world that any attempt to develop such a weapon would result in disaster for the country attempting it (which, one feels quite sure, the Soviet Union would not have hesitated to deliver, had it been the first to possess a usable nuclear weapon), which would have assured this country of a dominant military position in the world indefinitely at extremely modest expense, done nothing effective to prevent other nations, including our obvious and sworn enemies, from developing nuclear weapons; no, we had to demonstrate our good faith by letting the Soviet Union pass us by in overall military strength.

The same alienated, anti-American, no-enemies-to-the-left sort of mind has succeeded in playing on the Sunday school mentality of much of America in order to destroy the CIA as an effective force in the world. Just as the continuing Soviet arms buildup has been of no apparent concern to the enthusiasts of unilateral disarmament in the military area, so the obvious aggressiveness and vigor of Soviet operations in the area of covert operations have bothered the anti-CIA crusaders not a whit. If one operates on the assumption that these people are really sincere Americans who share the basic attitudes and concern for this country's welfare of the average American man-in-the-street, and his preferences as to what sort of world this country is to operate in, this attitude leaves us totally bewildered; if we recognize that many of these people dislike this country and basically all that it stands for, their desire to render it impotent, unable further to threaten, beyond its borders, the sorts of things that these people do believe in, becomes completely understandable. The delegation of Americans who as this is written are in Teheran denouncing their country would seem a case in point. What sort of American, again, would be motivated to so stand reason on its head as to blame the *United States* (because years ago we responded to communist activities within Cambodia by bombing and thus in a way added to Cambodia's involvement in the Vietnam conflict) for the ghastly atrocities carried out in 1979 by Cambodia's communist rulers? Here is a degree of hatred of country that can best be described as obscene.

Speaking of lambs and wolves, then, referring to the title of this chapter, the metaphor would represent quite an over-simplification of the nature of America's experiences as a part of the world, particularly since the end of World War II. Much of the situation no doubt involved a naive and idealistic country taken advantage of by the more cynical and self-seeking, around the time of World War I and its aftermath, but in the last thirty years there has been considerably more to the problem than that.

Perhaps the metaphor needs the element of false shepherds added to it. The interests of this country have been disastrously served by what has happened in the world since World War II, and to the extent that those responsible for handling our foreign policy and having an effect on the world beyond our borders *have* sought to advance the real interests of this country they have failed miserably; but in the case of many of those entrusted with that responsibility, they have succeeded all too well in their *personal* objectives for the world and its effect on America.

22

Conclusion

Where does all this leave us? First of all, we should clearly recognize that the terms "environment" and "ecology" have a meaning in our existence as part of an economic system and a socio-political system, not only in connection with physical nature (as rivers, forests, etc.). One can speak of a socio-economic system, combining the economic and what we have called the socio-political systems, and indeed it is in that combined system that we live and concerning which there is currently so much to complain of; for purposes of coming to grips with what the problems and their causes are, it is, however, helpful to distinguish the two and, to the extent appropriate, analyze them separately.

We should also recognize that the principle that applies to nature, of there being a way in which, in accordance with not always obvious natural laws, the elements interact in a certain fruitful harmony, so that tampering with the system from an external source is all too likely to be detrimental rather than harmful in its effects, also applies in the case of the economic environment. It can be seen that much harm has been done by disregard of this fact: if an "environmental impact study" is required before a dam or breakwater is constructed, the equivalent ought *a fortiori* to be insisted on before a government action impinges on the economic environment. It is foolishness to so impinge willy-nilly.

Given the economic environment, of which in this country the most fundamental element is the institution of private property and the concomitant of fundamental capitalist economics, a certain amount of the socio-political environment, particularly the social part, follows. The remainder, predominantly the political part, is understood to be subject to deliberate choice and change by those with the ability to make those choices and changes in accord with the mechanisms and procedures in existence. But the point that deserves stressing and understanding is that changes politically made in the socio-political environment that stem from beliefs and objectives at odds with those underlying the basic economic environment, resulting in people being motivated in ways that are at odds with the motivational system basic to the economic environment, bring disharmony and malfunctioning into the whole combined system.

It is well to discuss the economic and socio-political environments separately for several reasons. For one thing, the processes by which significant changes have been made in the two areas have been on the whole quite different, being legislation in the former case and judicial and administrative actions in the latter. For another, it is well to keep the "environments" somewhat separate: one the economic, where in terms of its objective, satisfying effective demand, in essence, hindrances and harmful interventions can be fairly objectively recognized and discussed, and the underlying premises explicitly taken note of; the other the socio-political, where far more subjective matters are involved. If there are premises underlying recent changes in the socio-political environment which are opposed to the premises on which the economic environment is based, it is well to be aware of that inconsistency in terms of assessing what our fundamental beliefs and principles are and what adjustments or improvements are appropriate in order to achieve, or perhaps rather restore, a better congruence between beliefs and principles and laws and institutions.

We have seen that intervention in the economic environment has done much harm; we have also seen that fundamental changes in the socio-political environment have in some cases been inappropriate given the economic environment (e.g., the attitude that much work is demeaning, rationalization of insubordination, racial quotas) and in other cases simply changes for the worse when measured against the obvious preferences of the general population. In terms of those preferences, involving a smoothly-running, safe, orderly society, where in the non-economic areas in essence virtue and industry are rewarded and vice and sloth punished and life, liberty, and the pursuit of happiness facilitated, it also becomes possible to say that, in terms of such an environment, a given change is or is not appropriate or "ecological," just as meaningfully as this can be said of changes in the economic environment that reduce the satisfaction of effective demand, *that* environment's *raison d' être*.

Just as the measure of what is ecological in the economic sphere is the satisfying of the people's material wants as reflected in effective demand, so the measure of what is ecological in the socio-political sphere is the satisfying of the people's desires as to the sort of society they wish to live in. It can be said that things are "going to the dogs," or that the environment is deteriorating, in either case, if these conditions are being met less well.

It is clear that political intervention in the economy has had, and is having, disastrous effects. The ultimate result of minimum wage laws, labor union strength, generous welfare (and unemployment) benefits, government spending, and regulation is misallocation and waste of resources on a vast scale (when huge amounts of labor and materials go into office buildings to house the bureaucracy and into anti-pollution "overkill," "misallocation" is clearly the right word; when millions sit around watching TV, supported by the taxpayers in one way or another, "waste" comes to mind: although, of course, waste can be considered a form of misallocation, so that the one term would be sufficient).

It would be hard, in the course of a normal day, for anyone to avoid personally encountering a multitude of instances of such misallocation: here a huge office building for an expanding bureaucracy under construction; there idlers, presumably taxpayer-supported in one way or another; here a street dug up for a billion-dollar sewage treatment project of no real value; there specialists working on extensive "environmental impact reports"; here an obviously overstaffed city street-repair crew; there a squad of lawyers heading for court with a promising piece of litigation spawned by recent legislation. Nowadays, with more and more efficient foreign competitors, these impediments to American productivity are causing an increasing amount of discomfort for the American people.

Their discomfort is also substantial, probably more so in fact, because of what has been done to the socio-political environment. Analysis of what has happened here and how it came about showed that the changes were almost entirely judicial and administrative in origin, rather than coming about through enactment of legislation;

and that the prevalence of what may be called "liberalism" among the articulate, "opinion-molding," "intellectual" community was the crucial factor in making feasible this remaking of society by fiat.

Note has been taken of several significant encouraging signs, which analysis led on to the disturbing fact that now, just as a desirable, or ecological, trend can be clearly seen to have developed within the United States with respect to our economic and socio-political environments, external developments are beginning to pose some very alarming questions as to the future well-being of the United States in the world—in its external environment, if one will.

Interestingly enough, when the process by which this situation had come about was analyzed, it became clear that what had happened was almost exactly parallel to what had happened with the harming of our domestic environments: that is, the articulate, "opinion-molding," "intellectual" community, marching again to different music than the country as a whole, had brought about, in some cases actively and in other cases by failing effectively to oppose, changes in our position vis-à-vis the rest of the world (or in the position of the rest of the world vis-à-vis us) emphatically not desired by Americans in general.

Indeed, in view of the many striking parallels between liberal attitudes toward elements at home and toward their analogous foreign counterparts, one may usefully say that the liberal drummer is the same in both cases and that what he plays is basically the same too, albeit transposed and varied slightly to fit the somewhat different instruments used.

The awakening of the American people that is needed to save, or restore, their environment, then, must be a twofold one, involving a determination to override the liberal-"intellectual" predilection for underdogism and socialism at home *and* abroad. The same feelings of "guilt" and distrust of and disdain for basic American institutions and values that have led to the fouling up of our domestic environment have done this country and its interests and values a titanic disservice with respect to the rest of the world.

Our foreign relations must be administered by people believing in what America believes in: in individual freedom, including the fundamental right of private property; in the capitalist, free-enterprise system, as the most effective engine of economic progress existing; in the resulting rightness of our cause in opposition to communism and socialism. People with their feet thus planted firmly on the ground—on *American* ground, that is—will not *approve* of imperfections in foreign governments that are fundamentally capitalist and pro-American, but they will not consistently prefer left-wing dictatorships to right-wing and follow policies that conduce to the replacement of a Batista by a Castro, a Shah by an Ayatollah Khomeini, and a Somoza by a Havana-directed revolutionary government.

Neither will they fuss and fret and condemn a Chilean, or Argentinian, or Rhodesian government while uncritically fawning over more serious violators of "human rights" of the communist or Marxist persuasion, such as Communist China and Tanzania. The reason many of those who have been handling our foreign affairs have pursued this one-sided course is, not that they are somewhat absent-mindedly inclined to be overcritical of our friends, as conservative commentators sometimes seem to assume when they repeatedly, devastatingly, point out the screaming inconsistency in liberal thought and policies, but, rather, that as far as those foreign-affairs people are concerned, *a socialist dictatorship is preferable to a capitalist one.*

It is this orientation that must be replaced: replaced with one that represents, rather than being at odds with, American views. The controlling and redirection and/or replacement of foreign relations personnel is to restoring to the United States a foreign policy that represents it what achieving a reoriented judiciary and bureaucracy is to restoring the domestic environment that Americans want.

The "how" is often more difficult than the "what." Part of the "how," of course, in fact a prerequisite to any real hope of achieving the necessary changes, is the knowledge of the "what": the realization, in the country, that significant changes are needed and a determination to effect them and not be sidetracked or misled by the articulate advocates of continued deterioration. These elements are becoming present to an increasing degree, and, given the mechanisms for effecting the people's will in a democratic country, this represents a major part of the battle.

In terms of specifics, a determination to elect sensibly oriented persons to office is critical; this determination must include a focusing on the fundamental issues of importance. In view of the immense importance that the judiciary and bureaucracy have taken on, elections to executive office are obviously the most important of all. Those seeking such office must evince an understanding that judicial appointments must be made, in every case, on the basis of a judicial philosophy that is, simply put, a *judicial* philosophy: a solid commitment on the part of the prospective jurist, consistent with and demonstrated by his or her past record, to administer the laws and interpret them on the basis of their meaning and the intent of those who enacted them, *not* to overrule or negate the laws and the Constitution on the basis of personal politics.

To those who use the argument that such a test involves "bringing politics into judicial selection," or "into the judiciary," the answer is that politics has always been involved in judicial selection; that *ideological* politics has long been involved as well and has resulted in an excessively political, and to a significant degree as a result a discredited, judiciary;* and that the whole idea is to bring into being a *depoliticized* judiciary, which will do its constitutional job without usurping or attempting to usurp the rightful functions of the legislative and executive branches: to select judges with that in mind is to *remove* ideological politics from judicial selection, not to introduce it; an understanding of the constitutionally proper sphere of the judiciary is a judicial, not a political, qualification for judicial office.

A handicap that seems inevitable, for the ecologists, is the need to fight their battles to the accompaniment of a hostile chorus, the "intellectual" community. For very fundamental reasons, analysis of which was attempted earlier, this element can be expected to be fundamentally wrong-headed on the whole. But the rest of the country does not have to supinely permit this element to propagandize to its heart's content, and it can reasonably be hoped that the current awakening will include a readiness to take appropriate action.

Education, for example, is in general under the control of private or elected public boards, and it is a safe bet, whether it is financed publicly or privately, that those who are footing the bills intend that educational institutions educate, not brainwash or propagandize. Rather than tamely countenance the most biased "teaching," such boards have every right (and, one would think, the duty) to insist that pedagogues confine themselves, in the classroom, to the job they are being paid to do. (This would seem a more simple and straightforward policy than one of seeking to balance one biased instructor with another from the "other side," but, particularly in the more subjective areas and advanced levels, some of that may be appropriate.)

The attempt by academics to use the term "academic freedom" to argue that no one has any business requiring them to do the job they are hired to do, in the classroom, is laughable. What if one read the following article in the newspaper:

CHICAGO (date) Attempts by a building owner to curb a controversial plumber here have led to an uproar in the local plumbing community. Denouncing the

---

*Not, obviously, that the average judge is a usurping activist; many a fine jurist feels keen pain at what those who are have done to the bench's reputation.

attempt as an "attack on plumbing freedom," plumbers have mobilized in defense of Angelo Marcus, an Associate Plumber at the skyscraper Mammoth Building here.

Building manager Roger Jones, whose company has attempted to prevent Mr. Marcus from carrying on plumbing at its building, claims that for some time now Marcus has ignored his wishes and instructions with respect to plumbing work at the Mammoth Building. "He has run pipes all over the place, some of the plumbing doesn't lead anywhere, and there is the most bizarre Rube Goldberg array of pipes and valves all over the halls and rooms that you ever saw," complains Jones.

Marcus acknowledges that his plumbing is unorthodox and that "some may call me controversial." He argues, however, that as a tenured plumber he is protected by traditions of plumbing freedom from any interference with his work by the building owners. "There is nothing more sacred to the plumbing profession than plumbing freedom," the earnest Marcus insists. "The expression of different viewpoints, no matter how controversial, must be protected, or we become like Nazi Germany."

The owners' contention that since they are paying the bills they are entitled to have the kind of plumbing they want in their building is challenged by Rupert Osgood, head of the local chapter of the American Association of Skyscraper Plumbers. "That just shows how pathetically little Jones and the others who would bring politics into plumbing understand about the basic principles of plumbing freedom. A plumber must be free to plumb the way he wishes, without outside interferences. It is only in this way that new innovations and the free flow of creativity can proceed." Osgood has threatened to have the Mammoth Building blacklisted by his organization if it makes good on its threat to fire Marcus.

Occupants of the Mammoth Building are divided, but a substantial number are strong supporters of Marcus. "He is the most dedicated, creative plumber we have ever had," declares Miss Ethel Lebensraum, an intent, bespectacled statistician at Churnem & Co., a brokerage house. "He has really made plumbing come alive for us. Sure, some of his work is a little disorganized, but maybe that is the price you have to be willing to pay for creativity and innovation." Oscar Zilch, a young attorney, feels that it would be "a tragedy" if Marcus were to be removed. "That would really destroy the confidence of the people here in the building management."

Some of the skyscraper's older tenants complain that the intricate array of valves and pipes in the building's rest rooms confuses them. However, Otis Wrench, dean of the building's plumbing department, backs Mr. Marcus wholeheartedly. "The man's work is brilliant," he told a reporter recently. "Jones ought to be thankful that he has a man of Mr. Marcus' caliber on the staff here. Angelo really puts his heart and soul into his work. Some of his valves and piping are the finest I've ever seen in all my years of plumbing."

A confrontation seems inevitable here between those who hold that "he who pays the piper calls the tune" and those who, like Wrench, feel that plumbing freedom must come first. "The building owners," he declares, "have no more right to dictate to their plumbers than a board of regents to control their professors."

Of course, the idea that a plumber, or a carpenter, has *carte blanche* to do whatever he wants is laughable. Plumbers don't write books and mold public opinion. But, in the last analysis, while an advanced scholar may in fact be paid to think and research and voice whatever conclusions he reaches (and, indeed, there is research and development in plumbing supply companies!), the high school civics or English teacher and the college instructor in freshman English, beginning French or political science is definitely not. There would be less of a problem in terms of young people having to go through a post-college process of growing out of half-baked liberal ideas if politics—which almost invariably, in this context, means left-wing politics—were more effectively kept out of the classroom; the beneficial effect would be greater, in fact, since (a) some never recover from exposure to their professor's biases and (b) the biases of tomorrow's teacher in large part come from what he absorbs in classrooms today.

"Witch-hunts in the classroom!" A cleverly worded phrase. But it is not witches, which are generally not considered to exist today, particularly in classrooms, that are objected to, but rather teachers whose biases distort their instruction; and of those we have a goodly number.

Another problem area where ecologists should not be helpless, in terms of reducing the handicap under which they labor, is represented by the media. Granted that a disproportionate number of those attracted to both the print and audio-visual media can be expected to be of liberal persuasion, it does not follow that better balance cannot be achieved in those who are employed, nor that liberal journalists, if employed, cannot be required to achieve greater objectivity in their work. There are such things as editors, who can see to it that news stories are not slanted and that slanting is not accomplished by the emphasis given various stories. Those who own the media, and those who use them to advertise their products and services, have every right to refuse to further the misleading of the public.

While the proprietors of television stations and newspapers, and the companies using them to advertise, have in general been slow to act against media bias, it may be hoped that they are not themselves immune to the general spread of sense among the people and that that general spread will encourage them to avoid offending viewers and readers with slanted coverage.

Particularly as and if steps are taken to mute, partially, the hostile chorus, prospects for progress in restoring the environment at home appears fairly good.

This is particularly true of the light of the successes recently enjoyed through the initiative process, which have encouraged increasing use of it and fostered tantalizing thoughts of somewhat analogous action at the national level through constitutional amendments. Such, of course, may be submitted to the states for ratification either by a two-thirds vote of Congress, as occurred with ERA, or by vote of a national constitutional convention. The latter, although provided for in the Constitution, has never been held, but the number of states that by their legislatures' votes have joined in the call for such a convention to consider an amendment requiring a balanced federal budget is now only three short of the thirty-three required.

It is intriguing to think of the many areas in which Constitutional amendments, carefully drafted and clearly enough worded to be unambiguous even to Supreme Court justices—fool-proof—could, virtually overnight once ratified, restore sanity to American institutions and society. A balanced federal budget except in some sort of *very* rigorously defined "emergency"; capital punishment; the end of the "exclusionary rule"; school busing; permitting school prayer; restoring the rights of the states to regulate abortion which they possessed until very recently; making clear that the "equal protection of the laws" precludes discrimination against *all* people.

It might even be possible to circumscribe the federal government's permissible sphere of activity, with respect to domestic matters, so as to force the federal government once again to concentrate on its proper area of responsibility and free the country from the plague of federal interference with just about everything. It is perhaps not realistic to entertain too high hopes for quick cures via the constitutional amendment route, but on the other hand, at the start few gave the Jarvis Proposition much chance of succeeding, and it should not be forgotten that the United States actually enacted the Prohibition Amendment.

As to America's world environment, gloomy though the situation may appear, it must be remembered that situations can turn around very quickly. The collapse of the Shah's government was swift; but so was the collapse of those of the Marxist Allende in Chile and of communist-influenced Sukarno in Indonesia. Just as the collapse of American will as to Indo-China happened relatively suddenly, so did the resurgence of British will not long after Munich. The recent defection of members of the Bolshoi Ballet reminds us, or should remind us, of the fundamental inferiority of the system which opposes us, being, as it is, built on a foundation that includes absolutely crackpot economics and a fundamentally wrong-headed view of the nature of man.

The values and principles on which this country's economic system and political system are built, and which the preponderance of Americans, the "heart of the country," share, are sound. With their confident reassertion, which now is under way, should come a restoration of domestic prosperity and tranquility and a securing of our position in the world.

Selected Bibliography

Anderson, Martin. *Welfare: The Political Economy of Welfare Reform in the United States*. Palo Alto, Calif.: Hoover Institution Press, 1978.

Banfield, Edward C. *Unheavenly City Revisited: A Revision of the Unheavenly City*. Boston: Little, Brown and Company, 1974.

Berger, Raoul. *Government by Judiciary: The Transformation of the Fourteenth Amendment*. Cambridge, Mass.: Harvard University Press, 1977.

Commonwealth Club of California. *Are the Courts Handcuffing the Police?* San Francisco: Transactions of the Commonwealth Club, Vol. LXVII, ''B,'' 1973.

Friedman, Milton, and Rose Friedman. *Free to Choose: A Personal Statement*. New York: Harcourt Brace Jovanovich, Inc., 1980.

Kendall, Willmoore. *The Conservative Affirmation*. Chicago: Henry Regnery Company, 1963.

Keynes, John M. *The Economic Consequences of the Peace,* reprint of 1919 edition. New York: St. Martin's Press, 1971.

Lambro, Donald. *Fat City*. South Bend, Ind.: Regnery/Gateway, Inc., 1980.

MacArthur, Douglas. *Reminiscenses*. New York: McGraw-Hill Book Company, 1964.

Nixon, Richard M. *The Real War*. New York: Warner Books, Inc., 1980.

Podhoretz, Norman. *Breaking Ranks: A Political Memoir*. New York: Harper & Row, Publishers, Inc., 1979.

Schumpeter, Joseph A. *Capitalism, Socialism and Democracy*. New York: Harper & Row, Publishers, Inc. (Colophon reprint edition).

Simon, William E. *A Time for Truth*. New York: McGraw-Hill Book Company/Reader's Digest Press, 1978.

————. *A Time for Action*. New York: McGraw-Hill Book Company/ Reader's Digest Press, 1980.

Smith, Adam. *The Wealth of Nations*. New York: E. P. Dutton and Company (Everyman reprint edition).

Sowell, Thomas. *Black Education: Myths and Tragedies*. New York, David McKay, Inc., 1972.

Von Mises, Ludwig. (Hans F. Sennholtz, trans.) *A Critique of Interventionism*. New Rochelle, N.Y.: Arlington House, Inc., 1977.

Index

224

226